John F. Kennedy, Barack Obama, and the Politics of Ethnic Incorporation and Avoidance

SUNY series in African American Studies

John R. Howard and Robert C. Smith, editors

John F. Kennedy, Barack Obama, and the Politics of Ethnic Incorporation and Avoidance

Robert C. Smith

Published by State University of New York Press, Albany

Printed in the United States of America

For information, contact State University of New York Press, Albany, NY
www.sunypress.edu

Production by Eileen Nizer
Marketing by Kate McDonnell

Library of Congress Cataloging-in-Publication Data

Smith, Robert Charles, 1947–
John F. Kennedy, Barack Obama, and the politics of ethnic incorporation and avoidance / Robert C. Smith.
p. cm. — (SUNY series in African American studies)
Includes bibliographical references and index.
ISBN 978-1-4384-4559-5 (hc : alk. paper)—978-1-4384-4560-1 (pb : alk.)
1. Minorities—Political activity—United States. 2. Political participation—United States. 3. Irish Americans—Politics and government. 4. Catholics—Political activity—United States. 5. African Americans—Politics and government. 6. Presidents—United States—Election—1960. 7. Presidents—United States—Election—2008. 8. Kennedy, John F. (John Fitzgerald), 1917–1963. 9. Obama, Barack. I. Title.

E184.A1S6645 2013
323.173—dc23 2012012852

10 9 8 7 6 5 4 3 2 1

In Memory of My Esteemed Mentor
and Friend, Ronald W. Walters
(1939–2010)

Contents

Tables

Acknowledgments

As with everything I have written in the last four decades, I would first like to thank my wife, Scottie, for her manifold assistance in preparation of the manuscript. Charles Henry of the University of California, Berkeley; Toni-Michelle Travis of George Mason University; and Hanes Walton Jr. of the University of Michigan read the entire manuscript and offered good suggestions for its improvement. I am especially grateful to my good buddy, collaborator, and fellow Howard University alumni Hanes for his spacious and detailed comments on the manuscript. We are coauthors of an American government textbook now in its seventh edition, and we read everything the other writes. For this manuscript he was particularly helpful in bringing to my attention obscure but illuminating sources and in urging me to develop in greater detail the concept of ethnic avoidance and its implications for democracy in America.

The anonymous reviewers SUNY Press selected encouraged me to pay more systematic attention to the relationships between race and ethnicity in minority group subordination in the United States. John Howard, the coeditor with me of SUNY's African American studies series, reviewed the manuscript with his usual discerning and critical eye, as he has done with each of the five books I have published in the series since 1992. I shall be forever grateful for his intellectual support and guidance. Michael Rinella and Andrew Kenyon, my in-house editors at SUNY Press, were critical, thoughtful, and timely from the origination of the idea for the project through the various stages of review, editing, and production. I should also like to thank Therese Myers for her very careful and discerning copy editing.

Parts of the manuscript were presented at the University of California, Berkeley, at a conference celebrating the fortieth anniversary of the publication of *The Black Scholar* on November 23, 2009. I also had the good opportunity to discuss the origins and research for the project in the works-in-progress section of the *National Political Science Review* (vol. 13, 2011). I am grateful to the editors, David Covin and Michael Mitchell, for extending the invitation.

Professor Matthew Platt of Harvard provided useful comments on chapter 7, which was presented as a paper at the forty-second annual meeting of the National Conference of Black Political Scientists in Raleigh, North Carolina, March 16–20, 2010.

The final draft of the manuscript was written while I was on sabbatical in the fall of 2011. The College of Behavioral and Social Sciences and the Department of Political Science at San Francisco State defrayed the cost of copying and traveling.

Finally, this book is dedicated to the memory of my esteemed mentor, friend, and colleague, Ronald Walters. Ron's death in September 2010 has left a void in my intellectual, political, and personal lives that can never be filled.

Robert C. Smith
El Sobrante, California
November 2011

Introduction

Barack Obama's election to the presidency represents the ultimate manifestation of the incorporation or integration of African Americans into the political system. This process of incorporation started in the late 1960s with the election of blacks to big-city mayoralties and appointments to high-level positions in the federal executive and judicial branches.

Obama's election represents only the second time in history that an "ethnic" American—a nonwhite Anglo-Saxon Protestant—has been elected president. When John F. Kennedy was elected, the Irish Catholic community had been fully integrated into American society. As Greeley writes, "The Irish were probably on the verge of making it when the Great Depression rolled the Nation into a decade of economic stagnation. It took the prosperity of World War II and the postwar economic boom, plus the G.I. Bill to enable the Irish to make it definitively into the ranks of the middle class."[1] Indeed, by the time of Kennedy's election, by most measures Irish Catholics were more successful than Anglo-Saxon Protestants, exceeded in social and economic status only by Jews.[2]

Related to Irish Catholic incorporation into the economy and society, by 1960 the once vibrant Irish group consciousness and identity created by "the strong tie of bearing one common wrong" had withered away.[3] And Moynihan concluded that there was "no possibility—not the most remote—that a distinctive Irish identity [could] be recreated in the United States."[4]

Not so with Obama's election and the African American community. As I wrote in 1996 about the process of incorporation of black leaders into the political system, "Compared to the experience of other ethnic groups in the United States this situation is near unprecedented. The integration or incorporation of Irish, Jewish, Polish and Italian American leaders into the institutions of the society and polity roughly paralleled the integration of their communities as a whole. In contrast, black leaders are integrated, but their core community is segregated, impoverished and increasingly in the post–civil rights era marginalized, denigrated and criminalized."[5] And when Obama was elected "blackness," a sense of group identity and consciousness—also created by a "strong tie of a common wrong"—remained vibrant.[6] As a result, unlike Kennedy and the Irish, when Obama was elected the black community still had significant group-specific demands on the state for redress of wrongs.

This book compares the Kennedy and Obama elections, and the Irish Catholic and African American experiences in the United States. Obvious similarities are found between Kennedy and Obama as "presidential characters" or personalities, as well as between their campaigns. For example, Caroline Kennedy, the President's daughter and his brother Senator Edward Kennedy in endorsing Obama explicitly said that Obama would be a President like their father and brother.[7]

The Irish and the African American experiences have been frequently compared.[8] Moynihan writes ". . .the twentieth century Negro experience is best understood in the context of the nineteenth century Irish experience."[9] Although Greeley exaggerates the similarities between the Irish and African experiences in America, it is true that "both lived in abject misery, the victims of political oppression and economic exploitation. The principal difference is that the Irish having white skins, were eventually given a chance to 'earn a place' in American society; the blacks were not permitted to do so."[10]

This book, therefore, fits within a broader body of literature on comparative ethnic politics in the United States. It is also a historical and comparative study in U.S. presidential politics.

Chapter 1 defines ethnicity and discusses its relationship to race in the United States, and then outlines the theory of ethnic incorporation used in the study. This theory draws substantially on Michael Hechter's 1975 work *Internal Colonialism: The Celtic Fringe in British National Development, 1536–1966.* Hechter's work is not only an important synthesis of theoretical material on ethnic incorporation in developed societies, but it is also useful because it draws explicit attention to the Irish and African American experiences.

Chapter 2 is a synoptic history of the Irish Catholic and African American experiences. The comparison focuses mainly on the American experiences, but some attention is paid to colonialism in Ireland and Africa. This comparison makes clear at the outset that systems of ethnic subordination based on race tend to be much more rigid than those based on religion.

Chapter 3 compares the development of Irish Catholic and African American ethnic group consciousness, identity, culture, solidarity, and power in the United States. Catholic Irish consciousness and identity in politics had substantially withered away by the 1960s, however, African American consciousness and identity was markedly revitalized with consequences during this decade that endure until today.

Chapter 4 looks at Boston and Chicago and the beginnings of the political careers of Kennedy and Obama. Of Boston, Thomas O'Connor writes that because of the militancy of "Anglo-Saxonism" it was "the one city in the entire world where an Irish Catholic, under any circumstances, should never, *ever* set foot."[11] Meanwhile, Chicago was the first big northern city that began the political incorporation of blacks and where they were first elected to office in significant numbers. Yet in Chicago African Americans were subordinated by probably the most oppressive Irish Catholic machine of any city. After examining Irish and African American incorporation in the cities, I compare the political careers of Kennedy in Boston and Massachusetts politics, and Obama in Chicago and Illinois politics.

Chapter 5 views the Al Smith campaign in 1928 and Jesse Jackson's in the 1980s as precursors to the Kennedy and Obama campaigns. The circumstances of the Smith and Jackson campaigns are quite different, but exploring the role of religion and race in both is illuminating. In addition, both Smith and Jackson were consciously "ethnic" in their presentations of self, whereas Kennedy and Obama were consciously postethnic candidates. In other words Smith was Irish and Catholic and Jackson was black, whereas with Kennedy and Obama, questions were raised about how Irish and Catholic Kennedy was and how black Obama was.

Chapter 6 compares the degree of incorporation and assimilation of the two groups in 1960 and 2008. In addition to comparing the social, economic, and political incorporation of the two communities, the chapter also studies the extent of integration of the groups in sport and popular culture. This comparison shows in a detailed way the more rigid character in the United States of pan-ethnic white racism as form of ethnic subordination with respect to African Americans, compared to Anglo-Saxon nativism with respect to the Catholic Irish.

Chapter 7 focuses on the two men; their personalities, and presidential character, as well as comparing them with respect to their ethnic consciousness and identity. In other words, how Irish and Catholic was Kennedy in 1960 and how black was Obama in 2008?

Chapters 8 and 9 offer detailed comparisons of the primary and general election campaigns of 1960 and 2008, focusing on the roles of religion and race. Although religion was more of an issue in 1960 than was race in 2008, the similarities between the two campaigns in their practice of the politics of ethnic avoidance are striking. The concept of ethnic avoidance as used in the book suggests that the first successful identifiable, consciously ethnic candidate for the presidency of any group is required to campaign and govern in ways that avoid close identification with their ethnic identity and the ethnic-specific interests of their group. In spite of their skillful practice of ethnic avoidance, both Kennedy and Obama suffered "ethnic deficits" at the ballot box, winning by narrower margins than they would have had they been Protestant or white.

Chapter 10 compares the presidencies of Kennedy and Obama. Both were pragmatic, liberal reform presidents, and as the first of their ethnic origins to hold the office, they had to balance the concerns of their ethnic communities within the broader mainstream of U.S. politics. In other words, they had to practice the politics of ethnic avoidance. Kennedy, partly because of the near full incorporation of the Catholics and the Irish, was more successful at this endeavor than Obama.

The last chapter examines the impact of Kennedy's presidency on anti-Catholicism in the United States and the role of religion in politics. The chapter concludes with a speculative analysis of the likely impact of the Obama presidency on the role of race in America, but more important, and unlike Kennedy, the impact of Obama on the need to fully incorporate his still substantially marginalized and oppressed ethnic people. The implications of the politics of ethnic avoidance for ethnic pluralism, diversity, and the American democracy are also discussed.

1

Understanding Ethnicity and Ethnic Incorporation in the United States

Generally, a group distinguishable on the basis of religion, race, language, national origins, immigrant status, or any combination of these *becomes* an ethnic group if it faces subordination or exclusion from a society's opportunity structures on the basis of these ethnic markers. The greater the degree or intensity of the subordination or exclusion, the greater the degree of the ethnic group's consciousness, identity, and tendencies toward ethnic solidarity. Hechter describes this process of creating ethnicity as a "cultural division of labor" where a "superordinate" or dominant group in a society "attempts to regulate the allocation of social roles such that those commonly defined as having high prestige are reserved for its members." Conversely, individuals from the less advanced (subordinate) group are denied access to the roles.[1]

Hechter used this formulation in his study of the "Celtic fringe" in British national development to explain why Wales and Scotland were incorporated into the United Kingdom whereas Ireland pursued nationalism and independence. The explanation for these differential patterns of ethnicity is the greater extent of oppression of the Irish; as Hechter writes, was due to "the especially brutal policies perpetrated by the English and Anglo-Irish settlers in Ireland."[2]

Hechter's formulation also explains why in the United States the Catholic Irish became an ethnic group and the so-called Scotch-Irish did not. The Scotch-Irish—Protestants—were the first Irish immigrants to the United States, coming in relatively large numbers from the colonial era to the 1830s. Confronting little oppression or exclusion from America's opportunity structures, they were fairly quickly incorporated into the Anglo-Saxon or WASP (white Anglo-Saxon Protestant) community and ceased to be ethnic.[3] And when their fellow Catholic Irish nationals began to immigrate in large numbers starting in the 1840s the Scotch-Irish were as hostile to them as they had been in Ireland and as were the Anglo-Saxons, whether in England or New England.[4]

This is not a study of the election of the first person of Irish ancestry to the presidency but the first person of Irish Catholic ancestry. Three Scotch-Irish have been president: Andrew Jackson, James Buchanan, and Chester Arthur (both of Jackson's parents were born in Ireland and one of Arthur's and Buchanan's).[5] But Jackson, Arthur, and Buchanan were not "ethnic" Americans. In 1960 the Scotch-Irish vote for Kennedy was indistinguishable, north and south, from the vote of other white Protestants.[6]

Finally, just as Hechter's understanding of ethnicity explains Irish nationalism compared to Scotch and Welsh incorporation on the British Isles, it also explains the intensity of Irish Catholic "nationalism" in the United States compared to other European immigrant groups with the exception of Jews.[7] At least in New England, Catholic Irish ethnic solidarity exceeded that of other Catholic groups because of the intensity of their exclusion from the opportunity structures in Ireland and the United States. Hechter's formulation also explains the intensity of black ethnic nationalism because in their homelands and in the United States no ethnic group has faced greater oppression and a more rigid cultural division of labor than Africans. For example, on the cultural division of labor specifically between Irish Catholics and African Americans, Ignatiev writes, "At every period, however, the 'white race' has included only groups that did 'white man's work.' But what was 'white man's work'? In the case of the Irish, 'white man's work' could be defined as work they did, when it was precisely their status as 'whites' that was in question. Since 'white' was not a physical description but one term of a social relation which could not exist without its opposite, 'white man's work' was simply, work from which Afro-Americans were excluded. Conversely, 'black man's work' was work monopolized by Afro-Americans."[8]

Ethnicity and Race

"It is superficial and inaccurate," Matthew Holden Jr. writes in *The Politics of the Black Nation*, and "implicit snobbery" to define Italian or Irish Americans as ethnics "but Anglo Protestants as non-ethnic. Each is as ethnic as the other. That implicit snobbery has made it possible for social scientists (and others) to suppose that 'ethnicity' was essentially abnormal, undesirable and would in due course disappear. Such estimates are wrong. Ethnicity is one of the fundamental bases of social organization and social division and is at least as persistent—and often more divisive politically—than social class."[9] Holden's observation highlights the fact that in the United States discussion of ethnicity in both popular and academic discourses often evokes strong feelings and biases.

Since Max Weber first defined the term in the 1920s, social scientists have defined ethnic group in multiple ways.[10] Weber's classic definition understood an ethnic group as "those human groups that entertain a subjective belief in their common descent because of similarities of physical type or customs or both, or because of memories of colonialization; the belief must be important for group formation, furthermore, it does not matter whether an objective blood relationship exists."[11] Most modern scholars of ethnicity accept Weber's definition, as for example, Schermerhorn's slightly modified formulation: "A collectivity within a larger society having real or putative common ancestry, memories of a shared historical past and a cultural focus on one or more symbolic elements defined as the epitome of their peoplehood."[12]

In Hechter's formulation, however, Weber's definition points only to the potential for an ethnic solidarity group, providing necessary but not sufficient conditions for its expression politically. The sufficient condition is subordination, oppression, or exploitation, real or perceived, on the basis of this subjective belief or identity.[13] In other words, "much of the dynamics of interethnic relations derive from the structure of dominance and subordination involved in the majority-minority relations."[14] If a group confronts little or no subordination based on its ethnicity then its manifestations of its ethnicity are likely to be largely symbolic or cultural. However, the more rigid the ethnic-based subordination or exclusion of a group, the more likely it is to express its ethnicity politically as well as culturally.

In the United States race has constituted the most rigid and the most exclusionary basis of ethnic subordination—much more than religion, national origin, or language. In the case of African Americans, the rigidity of their subordination was created and sustained on the basis of skin color, a physical type that made them distinctive and visible when compared to European ethnic immigrant groups.

The more rigid nature of the subordination of blacks has led many scholars of black politics to contend that race is not just another ethnic attribute like religion or nationality, but instead belongs in a separate analytic or theoretical category. Leslie McLemore, for example, writes: "The very foundation of a theory of black politics rests on the clear understanding that Afro-Americans are a *racial* group and not an ethnic group. . . . When we speak of a racial group we are referring to those minorities in a society which are set off from the majority not only by cultural differences but in a more profound sense by skin color (high visibility) and the near total inability of that group to assimilate into the larger society."[15] In this view blacks in the United States should not be considered an ethnic group because their black skin color combined with the tenacity of white racism makes their full incorporation into American society impossible. As Barnett puts it, "Racism, therefore, is a fundamental factor that makes the black situation distinctively different from that of all white ethnic groups."[16]

In the course of this study, considerable historical and empirical evidence are developed that demonstrates the difficulties of black incorporation in the United States when compared to the Catholic Irish. Nevertheless, whether black incorporation is impossible is an empirical question that should not be settled a priori. In the 1940s, Ralph Bunche wrote that it was inconceivable that an African American could ever be elected president; a governor, a senator, a cabinet officer perhaps, but president, never.[17] In 2008 the impossible happen. The near full incorporation of blacks into sport and popular culture (discussed in chapter 6) was considered impossible in the 1940s when Jackie Robinson became the first major league baseball player.

As a scholar of black politics for almost four decades I am pessimistic about the likelihood of the full incorporation of African Americans into U.S. society, polity, or economy, and the evidence from this study tends to confirm that pessimism. However, awareness of the differences in the experiences of African Americans and the Catholic Irish should not blind us theoretically to how much they have in common not only with each other but also with other bases of dominance—subordination such as class, gender, and sexuality. As Isajiw writes, "The scholar of ethnicity must be as aware of the varying conditions of ethnicity over time as of all the conceptual and theoretical possibilities of it."[18] Ultimately, whether African American ethnicity constitutes an impossible barrier to full incorporation is an open question. Theoretically, historically, and empirically this book is a contribution to answering that question.

A Theoretical Model of Ethnic Group Incorporation

Social scientists have generally assumed that, at least in developed societies, over time ethnic groups will wither away as cultural divisions of labor are eliminated, and opportunity structures are opened to all on the basis of individual attributes.[19] In this view, in well-ordered societies rational individuals will organize their politics based on class interests rather than irrelevancies such as race or religion. Hechter models this process of the "deethnicization" of groups into "three analytically separate black boxes," which I use—slightly modified—to compare Irish Catholics and African Americans.[20]

The first is cultural integration or incorporation, which involves the erosion of distinctive ethnic group cultures and the absorption of elements of their cultures into the mainstream or national culture. Evidence of this process includes a common national language and symbolism, and the decline of racism, nativism, and invidious ethnic stereotypes. It also includes the integration of members of the group into the arts, universities, sports, popular culture, and other institutions that "govern the aspirations and values of the masses."[21] Finally, interethnic marriage may be one of the most important indicators of cultural integration.

The second box is economic incorporation. Inclusionary opportunity structures overtime should result in similarities among religious, nationality, and racial groups in education, occupation, income, wealth, and poverty. This does not require exact equality or correspondence between the groups, but it precludes the existence of wide socioeconomic disparities as manifested in concentrated poverty among any particular group.

The third box is political incorporation in which ethnicity ceases to play a significant role in the formation or expression of the group's political attitudes and behavior. Instead, such attitudes tend to be shaped by social class. Second, ethnicity ceases to play a major role in the group's claims on the state. Rather citizens make demands based on their class positions or interests deriving from other than their ethnic origins. Finally, political incorporation requires some rough degree of parity in holding elective and appointive offices, or at least ethnicity is not manifestly a bar to holding appointive or elective office at any level of government. As Domhoff puts it, "When it is determined that a minority group has only a small percentage of its members in leadership positions, even though it comprises 10 to 20 percent of the population, then the basic processes of power inclusion and exclusion are inferred to be at work."[22]

Although not included explicitly as one of the analytical boxes in Hechter's model, residential integration is also an important indicator of a group's incorporation. Residential segregation sustains a "geography" for ethnic consciousness and solidarity. In particular "the concatenation of residential and occupational segregation gives a decisive advantage to the development of ethnic rather than class solidarity."[23] Ethnic ghettos, in other words, both create and sustain ethnic consciousness and perhaps are the most impressive evidence of the lack of incorporation along all three dimensions.

In summing up his model, Hechter advanced three propositions on the prospect for the maintenance of ethnicity. First, the greater the inequalities between groups, the greater the likelihood the disadvantaged group will embrace ethnic solidarity. Second, the greater the frequency of intraethnic relations, the greater the embrace of ethnicity. Third, the greater the differences in culture, real or imagined, the greater the degree of ethnic solidarity. These three propositions are at the same time indicators of the absence of ethnic incorporation, as well as a wish for a degree of autonomy or nationalism on the part of the unincorporated group. These indicators will be of some utility in understanding the ethnic forces shaping the presidential campaigns and presidencies of Kennedy and Obama.

An American Model of Ethnic Incorporation

As indicated, Hechter developed his understanding of ethnicity mainly as a tool to explain the political incorporation of Wales and Scotland into the United Kingdom compared to the path of national independence the Irish pursued. Yet, he was theoretically aware that understanding the situation of the British Isles was related to explaining ethnic change in the United States, especially the failure of African American incorporation.[24]

In *Who Governs?* the American political scientist Robert Dahl developed a three-stage model to explain specifically the incorporation of ethnic immigrant groups and blacks into the U.S. polity.[25] In the first stage, because of the cultural division of labor, the immigrants are disproportionately poor and working class, living in ethnic ghettos. They practice in this stage a ghetto-specific ethnic politics. In the second stage, a sizeable middle class develops, and ethnic solidarity declines, however, it does not disappear because the group as a whole is not incorporated and its middle class "retain[s] a high sensitivity to their ethnic origins."[26] In the third stage, ethnic solidarity withers because the group as whole is fully incorporated with a high degree of socioeconomic differentiation including an upper class as well as a middle class. For the ethnic middle and upper classes, "ethnic politics is often embarrassing" although "a middle-class or upper-class candidate who happens to be from an ethnic group may use this tie to awaken sentiments of pride,"[27] but in the main such candidates run "de-ethnicized" campaigns, emphasizing issues of concern to the broad, mainstream electorate.

Based on an analysis of occupations, residence, and voting patterns in New Haven, Connecticut, Dahl estimates that the Irish Catholics, arriving in the 1840s, remained in the first stage for fifty years—until 1880. They remained in stage two for forty years, entering stage three in the 1930s. African Americans in New Haven entered the first stage in 1784, almost sixty years before the Catholic Irish arrived, and they remained in this first stage for more than a century and half before entering the second stage in the 1950s more than twenty years after the Irish Catholics entered the final stage. Thus, the Catholic Irish took ninety years to move from poor, impoverished ghettoized ethnic immigrants to middle-class to upper-class, fully incorporated Americans.[28] African Americans, conversely, took 166 years to move from a partly free, partly enslaved (slavery was abolished in Connecticut in 1848), impoverished ethnic group to partial incorporation with an incipient middle class along with a still large, impoverished ghettoized core.

Dahl does not explain the anomaly of the African American situation in New Haven presumably because it was obvious that it "emanated largely from the racist perspective of the American social system."[29] That is, it is the intensity of racism directed toward the black ethnic collectivity compared to the Irish and other European ethnic immigrant groups in New Haven that explains the persistence of their exclusion from the city's opportunity structure and their persistence as the most ethnic nationalist of the city's ethnic groups. As the following chapters demonstrate, this pattern of intense exclusionary racism compared to a more benign nativism against Irish Catholics also characterized Boston and Chicago. This differential indeed characterizes the whole of America and constitutes one of the major differences in the history and context in which Kennedy and Obama sought the presidency.

The first Catholic Irish mayor of New Haven was elected in 1899, near the beginning of their entry into the second stage of incorporation. The first African American mayor of New Haven was elected in 1989, almost a half century after blacks entered the second stage of incorporation. Although sensitive to the ties of ethnic origins, John Daniels—the city's first black mayor—ran a deracialized campaign that appealed to the broad mainstream of New Haven's electorate.[30] With a population only one-third black, he had no choice except to downplay his ethnic ties and interests. However, like U.S. cities elsewhere, New Haven's core black community is segregated and impoverished with some conditions "reaching Third World proportions."[31]

When Obama was elected president, African Americans nationally were in the second stage of incorporation, entering it in the late

1960s. When Kennedy was elected in 1960, Irish Catholics were in the third stage nationally, entering it in the 1930s. Understanding the consequences of this on their campaigns and presidencies is the central concern of this book. But first we need to go back to the histories of the Irish Catholic and African peoples in their homelands—and in America, which will help us understand their stages of incorporation.

2

The Subordination of Irish Catholics and African Americans

The Colonial Experience

Ireland

The oppression of the Catholics of Ireland has been described as an almost "ideal-typical" case of colonialism, providing the English valuable experience that they later used to colonize Africa and other parts of the world.[1] The English conquest of Ireland in the twelfth century inaugurated centuries of subordination that did not come fully to an end until the establishment of the Irish Free State in 1922 and continues to some extent even today with British control of northern Ireland. Although phenotypically identical, English attitudes toward Irish Catholics resemble in some ways those displayed toward Africans and other peoples of color. David Brion Davis writes, "However unflattering the usual African stereotype may have been, it was probably less derogatory and venomous then that applied at this time to the Irish, who were undoubtedly white."[2] The English generally regarded the Catholic Irish as a barbaric, inferior people who were an embarrassment to the race. A nineteenth-century Cambridge University historian traveling in the Irish countryside wrote, "But I am haunted by the human chimpanzees I saw along that hundred miles of horrible country. I don't believe they are our fault. I believe there are not only many more of them than of old, but they are happier, better, more comfortably fed and lodged under our rule than they ever were. But to see white chimpanzees is dreadful; if they were black, one would not feel so much, but their skins, except tanned by exposure, are as white as ours."[3]

In 1695 the English imposed on Ireland the Penal Laws. Not fully repealed until Catholic emancipation in 1829, the aim of these laws was the destruction of Catholicism in Ireland. Edmund Burke wrote of the

Penal Laws, "A machine as well fitted for the oppression, impoverishment and degradation of a people, and the debasement in them of human nature itself, as ever preceded from the perverted ingenuity of man."[4]

The Penal Laws have in their depravity sometimes been compared to the slave codes in the United States.[5] Although the English in Ireland for sure did not go as far as their cousins in the American South, "there did sprang [*sic*] up in those days the infamous trade of priest-hunting, 'five pounds' being equally the government price for the head of a priest or for the head of a wolf."[6] Among the provisions of the comprehensive code, the Catholic Irish were forbidden to:

> receive education; exercise his religion; enter a profession; hold public office; engage in trade or commerce; live in a corporate town or within five miles thereof; own a horse of greater value than five pounds; purchase land; lease land; accept a mortgage on land in security for a loan; vote; keep any arms for his protection; hold a life annuity; buy land from a Protestant; receive a gift of land from a Protestant; inherit land from a Protestant; rent any land worth more than thirty shillings a year; reap from his land any profit exceeding a third of the rent; be a guardian to a child; leave his infant children under Catholic guardianship when dying; attend Catholic worship; and [were] compelled by law to attend Protestant worship. The priest was banned and hunted with bloodhounds. The schoolmaster was banned and hunted with bloodhounds.[7]

While not seizing the bodies and babies of the Catholics as their counterparts did with respect to the Africans in the United States, the English in Ireland did seize the land and destroy the language. By the mid-eighteenth century, the English held more than 90 percent of the land of Ireland,[8] and in order to accommodate English dominance, the Irish had to gradually abandon Gaelic and embrace the English language in order to survive.

In one sense the penultimate manifestation of English oppression came with the "Great Hunger." Although not a genocide (in the strict sense of an effort to eliminate a specific ethnic group), from 1846 to 1851 experts estimate that between 1 million and 1.5 million Catholics died from starvation or from diseases related to malnutrition.[9] The spectra of genocide are raised because while the people of Ireland were "eating the bark off trees," huge amounts of food were shipped from Ireland to England.[10] Although the British government may have made some genuine efforts to deal with the famine,[11] exporting food from the land of a starving people if not genocide is at a minimum criminal indifference to misery and death on a massive scale of an oppressed people different in ethnicity.

In a sense though it does not matter what the British did substantively during the famine to relieve the misery because the millions of dead became a symbol of the long Catholic Irish memory of centuries of English oppression. "Deeply engraved on the memory of the Irish race," Woodham-Smith writes, so that "all hope of assimilation with England was then lost, and bitterness without parallel took hold of the Irish mind."[12]

Although Irish Catholic immigration to the United States goes back to the colonial era and there was a steady flow between the 1830s and 1840s, after the famine more than one million came in a single decade.[13] On their journey across the Atlantic an estimated one-third died on the "coffin ships."[14] The Catholic Irish sojourn is often compared to the middle passage of the African slave trade. Indeed, Whalen writes, "The Negro, as valuable property, probably fared better than the Irishman, who was looked upon as worthless chaff."[15] In his memoir *Man of the House*, Tip O'Neill recalls that he still had the deed to a cemetery plot his grandfather purchased when he arrived in Boston: "The immigrants had seen such death during the potato famine that the first thing they did when they came to America was to buy a plot to be buried in—just in case."[16]

Memories of English colonialism shaped Catholic Irish consciousness, identity, solidarity, and politics in the United States. This heritage shaped their attitudes and behavior throughout the United States, but especially in Boston where they confronted Americans who in their attitudes and behavior resembled the Anglo-Saxons who had so brutally oppressed them in Ireland.

Africa

At a conference in Berlin in 1884 the leaders of Europe divided the land and peoples of Africa among themselves. The British took the larger share, but Germany, France, and Portugal also colonized large areas of the continent. Perhaps the most egregious case of European colonialism in Africa was Belgian rule in the Congo. One of the great mass killings of all time, the "Congo holocaust" between 1885 and 1910, may have resulted in the death of more than 10 million people, reducing the population of the Congo by at least half.[17]

Unique among the European colonies, the Congo was the personal property of Belgian King Leopold, whom the international community (with the United States taking the lead) recognized as the "King Sovereign" of the territory.[18] The Penal Laws, as Burke said, constituted a perverted form of oppression and degradation, but they do not compare in depravity to the "rubber terror" in Leopold's Congo.

In pursuit of profits from the harvesting of the Congo's huge rubber resources, the Belgians systematically worked people to death; women were seized to force their husbands to work; young men were forced to rape and kill their mothers and sisters; the "chicottee," a whip of raw sun-dried hippopotamus hide, was used in "relentless" floggings; and salt was literally rubbed into the wounds.[19] The practice of "priest hunting" shocks the conscience, but in the Congo "murderous head collectors" engaged in a systematic policy of cutting off the heads of Congolese people.[20]

The Congo is the worst example of European colonialization of Africans but Hochshild concludes, "the sad truth is that the men who carried it out for Leopold were no more murderous than many Europeans then at work or war elsewhere in Africa," including Kenya.[21]

Unlike the Catholics in Ireland, the Congolese could not immigrate to America to escape their oppression. On the contrary, one of every four enslaved African transported to the United States came from the Congo region.[22] The oppression that the Catholic Irish and Congolese Africans would face in the United States would be almost as different as the oppression they faced in their homelands.

Before turning to these experiences, the Congo shows in another way the relationship between the African American and Irish Catholic experiences. Roger Casement, a British consular officer, is credited with yeoman's work in exposing Leopold's terror. A native of Ireland, Casement as a result of his work in the Congo came to realize that Ireland too was a colony and joined in the struggle for the liberation of his homeland. Casement concluded, "It was only because I was an Irishman that I could understand *fully*, I think the whole scheme of wrong doing at work on the Congo. . . . I realized that I was looking at the tragedy [in the Congo] with the eyes of another race of people once hunted themselves."[23]

This sense of solidarity of the oppressed, as we shall see, did not survive the journey of the Irish across the Atlantic. In the United States the Catholic Irish became leading opponents of the abolitionist movement and of the war that would liberate the enslaved Africans. In other words, the oppressed Catholics joined with their English oppressors to oppress the Africans in order to "become white."[24]

The American Experience

The Catholic Irish

In his classic account of nativism—the tradition in the United States of intolerance of foreign-born persons—Higham contends that anti-Catholicism, the oldest and most powerful element of the tradition, has been so pervasive that historians have frequently regarded the two as synomous.[25] Anti-Catholic nativism in the United States was, as Higham understands it, an important part of the "British national consciousness." Growing out of the "shock of the Reformation" and British rivalry with the Catholic powers of Europe, disdain of Catholicism and the Pope formed a part of the early British heritage of the American colonies.

Although two Catholics were among the signers of the Declaration of Independence (including Charles Carroll, brother of John Carroll the first Catholic bishop in the United States) and many fought in the Revolutionary War, repression of Catholicism was widespread in colonial America. Of the colonies only Rhode Island granted full legal equality to Catholics, and even there, Roger Williams, its founder, declared the Roman church a "wolf" and a "popish leviathan."[26] In 1649 Virginia declared that "no popish followers" could hold office or vote, and priests were forbidden to enter the state.[27] The Massachusetts General Court in 1647 legislated that any "Jesuit or priest coming within the colony was to be 'banished,' and if returned executed."[28] Most Catholics in the colonial era lived in Maryland where, under a 1632 charter granted to Lord Baltimore, religious tolerance was the law. But soon after Protestants gained power in the state they repealed the acts of tolerance and passed legislation declaring "none who profess the exercise of the popish religion . . . can be protected in this province."[29] Although the U.S. Constitution specifically prohibited any religious test for holding federal office, seven state constitutions barred Catholics from holding office.[30]

Anti-Catholic nativism was not in the colonial era based on Anglo-Saxon racism or a developed sense of the inherent inferiority of Catholics. This was to come later. Rather, hostility to Roman Catholicism was rooted in the Reformation; the Pope's alliance with the feudal, monarchical powers of Europe; and the view that the Pope was an authoritarian monarch bent on undermining republican values and institutions. To many, perhaps most, Americans, then, Catholicism "was not just another Christian denomination, another way of interpreting God and Christ but a mélange of superstition, corruption and authoritarianism,"[31] and the Pope was not just another preacher but the "whore of Babylon," the "Great Harlot," and the "Anti-Christ."[32]

This bigotry was reinforced when in 1864 Pope Pius IX promulgated the Syllabus of Errors, which condemned freedom of religion and the separation of church and state, and in 1887 when the Vatican articulated the doctrine of papal infallibility. The ideas that the Roman church and its leaders were a threat to democracy, and that Catholics in America were more loyal to Rome than Washington, were thereby reinforced.

There was also fascination with "popish brothels" and "priest harems," as reported in pamphlets and from pulpits that priests and nuns in convents were engaged in pathological sexual activities. The most infamous example of this genre was the 1836 bestseller, Maria Monk's *Awful Disclosures of the Hotel Dieu Monastery.* This fabricated work, by a mentally retarded woman who claimed to be a nun, proclaimed that priests forced nuns to have sex, and then baptized, strangled, and buried the babies in the church basement.[33]

These patterns of anti-Catholic nativism were extant in the culture when the Catholic Irish began to arrive in the millions after the famine. Unlike subsequent Catholic immigrants, the Irish came from "the most devoutly and uniformly Catholic country in the modern world."[34] In addition, unlike the Italians or Poles, the Irish had faced systematic Anglo-Saxon oppression because of their religion, forging a bond of ethnic identity, consciousness, and solidarity unique among immigrant groups. As a result in the United States, religion and the church became integral parts of Catholic Irish culture, a haven in a heartless world. Finally, as the first large group of Catholic immigrants, the Irish quickly came to dominate the church hierarchy (as late as the 1950s all but one of the ten native-born Cardinals in the United States were of Irish origins). In other words, for a long time the Catholic Church in America was the Irish Catholic Church. The Irish became the symbol of Catholicism, and this link reinforced Anglo-Saxon nativism.

The Catholic Irish came mainly from the rural bogs of Ireland, but in America they became the quintessential urban people. Efforts to settle them in the rural Midwest and upper Middle West failed. The result was that the prejudices of rural, small-town America toward the big cities could be focused on the Irish Catholics. The saloon, crime, "pauperism," ghettos, and the corruption of the big-city machines congealed into an ethnic-religious stereotype—the Irish Mick or Paddy—rather than the Jeffersonian idea of the self-reliant artisan and yeoman farmer.[35]

If the church was the most important formation in the institutional culture of the Catholic Irish community in America, close behind was the parochial school. In order to maintain their religious heritage in a hostile Protestant environment, Catholic clergy and parents early on decided they needed schools of their own. Soon thereafter these parents and clergy concluded that if their taxes were used to support "Protestant" public schools then fairness required public support for their schools. Perhaps no other decision had a more important impact on furthering the divide between Catholics and Protestants than the decision to create a separate system of education for Catholic children. Many Protestants viewed the schools as un-American, authoritarian, anti-intellectual parochial institutions, and were outraged when Catholic leaders sought public support for them. As early as 1875, President Grant in his annual message to Congress thought the issue so important that he proposed an amendment to the Constitution to prohibit appropriations of public funds for "denominational schools."[36] Federal aid to parochial schools was the major "Catholic" issue of the 1960 election.

In the 1840s the anti-Catholic Know-Nothing movement emerged. Urging strict limitations on Catholic immigration and restrictions on the right of immigrants to hold office, the movement was able to elect seventy-five members of Congress in 1854.[37] In Massachusetts the Know-Nothings in the 1850s elected governors and a majority of the state legislature. The Know-Nothings had little success in enacting their program and declined as a force in national politics as the Civil War approached, but their strident attacks on Catholicism helped to strengthen bonds of solidarity among the Catholic Irish.[38]

Nativist agitation against Catholics and Catholicism continued with the formation in 1887 of the American Protective Association (APA). Like the Know-Nothings, the APA sought to restrict immigration and prohibit Catholics from holding office.[39] In the 1920s the Ku Klux Klan was revitalized. Unlike the old Klan, this new incarnation limited membership to native-born white Protestants and along with white racism it embraced an all-encompassing "Anglo-Saxon nationalism" that was anti-Semitic and anti-Catholic. Partly because "the Negro had been successfully put in his place," anti-Catholicism for this new Klan surpassed racism as a concern.[40]

Also during this period, within the Anglo-Saxon establishment, a new "semi-scientific racism" was developing that defined non-Nordic "races" as inherently inferior.[41] This "Anglo-Saxon racism" extended to Jews and Catholics "that sense of absolute difference" that divided white from black.[42] For example, in his 1923 book *A Study of American Intelligence*, Carl Brigham concludes that the "Alpine races" such as the Catholics were the "perfect slave" because of their "lack of coordinating and reasoning power."[43] This racist, nativist propaganda fueled the passage of the Immigration Act of 1924, which restricted immigration from the non-Nordic parts of Europe.[44]

In 1919, partly as a result of the agitation of the Klan and fundamentalist Protestant clergy against "papist owned saloons," the Eighteenth Amendment, which banned the use of alcohol in the United States, was adopted.[45] In 1928 prohibition became an issue in the defeat of the first major party Catholic nominee for president.

Meanwhile, however, Catholic voting power was growing in all regions of the United States outside of the South, but especially in the electorally crucial Northeast and Middle Atlantic states. The growth of Catholic power at the ballot box by the beginnings of the twentieth century inevitably became a part of the strategic calculus of the elites of both major parties as they competed for office at local, state, and national levels.

The African Americans

"Nothing," James Melton writes, compares with the "cosmic arrogance of slavery" because "even the most brutal, most unabashedly nihilistic of tyrants of the twentieth century have stopped short of claiming their victims as personal property . . . to be physically owned . . . traded for a mule or a cow or simply lost by one's owner in a card game."[46] Slavery and the oppression of the "free" Africans is thus the ultimate expression of Hechter's cultural division of labor.

As Kenneth Stamp's classic work shows, slavery in the United States was above all else a labor system designed for the super exploitation of black bodies and souls.[47] W. E. B. Du Bois estimated that 15 million Africans were transported to the Americas;[48] others put the figure as high as 20 million, and Phillip Curtin, in what is generally considered the most authoritative estimate, puts the figure at between 9 million and 10 million.[49] Whatever the number, scholars generally agree that one-third died on these first "coffin ships" or duing the "seasoning process"—the system of dehumanization designed to turn people into property. This ethnic division of labor, however, was made near immutable by the differences in color between the oppressed and oppressor.

In southern law and custom this division of labor for the enslaved was clearly defined as work from "day clear" to "first dark" and to "breed prolifically" for the profit of the owner.[50] As in the Congo this system was enforced by the whip. This "savage instrument" made of "three feet un-tanned rawhide, an inch thick at the ball end" was routinely employed to terrorize.[51] In his interviews with surviving enslaved persons conducted in the 1930s, Melton found that their most common grievances were being separated from their families and the "bullwhip days." President Lincoln acknowledged the pervasiveness of the bloody instrument when he admonished his countrymen in his second inaugural, "Fondly do we hope, fervently do we pray that this mighty scourge of war may speedily pass away. Yet, if God wills that it continue until all the wealth piled by the bondsman's two hundred and fifty years of unrequited toil shall be sunk, and until every drop of blood drawn with the lash shall be paid by another drawn with the sword, as was said three thousand years ago, so still it must be said 'the judgments of the Lord are true and righteous altogether.'"

Although blacks were not forced to labor and breed like animals, the color-coded division of labor in the North was otherwise almost as rigid as in the South. Theodore Hershberg and his colleagues at the Philadelphia Social History Project at the University of Pennsylvania have studied this northern division of labor in detail,[52] comparing the experiences of Irish and European ethnic groups with African Americans living in nineteenth-century Philadelphia. They conclude, "During the antebellum years, blacks were not only excluded from the new and well paying positions, they were uprooted as well from many of their traditional unskilled jobs, denied apprenticeships for their sons, and prevented from practicing the skills they already possessed."[53] During this period the authors also note blacks were denied the right to vote and were the victims of frequent race riots in which their homes, churches, and schools were repeatedly destroyed, experiences unlike those of the Irish or any other ethnic group in Philadelphia.

Ignatiev notes there were *only* "nine major mob attacks on the black people of Philadelphia in the years 1834–1849" (emphasis in original).[54] And what he describes as a "by-now familiar pattern," the Catholic Irish were in the vanguard in the riots and pogroms perpetuated against Africans.[55]

The Catholic Irish also figured prominently in the opposition to the abolitionist movement. Although prominent Irish leaders in Ireland issued a series of forceful declarations against American slavery, they were overwhelmingly rejected by Irish American media, leaders, and public.[56] In one of the worst riots in U.S, history—the so-called New York City draft riots of 1863—the Irish Catholics attacked African people as part of a rebellion against fighting in Lincoln's war of emancipation.

Understandably the long, stalled process of full black incorporation it is necessary to emphasize that the enslaved Africans were not emancipated because whites, whether North or South, Catholic Irish or Protestant, leaders or ordinary people, came to believe that African slavery was morally unjustifiable. Rather, slavery came to an end as a byproduct of the war to preserve the union. Although Lincoln personally believed that slavery was wrong (writing, "If slavery is not wrong, nothing is wrong"), he steadfastly refused entreaties to wage the war as a moral crusade against slavery. Indeed, he was willing to allow slavery to be maintained forever in the southern states if only they remained in the union.[57] As he famously wrote, "What I do about slavery and the colored race, I do because I believe it helps save the union." As commander-in-chief Lincoln, midway through the war, came to believe that in order to save the union, some of the slaves had to be promised freedom. As he put it he was "driven to the alternative of either surrendering the union or laying strong hand upon the colored element . . . to gain. . . a hundred and thirty thousand soldiers, seamen and laborers."[58] In issuing the famous proclamation, Lincoln decreed freedom only for those enslaved in the rebellious South. Written by the most eloquent of American presidents, Richard Hoftstadter said the proclamation had "all the moral grandeur of a bill of lading," and the *London Speculator* scorned the proclamation as asserting "not that human beings cannot fully own another, but that he cannot own him unless he is loyal to the United States."[59]

Thus, from the outset, whites were ambiguous about liberating African Americans. Indeed, if the southern states had accepted Lincoln's offers and stayed or returned to the union, slavery probably would have been maintained in places like Alabama, Mississippi, and Louisiana well into the twentieth century. This ambiguity may be seen in the adoption of the Thirteenth Amendment. Fearing that his proclamation might be reversed after the war, Lincoln urged the Congress to constitutionally abolish slavery by passing the Thirteenth Amendment, proposed in April 1864. It easily passed the Senate, but it was defeated in the House 95–66, a House we should note that was composed almost entirely of representatives from the northern states. (The amendment passed the House in January 1865, 119–56.) Similarly, the Fourteenth Amendment—declaring liberty and equality under law for the emancipated—would not have been ratified if its ratification was not a precondition for the readmission of southern states to the union.

This grudging, reluctant, ambivalent abolition of slavery is worth underscoring because it helps explain the still-not-complete incorporation of African Americans. Why? Because at emancipation and afterward, most whites still could not "conceive of Negros as men."[60]

After the war the Congress attempted to reconstruct the South on the basis of the equality of all men and build a biracial southern democracy. But the southern rebels waged what was in effect guerrilla war and within a decade overthrew the Reconstruction governments and established a rigid regime of apartheid. Maintained by Ku Klux Klan terror in the south, in the northern states a less rigid cultural division of labor was maintained by riots and pogroms until the 1940s.

In the early twentieth century, W. E. B. Du Bois and Joel Spingarn led a small band of interracial liberals (Jews and upper-status Anglo-Saxons but no Irish Catholics) to begin what would be a decade's long effort to inaugurate a second reconstruction. In the face of southern terror and northern riots, they persisted using lobbying, litigation, marching, and voting (where they could) forcing the President and Congress during the 1960s to once again reconstruct the South on principles of racial equality.[61] However, we should once again underscore that this second reconstruction was like the first and like the abolition of slavery slow, grudging, and ambiguous; undertaken as much out of concern about stability of the system as for moral imperatives.

The first Catholic Irish president was in office when the civil rights movement reached its apogee. President Kennedy's attitudes and actions on civil rights are discussed in chapter 8; suffice it to note here that, like Lincoln's, they were morally obtuse, politically calculating, and hesitant.

With Lyndon Johnson's committed and strategically sophisticated leadership, civil rights legislation and more were enacted after Kennedy's death. President Johnson, however, recognized that more than 300 years of a rigid cultural division of labor had rendered the blacks a severely disadvantaged group requiring extensive government remedial actions to fully incorporate them into the society. As he told Howard University's 1965 graduating class, "you do not take a person who, for years, has been hobbled by chains and liberate him, bring him up to the starting line of a race and then say 'you are free to compete with others,' and still justly believe that you have been completely fair."[62]

Pursuant to the objectives outlined in the speech, the President initiated the Great Society, the war on poverty, and the beginnings of affirmative action as a strategy to accelerate processes of incorporation. By 1968, however, a neoracist, conservative movement was beginning to take hold and by 1980 it was ascendant. Its ascendancy did not bring an end to the second reconstruction, but it did effectively end the war on poverty and other efforts to facilitate social and economic incorporation.[63]

In the "Age of Reagan" the national consensus became that the failure of blacks to achieve full incorporation like the Catholic Irish was their own fault. In other words, the white ethnic policy consensus was that African Americans were morally inferior, lacking family values, individual initiative, and an ethos of hard work and communal self-help.

From slavery through the first and second Reconstructions, the race-based cultural division of labor and apartheid was justified on the basis of the ideology of white supremacy. This ideology, based on philosophical, religious, scientific, and cultural elements, defined the African American ethnic group. It is within the context of this ideology, the conservative policy consensus on race and only second stage incorporation, that the first of the group won the presidency, a context wholly unlike the election of the first Catholic Irish president. Chapter 6 compares the state of incorporation of the Catholic Irish and the blacks in 1960 and 2008. But first I return to the time when the Catholic Irish were also unincorporated, stigmatized, and stereotyped as an inferior people, and a comparison of the development among the two groups of consciousness, identity, and solidarity.

3

Identity, Consciousness, Solidarity, and Culture

Irish Catholics and African Americans

The classic weapon of the ethnic oppressed is solidarity, derived from consciousness of one's identity and the need to organize on that basis to survive in a hostile environment. Individuals in solidarity groups think in terms of the effects of societal decisions on the group and feel they are in some ways personally affected by what happens to the group.[1] This solidarity is always accompanied by some consciousness of another group—defined as ethnic—as adversarial or hostile. Real or imagined cultural differences also distinguish the groups. Depending on the extent of cultural differences, the extent of oppression, or both, solidarity groups exhibit varying levels of "institutional completeness."[2] Finally, ethnic solidarity groups establish boundaries—social, cultural, and political—that, if individuals cross, they face isolation, marginalization, and contempt. This boundary maintenance function is often viewed as essential to the maintenance of the group's ethnicity.

Each of the foregoing aspects of solidarity groups has marked the experience of the Catholic Irish and African Americans in varying degrees depending on historical time and place. In other words, the ethnic politics of the two groups has been a function of the particularities of their subordination at various times and places in the United States. It is also a function of the relative populations of the two groups in relationship to Anglo-Saxons and whites. Catholic Irish solidarity, for example, may have been stronger in Boston and New England, whereas black solidarity may have been most attenuated in that city and region.

In his classic analysis of nineteenth-century Boston, Handlin writes, "only the Negroes developed a group consciousness comparable to that of the Irish."[3] However, he pointed out that black ethnic consciousness was more contingent and ambivalent than the Catholic Irish because black ethnicity derived not from cultural differences they desired to maintain, but from racial segregation and exclusion they desired to abolish. Thus, for example, as soon as school segregation was prohibited in Boston African Americans closed their separate schools.[4]

This ambivalent black identity and skepticism about separate institutions in Boston characterized black ethnicity throughout the United States with the dominant integrationist black leadership opposing institutional completeness arguing it was a form of self-segregation to be embraced only as a last resort. As Meier puts it, "On the one hand white hostility has led Negroes to regard the creation of their own institutions as either necessary or wise, on the other hand these institutions reinforced and perpetuated thinking favorable to group separatism."[5] No such ambivalence marked Catholic Irish ethnicity in Boston. They embraced ethnic identity because of Anglo-Saxon hostility but also because they wished in nineteenth-century Boston and elsewhere to preserve their cultural heritage. At the core of this heritage was Catholicism. Excluded from participation in many aspects of secular life in Boston and unwilling to participate in its religious life, the Catholic Irish, unlike the blacks, eagerly embraced institutional completeness in an effort to "erect a society within a society."[6]

Unlike African Americans, many Catholic Irish immigrants considered integration with Protestants a betrayal, an unforgiveable breach of ethnic boundaries. As the *Boston Pilot*, the city's leading Catholic Irish newspaper assessed, in words that echo Elijah Muhammad in the 1960s, "cooperation for any length of time in important matters between *true* Catholics and *real* protestants is morally impossible . . . tantamount to loss of faith."[7]

African Americans and Irish Catholics have displayed relatively high degrees of ethnic identity and consciousness. The two groups also exhibit other similarities, including placing high value on religion, the church, and clergy. Both groups have also exhibited a proclivity for politics, especially urban politics. An emphasis on oratory has also been an important feature of their political cultures, and each group has exhibited a tendency toward "centrifugalism" or tensions between the "bourgeoisie" and the "folk."[8]

As oppressed peoples the Irish Catholics and the blacks turned to the "solace of religion." Holden describes faith, the belief that "God will deliver us some day" as the single most common theme in African American culture.[9] Wittke describes the Catholic Irish as "a people of the parish" who in the midst of poverty and oppression could always rely on the "solace of religion."[10] Since both groups were for a time excluded from mainstream political processes and leadership positions, the church or parish also became political arenas and the clergy important political leaders.[11] Oratory or an appreciation of "men with a gift for words" or "blarney" was characteristic of Catholic Irish culture,[12] and Holden writes a black leader had better be a "good talker" because "the black culture is a culture in which, relatively speaking, oratorical-debating competence is far more praise worthy than technical bureaucratic skill or the investment of oneself in the tedium of organizational detail."[13]

Levine writes, "For most of their history . . . politics has been as vital a part of the Irish social structure, as important to their identity and way of life as was Catholicism."[14] From Reconstruction until the post–civil rights era, African Americans—excluded from business, the professions, the academy, and trade unions—turned to politics.[15]

Whether from the boggy countryside of Ireland or the backwaters of the rural South, the Catholic Irish and the blacks came to the cities and urban became almost synonymous, at different times, with being Irish or black. From the late nineteenth century until the 1950s, urban politics became almost synonymous with the Catholic Irish and thereafter with African Americans. The urban political machines were important bases of power, facilitating the initial political incorporation of the Catholic Irish and the blacks,[16] although their role in the economic incorporation of the groups is less clear.[17]

The two groups at the national level both developed parallel organizations for virtually every Anglo-Saxon or white organization in the United States. This relatively high level of institutional completeness is indicated by the existence of separate Catholic and black organizations in the professions, medicine, law, arts, and sport, as well as for women and youth. The United States has more than 100 historically black colleges and universities and more than 200 Catholic colleges and universities. Blacks initially organized these parallel institutions because they were excluded from or segregated in the "white" organizations, however, as discussed later, in the 1960s they organized along these lines separately purely for solidarity reasons.

Two institutions are distinctive to Catholic Irish ethnicity in the United States: the parochial school system and the saloon.

Most schools in the United States were Protestant—aggressively so—including the great universities such as Harvard, Princeton, and Yale. In Boston in 1859, a young Catholic boy was beaten by his teacher because he refused to read the Protestant Bible, sparking the movement to establish a Catholic school system.[18] In 1880 the archbishop of Boston said that wherever possible the church would withdraw all children from the public schools.[19] In 1884 the Third Plenary Council at Baltimore "laid down the first rule that every parish priest must have a Catholic school attached to his church."[20] The Catholic school system is therefore partly a reaction to Protestant prejudice, but it was also established as a "self-contained social system which Irish solidarity drew much of its strength."[21]

Although many Catholic families could not afford to send their children to church schools, the admonition to attend and the existence of the schools were symbolic of the intent of the Catholic Irish to remain Catholic and Irish in America. The parochial school system to Anglo-Saxons became a symbol of Irish Catholic unwillingness to Americanize and, once the demand for public support became an issue, a source of anti-Catholic sentiments.

The Catholic Irish saloon has been often described as the "poor man's club" and the "club of the laboring class."[22] Early in their sojourn the saloon became for Catholic Irish men a center of community life and political networking and mobilization, with the prosperous saloonkeeper (such as President Kennedy's fraternal grandfather) becoming an informal banker and political broker. These "instrumental agents in reinforcing solidarity" also were instrumental in the "maintenance of the tradition of excessive alcohol consumption."[23] A dominant social fact of the Irish community, Daniel Patrick Moynihan wrote, "[Great] is the number of good men who are destroyed by drink."[24]

Alcohol consumption or the use of mind-altering substances has frequently marked the cultures of poor, oppressed peoples.[25] In Ireland prior to the famine, alcohol consumption was a minor irritant, but the terrible conditions of the famine turned it into a serious problem, which was exploited in the United States. In America whiskey was cheaper (employers often used it as partial compensation for labor) and more accessible than in Ireland. Its consumption therefore became more widespread because it was a ". . . tonic, a restorative. To men desperate and despairing, it offered a temporary escape. Many Irish males (and some females) drink to endure their miserable lot or forget it."[26]

Although hard drinking declined as socioeconomic conditions improved, the stereotype of the drunken, fighting Irishman became the "shame of the cities," and was one of the factors in the Anglo-Saxon nativist push to impose prohibition. Levine writes:

> There is an interesting parallel between the Irish, prior to the time significant numbers of them reached middle-class status, and Negroes of the past as well as of today. The vocabulary of both groups contain terms ("lace-curtain" for the Irish, and "hincty" and "dicty" for the Negroes) used exclusively to describe those who have or pretend to have "achieved."

> These terms have no counterparts which accord distinction or recognition to the individuals who have risen to the socioeconomic level of the dominant, but strongly resented, society. The implication for both the Irish and the Negroes has been that such success irrevocably severs one from his group because it requires "conversion" to the values of the "enemy."[27]

The "lace-curtain" Irish in the eyes of the "shanty" were sellouts who ostentatiously displayed the lifestyles of the Anglo-Saxons while disparaging those left behind in the old neighborhoods as "ghetto" or "shanty." As the *Boston Pilot* editorialized, "No people have been more neglectful of its poor than the rich and educated Irish of America."[28]

This kind of centrifugal force always characterizes the culture of an oppressed ethnic community. Randall Kennedy writes, "A long-oppressed minority situated in the midst of a dominant white majority, blacks fear that whites will favor and corrupt acquiescent Negroes, who from a position of privilege, will neglect struggles for group elevation."[29] Thus, in African American culture, one observes "the ritualistic condemnation of Negro leaders" and the "black bourgeoisies" as "sellouts" and "Uncle Toms."[30] Unlike the Catholic Irish, in the African American community this phenomenon is exacerbated by "color snobbery" because the black middle class and leadership historically have tended to be mulattos or persons of light skin color.[31]

John F. Kennedy was the epitome of lace-curtain Irish when he ran in 1960; indeed an Irish Brahmin. Barack Obama was the essence of the dicty mulatto when he ran in 2008. Questions were raised in both cases about how ethnic they were; how Catholic and Irish Kennedy was and how black Obama was.

Interethnic marriage is for many the ultimate sell out, the ultimate going beyond the boundaries of ethnicity. Conversely, interethnic marriage is also perhaps the ultimate indicator of ethnic group incorporation.

In Handlin's nineteenth-century Boston, "the percentage of Irish intermarriage was lower than that of any other group including Negroes, 12 percent of whose marriages were with whites."[32] In the 1920s when her oldest daughter became engaged to a Protestant (and a member of the English nobility, the Duke of Devonshire) Rose Kennedy, having always taught her children to "Be Irish, Be Catholic," was said to have been "heartbroken and horrified."[33] She worried that it would not only set a precedent for her other children, but more important for Irish Catholic children throughout the country. "I thought," she said, "it would have such mighty repercussions in that every little young girl would say if Kathleen Kennedy can, why can't I . . . everyone pointed to our family with pride as well-behaved, level headed and deeply religious. What a blow to family prestige."[34] Although Joseph P. Kennedy was not as horrified as his wife at his daughter's marriage, he insisted, for political reasons, that his sons marry nice, lace-curtain Catholic girls.[35]

Because of the ambivalence about integration, the prohibition on interracial marriage in the African American community was not as strong as among the Catholic Irish.[36] But it was nevertheless a powerful sentiment as revealed in the controversies involving the interracial marriages of Frederick Douglass in the 1880s and the National Association for the Advancement of Colored People (NAACP) head Walter White in the 1940s, and it would have been more difficult—probably impossible—for Obama to have won the overwhelming support of blacks—especially women—if he had been married to a white woman or even a white-looking black woman.

Postscript: The Irony of Black Power

By the 1960s the processes that would result in the full incorporation of the Catholic Irish—social, economic, cultural, and political—were near complete. Consequently, Catholic Irish identity, consciousness, and culture were also disappearing. For African Americans the 1960s represented the beginnings of the processes to remove the legal barriers to incorporation. The irony is that these processes resulted in a revitalized black ethnicity that forthrightly and successfully challenged the ambivalent, integrationist ethos of the earlier black ethnicity. Thus, as Catholic Irish ethnicity was withering away black ethnicity was flowering. The withering of the one and the flowering of the other shaped both the Kennedy and Obama campaigns.

Scholars have identified multiple origins and consequences of the 1960s black power movement.[37] Fundamentally, however, it was a rejection of the dominant interracial, integrationist ideology of the civil rights movement. It was, in other words, a call for a consciousness and affirmation of a *black* ethnic solidarity. The black power advocates also created a new set of racially exclusive, autonomous parallel black organizations, which included groups like the Congressional Black Caucus, National Conference of Black Political Scientists, National Association of Black Lawyers, and the National Association of Black Journalists.

Paradoxically, advocates viewed black power as the most efficacious means to achieve full social, economic, and political incorporation. As

Carmichael and Hamilton wrote, "Before a group can enter the open society, it must close ranks."[38] Contending this was the path the Irish and other European ethnic groups followed, black power advocates were proponents of a militant ethnic solidarity and pluralism.

In the late 1960s and early 1970s, scholars observed a substantial increase in black ethnic solidarity at the mass level, noting that as a "result of black power the appropriate dimension for understanding the political behavior of black citizens may have changed. Contemporary black leaders may have helped shape the political meaning of being black in ways black leaders two decades before could not. Certainty, racial identity is now the most useful prescriptive measure of the political choice of many citizens."[39] Black power also resulted in a revival of cultural nationalism with the black arts movement, Afrocentrism, and African American studies.[40]

This racial group consciousness, identity, and solidarity cut across class lines to include all strata of blacks:

> Upper status blacks who have broken free from traditional moorings have become part of a *black political community* which includes persons from all social classes. The response of these upper status blacks to questions about the interpretations of significant events and the evaluation of leaders are more strongly affected by their sense of empathy and identification with their racial community than by their feelings of achievement or even their personal expectations for the future. They share a set of beliefs and a mood of protest about racial issues with those lower status segments of the black community who have also assimilated the secular culture typical of the urban north.[41]

This revitalized African American ethnic tradition contributed to the continuing significance of race, culturally and politically, in American life and established new boundaries of blackness in the community. Barack Obama came of age within these new boundaries and had to closely negotiate them in his personal search for identity and throughout his political career, but especially as he sought to become the first black president. As Ronald Walters argued at the outset of the 2008 campaign, "It is legitimate that Black Americans raise questions about Obama's 'blackness' as an objective issue, because it is the core concept that defines the basic cultural identity of Black people."[42] These questions were raised, and in answering them Obama secured the ethnic base essential to his winning the nomination and the presidency.

4

Boston, Chicago, and the Rise of Kennedy and Obama

Boston has been described as a "caste-ridden city" where the aristocratically pretentious "Brahmins," tracing their ancestry to the English founders of the city, "generally regarded the Irish as members of a barbaric, inferior and unmanageable race and who saw themselves as representatives of a superior English culture."[1] Boston's Brahmins, however, were relatively sympathetic to enslaved Africans and the city became something of a haven for free blacks and a citadel of abolitionism.

The Boston Brahmins, the African Americans, and the Irish Catholics

By the 1860s, Handlin contends that blacks were better off economically and politically in Boston than any other place—in the United States.[2] Better off than the Catholic Irish who were "unquestionably" lowest in the occupational hierarchy.[3] In Handlin's Boston, blacks were more socially incorporated with their 12 percent intermarriage rate vastly exceeding the Catholic Irish.[4] In 1866 blacks were elected to the state legislature and thereafter they were frequently elected to office, always from majority white constituencies.

Frederick Douglass described Massachusetts Senator Charles Sumner as the greatest friend the Negro ever had in public life. Nearly beaten to death on the Senate floor for his outspoken championing of the cause of African freedom, Sumner, with the evident support of his constituents, led the fight in Congress after the Civil War for civil rights legislation and passage of the Fourteenth and Fifteenth Amendments. With Congressman Thaddeus Stevens of Pennsylvania, Sumner was also responsible for the idea of "Forty Acres and a Mule," introducing legislation to confiscate the slaveholders' plantations, divide them up, and give them to the Africans as compensation or reparation, and as a means to punish the slaveholders for treason.

In 1850, Sumner filed the first school desegregation suit in the United States. Although *Sarah v. Roberts* was unsuccessful, in 1853 the Massachusetts legislature abolished segregation in public schools and in 1865 adopted a stature prohibiting racial discrimination in all public places.

Blacks in antebellum Boston by no means enjoyed complete incorporation and Handlin does not suggest otherwise, but he writes they were far better off than the Catholic Irish, who were "segregated in their murky slums, in their lowly occupations and their dread of losing religion."[5] The Catholic Irish immigrants to Boston during the antebellum era faced discrimination in employment, housing, schooling, and policing in an atmosphere of pervasive Anglo-Saxon bigotry and chauvinism. Occasional anti-Catholic riots also broke out, giving rise to what House Speaker Tip O'Neill described as a "tremendous hatred of the English in Irish neighborhoods."[6]

The worst case of Protestant anti-Catholicism in Boston was the 1834 burning of the Ursuline Convent in nearby Charlestown. Described by one historian as "one of the darkest incidents of religious persecution to be recorded in the new world,"[7] the convent was burned by a mob after an inflammatory sermon by the Reverend Lyman Beecher.[8]

An elite boarding school for young, mostly Protestant women, the convent was destroyed by a mob led by John Buzzell, who was acquitted and later became something of a folk hero throughout New England eventually winning election to the New Hampshire legislature. Burned into Catholic Irish consciousness Tip O'Neill recalls that the incident was a "favorite topic" in his neighborhood during his youth; "what those Protestant Yankees did to those poor Irish Catholic nuns" could stir the men into a "frenzy . . . as though it happened the day before yesterday."[9]

This kind of overt, blatant oppression of the Catholic Irish, however, began to wither away after the first generation, and the succeeding generations rapidly incorporated leaving the African American in Boston far behind. Indeed, as the Catholic Irish ascended in Boston and the influence of the Brahmins declined, the subordination of African Americans intensified.[10]

Economically, Thernstrom contends that the lowly occupational status of first-generation Catholic Irish may have been due as much to the culture of the group as Anglo-Saxon discrimination.[11] However one understands the causes of the initial Catholic Irish lag, by the second generation it was largely a thing of the past. Thernstrom writes that almost one-fourth "of the American born youths of Irish parentage found their way into middle class jobs; white-collar callings were twice as accessible to the second generation as to their fathers."[12] The second and third generations of blacks, however, made hardly any progress. Thernstrom concludes, "The northern-born son of a black migrant from the South, by contrast, had but a slight chance of ending up in a better job than his father. Indeed, his children—unless they were mulattos—were no closer to arriving in the white-collar world than their grandparents."[13]

Indeed, almost no improvement—none—was had in the occupational status of black men in Boston until World War II.[14] Consequently, by the 1940s the Catholic Irish middle class was four times as large as the black middle class in Boston.

Thernstrom is careful to conclude that unlike the initial Catholic Irish lag in occupational attainments, the long African American lag had little to do with culture. Rather, he writes, ". . . it appears that the main barriers to black achievement have not been internal but external, the result not of peculiarities in black culture but of peculiarities in white culture."[15] In other words, the main effects of Anglo-Saxon anti-Catholicism in Boston withered away economically after the first generation whereas the combined effects of overt Catholic Irish and other white ethnic group racism endures even until today.[16]

We have no better exhibits for second-generation Irish Catholic incorporation in Boston than the Kennedys and Fitzgeralds—P.J. and John F.—the grandparents of President Kennedy. We examine their rapid rise to lace-curtain and, in Kennedy's case "cut-glass" or Irish Brahmin status below, but we first examine the political incorporation of the Boston Irish.

The Political Incorporation of the Catholic Irish

As indicated earlier, Massachusetts elected blacks to office as early as the 1880s. Always a small percent of the state's population (in 2000 only 5.7 percent), Massachusetts continued this tradition into the twentieth century, electing the first black to the U.S. Senate in 1966 and only the second African American governor in 2006. This early history suggests the Protestants of Massachusetts may have been more anti-Catholic than anti-black. Whether this is true or not, by the 1880s the Catholic Irish population had far outpaced the black. Without the support of Anglo-Saxons and even in the face of their opposition, their numbers inevitably resulted in their rapid political incorporation. The only way to avoid this would have been to deny the franchise. And this even the most obdurate of Boston's Brahmins were unwilling to propose, although there were musings about denying suffrage to newly arrived immigrants.

By the 1880s the Catholic Irish were a near majority in Boston.[17] In 1857 the first Irish Catholic city councilman was elected, in 1870 the first aldermen, in 1882 the first congressman, and in 1884 the first mayor.[18] By 1899 Irish Catholics constituted a majority of the city council. At this point the political incorporation of the group was virtually complete; between 1884 and 1979 nine of the city's mayors were Catholic Irish, and between 1901 and 1980 they controlled the mayor's office for all but ten years.[19]

The first two Catholic Irish mayors—Hugh O'Brien and Patrick Collins—were conciliatory, conservative business-oriented executives who were more or less acceptable to the Anglo-Saxon establishment;[20] in other words, "good Irishmen." They neither emphasized their ethnicity, nor did they attempt to exploit the long years of Protestant domination.[21] Their successors—John F. Fitzgerald and the legendary James Curley—were different. Both were ethnic men who clearly sought "Irish power" and did not hesitate to attack "Yankee" arrogance, exploit the grievances of the Irish in their campaigns, and use the office to serve ethnic group interests.

Fitzgerald, the maternal grandfather of the President, was the more conciliatory of the two. Representing the emerging lace-curtain Irish, Fitzgerald appealed to ethnic solidarity and was ethnic in his oratory and campaigns. Kearns Goodwin describes him as friendly to business interests, and on the whole, Shannon writes that the amiable "Honey Fitz" was a rather urbane expression of Irish protest and unrest.[22]

Not so with his successor, James Michael Curley, one of the most controversial figures in Massachusetts political history. Curley, the basis of the fictional Catholic Irish political boss in Edwin O'Connor's novel and movie *The Last Hurrah*, relished expression of the resentments of the Catholic Irish working class against the Protestant establishment. In his first campaign against a conciliatory Catholic Irish establishment candidate, he played the "ethnic card," questioning his opponent's "Catholicness," accusing him of, among other things, attending an upscale Protestant church and eating a roast beef sandwich on Friday.[23] He lambasted those who attended Harvard rather than a Catholic university; mocked Yankee and lace-curtain Irish aristocratic pretensions; and made clear he intended to use the powers of the office to serve the needs of the Irish poor. With a gift for blarney and a sensitivity to the culture of the shanty Irish, Curley personalized politics (he served sixty days in jail for taking a civil service exam for a poor constituent). As mayor he employed thousands of poor Irishmen in building roads, schools, libraries, and clearing slums.

A former saloonkeeper, Curley had no formal education. The classic ethnic political leader, although he antagonized the Anglo-Saxon establishment and embarrassed the lace-curtain Irish, his great strength as a leader was his ethnic identity and consciousness, which allowed him in a unique way to "define, dramatize and play upon the discrimination, resentments and frustrations suffered by the Irish community in its long passage from despised immigrant minority to a politically irresistible but economically blocked minority."[24]

Curley was elected mayor four times (once from jail), elected to Congress twice, and served one term as governor. In 1936 he ran unsuccessfully for the U.S. Senate against Henry Cabot Lodge Sr. He was defeated partly because the suburban lace-curtain Irish voted against him because he was too Irish, too Catholic. In 1947 he was convicted of mail fraud and sentenced to federal prison. After serving five months, he was pardoned by President Truman and returned to Boston and twice again tried to become mayor. By then, however, the third generation, the economically and socially incorporated Catholic Irish community, was embarrassed by ethnic politics and ethnic politicians.

Tip O'Neill writes that Curley was undoubtedly corrupt, but he was a "great Irish folk hero," and although "the Yankees looked down on him as a shanty Irish rogue," he "hated them with a passion campaign[ing] for decades against what he called our Brahmin Overlords."[25]

To O'Neill and many other Irish Catholics, however, Curley was a hero, but to the Irish Brahmin John F. Kennedy, he was an embarrassing shanty Irish rogue. Tellingly, Kennedy was alone among Massachusetts Catholic Irish politicians in refusing to sign a petition requesting a pardon from President Truman.[26]

Although the Irish Catholic ascendancy in Boston politics was inevitable, the Protestant establishment resisted it. Routinely the legislature passed laws to disempower Boston's city government once it came under Catholic Irish control, including state assumption of some local powers, metropolitan government, and limitations on the city's capacity to tax and incur debt.[27] But as the Catholic Irish population increased statewide, even the most Anglophile of the Brahmin politicians began to have a change of heart.

In the Senate, Henry Cabot Lodge Sr. blamed the Catholic Irish for corruption and debt in Boston and was a leading supporter of restrictions on immigration; in the 1880s he described the group as "a very undesirable addition" to the population because they were a "hard drinking, idle, disorderly class."[28] But as the Catholic Irish population became a larger percentage of the state's electorate Lodge's rhetoric became more conciliatory. For example, in a 1909 speech he invidiously compared the new immigrants from eastern and southern Europe to the Irish, writing that the latter was a "race closely associated with the English speaking people . . . who presented no difficulties of assimilation."[29] By this time St. Patrick's Day was regularly and officially celebrated in Boston, and the holiday that once enraged Protestants was noted as symbolic of the Irish becoming a part of the mainstream. And as is frequently the case in interethnic situations of subordination, the Catholic Irish began to identify with the Protestant establishment and join in the disparagement of their co-religionists from southern and eastern Europe.[30]

The Kennedys and Fitzgeralds

President Kennedy's grandparents arrived in Boston in the late 1840s shortly after the famine. Penniless, within a generation the Fitzgeralds were lace-curtain and his maternal grandfather was a confidant of cardinals and mayor of the city. The second-generation Kennedys were near lace-curtain and the paternal grandfather was a prosperous saloon keeper, member of the state Senate, and an informal political boss of the city.

Although Thomas Fitzgerald and Patrick Kennedy came to Boston as poor immigrants and spent their lives as workingmen, their sons—John Francis and Patrick Joseph—both attended Harvard and established themselves as leading figures in the city's political life within a generation. After graduating from Boston Latin, John Fitzgerald entered the Harvard Medical School. Shortly thereafter, however, his father died and he withdrew from the university and began a political career that saw him become the first son of immigrant parents to be elected mayor. "Honey Fitz" was also twice elected to the House from the same district that in 1946 would send his grandson to the Congress.[31] In 1899 as the lone Catholic in the House he immediately became involved in an unsuccessful effort to allocate federal funds to schools on Indian reservations the Catholic Church operated.[32]

"P.J.," as the president's fraternal grandfather was known, became a prominent saloon keeper and whiskey dealer. Operating the saloon allowed him to establish a political base in the city, and in 1886 he was elected to the Massachusetts House and six years later to the Senate. After eight years in the state legislature he left elective office, became a partner in a local bank and "the unquestioned boss of his local ward."[33] As a local ward boss P.J. was part of the "unofficial board of strategy" that dominated Boston politics, picking candidates, distributing patronage, and pretty much running the city as an Irish catholic political machine.[34] Kennedy and Fitzgerald had their political differences, but they were more often allies than adversaries in state and local politics.[35]

By now both the Kennedys and Fitzgeralds were lace-curtain, far removed from the shanty background of their parents. Both married lace-curtain Catholic Irish girls and distanced themselves from the Irish poor, both culturally and residentially. Having attended public schools themselves, both men ignored the directive of the Boston Archdiocese that all Catholics send their children to church schools and universities because, as Fitzgerald said, Protestant institutions "were the training ground for success in the world."[36] Only after the personal intercession from the archbishop did Fitzgerald grudgingly agreed to transfer his oldest daughter, Rose, from Wellesley College to Manhattanville, the elite New York college for Catholic women, and later to the Academy of Sacred Hearts, the aristocratic German school for the daughters of the leading Catholic families from around the world.

With the assistance of his father, Joseph P. Kennedy, after graduating from Harvard, went into the banking business and was soon hailed as one of the youngest (at age twenty-five) bank presidents in the country. From this he went on through investments on Wall Street, in real estate, Hollywood, and whiskey to amass one of the largest fortunes in the nation and to become a prominent Catholic philanthropist and political leader.

In 1914, Joe Kennedy married Rose Fitzgerald, uniting two of the city's most prominent Catholic Irish families. Although Honey Fitz thought that Joe Kennedy was less than a suitable mate for his oldest daughter, they were married in the private chapel of Boston's Cardinal O'Connor. As a young Catholic entrepreneur on the make, Kennedy desperately wanted the approbation of Boston's Anglo-Saxon establishment: "To prove that he was above the ordinary Irishman, Kennedy found it necessary at times to disassociate himself from Irish ways, yet try as he might he could never escape the fact that his emotional roots were deeply sunk in the old Irish section of Boston. It was a confusion he would never resolve."[37]

At Harvard, Kennedy had been rejected for the membership in the Porcellian Club, and 1922 in a cause célèbre he was "blackballed" from the prestigious Cohasset Country Club.[38] Kearns Goodwin writes, "The women of Cohasset looked down on the daughter of Honey Fitz," and "who was Joe Kennedy but the son of Pat, the barkeep."[39]

Joe's desperate search for status, Kearns Goodwin suggests, may even be an explanation for his ostentatious affair with Gloria Swanson, the Hollywood actress, because she was a "badge of social acceptance . . . for the saloon keeper's son."[40]

Ultimately Kennedy concluded that Boston was too hidebound, too caste-like to ever incorporate fully the Kennedys, so in 1926 he left the city and moved to Bronxville, a fashionable, upscale Protestant suburb of Manhattan. Never to live permanently in Boston again, he established residences in Miami, Maryland, New York City, and Hyannis Port. Citing anti-Catholic and anti-Irish prejudices, Kennedy later said of Boston "it was no place to bring up Irish Catholic children. I didn't want them to go through what I had to go through when I was growing up there. . . ."[41]

The move to Bronxville further detached the Kennedys from Irish culture and Catholicism. This process of deliberate deethnicization started when the family moved to the Boston suburb of Brookline where "very few of the strong, collective bonds" of the Irish heritage could be maintained.[42] In Bronxville, except for daily mass, little of this heritage was a part of the lives of the Kennedys.

Like his father, Joe too ignored the admonitions of the church and sent his sons to Protestant schools and universities. Rose, always wanting the children to "Be Catholic, Be Irish," expected them to attend Catholic schools. Joe relented with the girls, but the boys attended exclusive Protestant prep schools and universities. (At Dexter, the elementary prep school that the President and his older brother attended, they were probably the only Catholics enrolled.) As Joe later quipped, "I'll send my girls to church to believe, my sons to the marketplace—to know better."[43]

More seriously, Kennedy was seeking to facilitate his son's incorporation into Anglo-Saxon society at its highest level. He wanted to transform his sons from mere lace-curtain into Brahmins with the "aristocratic ease of manner which he had first observed among the Brahmin students at Harvard when he was a freshman."[44]

Wealthy beyond the imagination of his parents, Kennedy began to use his money to systematically build a political career for himself and his sons. "Few wealthy men," Whalen writes, "ever approached Kennedy's mastery of the techniques of using money to satisfy personal ambitions."[45] Early on he began to cajole and bribe a "claque of newspaper sycophants" to advance his personal and family ambitions.[46] He also became a major contributor to Catholic charities and the Democratic Party.

In 1932 he raised a substantial amount of money for Franklin Roosevelt and was rewarded with appointment as the first chair of the newly established Securities and Exchange Commission (SEC). Kennedy wanted to be Treasury secretary, but settled for SEC chair; however his appointment to a leadership position regulating Wall Street was controversial especially among liberals given Kennedy's reputation for unsavory, corrupt stock practices. But Roosevelt quipped, "It would take a thief to catch a thief."[47] Although he was becoming increasingly uneasy with Roosevelt's liberal New Deal policies, Kennedy supported him for reelection in 1936. Offered a position in the cabinet as Commerce secretary, Kennedy instead opted for appointment as ambassador to Great Britain. Ambassador to the Court of St. James was by far the most prestigious position in the diplomatic corps. The status-conscious Kennedy and to some extent the entire Irish Catholic community viewed the appointment as a sign of "making it" in the Anglo-Saxon world.

The ethnic pride in the appointment, however, was to "end in humiliation, defeat and eclipse for the Kennedy name" as he was to be forced from the post amidst charges of cowardice, isolationism, profiteering, and anti-Semitism.[48] During the 1960 campaign, John Kennedy was frequently accused of being merely his father's son, and therefore linked to his controversial wartime views. For example, during the 1960 primary contests, President Truman expressed his opposition to Kennedy's nomination by quipping, "It's not the Pope I'm afraid of, it's the pop."[49] And Lyndon Johnson remarked, "I never thought Hitler was right. I was never a Chamberlin umbrella man."[50]

In the lead up to World War II, Ambassador Kennedy supported Neville Chamberlin's policy of appeasement and opposed U.S. intervention in the war. Kennedy was also accused of anti-Semitism because of his seeming indifference to Hitler's assault on the Jews (and his alleged disparagement of "the Jews" in private conversations and correspondence).[51] During the Nazi air attacks on London, critics called Kennedy a coward because he left the city for the hinterlands, and some alleged, but it was never proved, that he used his diplomatic prerogatives to import whiskey into the United States illegally.[52] A rambling interview with the *Boston Globe* in November 1940, however, effectively finished Kennedy's diplomatic and political career. In the interview he once again attacked Franklin Roosevelt's support for Great Britain and exclaimed, "Democracy is finished in England. It may be here."[53] In the midst of the national firestorm his remarks caused, Kennedy submitted his resignation and returned to the United States.

Assuming that Franklin Roosevelt would not seek a third term, Kennedy mused about running himself but soon realized that his controversial tenure as ambassador, rumors about his involvement in bootlegging liquor, his reputation as stock manipulator, as well as his Catholicism made a viable candidacy impossible.[54] Kennedy then stepped back from public service to concentrate on increasing his wealth. His presidential ambitions were bequeathed to his sons, and after the death of his oldest son, Joe, in a bombing mission in Europe, the duty fell to John to take Joe's place, enter politics, and if things went well, become the first Catholic president.

Joe Kennedy and his children eventually gained entry into the American establishment. C. Wright Mills wrote of the late 1950s establishment that it was "still 'pure' by race, by ethnic group . . . protestant . . . moreover, protestants of class church denominations Episcopalian or Unitarian or Presbyterian."[55] But Mills also wrote, "The one firm rule [of the American status system] is that, given persistent inclination, any family can win out on whatever level its money permits" because "money—sheer, naked, vulgar money—has with few exceptions won its possessors entrance anywhere and everywhere into American society."[56]

By the late 1950s Kennedy had bought his way into the Anglo-Saxon establishment, but he still chaffed at the slights. When a reporter in 1957 referred to him as an Irishman Kennedy exploded, "I was born here. My children were born here. What the hell do I have to do to be called an American?"[57] One thing the son of Pat the barkeeper could do was get out of the whiskey business. In 1946 as John Kennedy began his political career, Joe sold his interest in the liquor business because "the trade was vaguely embarrassing and not . . . keeping with the . . . dignity that Kennedy wished to achieve."[58]

John F. Kennedy Enters Politics

All of the elements of John Kennedy's subsequent campaigns—his father's influence, the role of money, organization, personality, courage, sophisticated polling, and marketing and manipulation of the media—were observed in his first campaign for Congress in 1946.

John Kennedy considered careers other than politics including journalism (he briefly worked as a journalist covering the founding of the United Nations in San Francisco) and the academy. His father considered buying a newspaper for him to edit, or even the Brooklyn Dodgers and installing him as president. But after his older brother's death, a career in politics probably became inevitable, given the entreaties of his father. Joe Kennedy recalled, "I got Jack into politics, I was the one. I told him Joe was dead and it was therefore his responsibility to run for Congress. He didn't want to do it. He felt he didn't have the ability and still feels that way. But I told him he had to."[59] John Kennedy said, "It was like being drafted. My father wanted his oldest son in politics. Wanted isn't the right word. He demanded it. You know my father."[60] This is not to say John Kennedy was merely a pawn of his father without ambitions of his own. Rather, in the course of considering what he might do with his life at the end of the war, he most likely came to agree with his father that a career in politics was not a bad way for a man with everything to do something meaningful with his life.

When Kennedy returned to Boston to run for the House in 1946 his opponents dubbed him the "Miami candidate" because for the last two decades he had lived mostly in Miami or at the other Kennedy residences scattered around the country. But the young Kennedy was not an unknown in Boston. The city's media had had extensively covered the lives of the Kennedy family for decades, and his father-in-law was the legendary "Honey Fitz," still alive at age eighty-six.

Joe Kennedy had worked tirelessly to make his son's reputation. In 1940 Kennedy's Harvard undergraduate thesis was published as a best-selling book, *Why England Slept*. The book was written on the basis of volumes of material supplied to him by the American embassy in London and with the assistance of a personal secretary. Harold Laski described the work as "immature" and told the ambassador in a letter, "I don't honestly think any publisher would have looked at that book of Jack's if he had not been your son and if you had not been ambassador."[61] Described by Garry Wills as a "passable undergraduate paper," Joe Kennedy had *New York Times* reporter Arthur Krock rewrite the manuscript; he persuaded Henry Luce, the publisher of *Time*, to write an introduction; and the book became a bestseller, with the young Kennedy hailed as "promising young thinker."[62] Joe Kennedy was aware of the significance of his son publishing a book, telling him, "You will be surprised how a book that really makes the grade with high-class people stands you in good stead for years to come."[63] In addition the young candidate was a genuine war hero, as a result of the courage displayed in the rescue of his PT boat crew during the war.[64] Kennedy's courage in this incident, again thanks to the intervention of his father, was widely publicized—published in the *New Yorker*, condensed in *Reader's Digest*, and reprinted countless times.[65]

Joe Kennedy was in effect Jack's campaign manager during this first campaign, although he worked behind the scenes.[66] The entire Kennedy family—grandpa Honey Fitz, his mother Rose, and brothers and sisters—were active campaigners, walking the tenements and holding elegant teas for the ladies of the largely working-class Catholic district. Guided by a well-staffed organization, the campaign was perhaps up to that time the most expensive and sophisticated ever conducted for a

House seat. State-of-the-art polling and campaign ads were employed. Although the precise amount spent in the campaign cannot be known, estimates range from $250,000 to $1 million.[67] The seat was held at the time by the legendary James Curley, perhaps not an easy person to defeat, the Kennedy name and money notwithstanding. Hamilton contends that Joe Kennedy bribed Curley to vacate the seat and run again for mayor.[68] And in what looked like a bribe, the *Boston Post* endorsed Kennedy after receiving a $500,000 loan from Joe, an endorsement Dallek suggests was worth 40,000 votes.[69]

Although his campaign rhetoric did not exhibit the sophistication and elegance that would come later with the hiring of Theodore Sorensen, Kennedy was a tireless campaigner. And as would be the case in all his subsequent elections, he often campaigned while in excruciating pain (as a result of back problems aggravated by war injuries). He easily won the nomination, securing 40 percent of the vote in a ten-man race. On election night, the aging Honey Fitz reportedly danced a "stiff-legged jig" and sang "Sweet Adeline," but election of his son-in-law clearly represented a new generation and a new kind of Catholic Irish politician—suave, sophisticated, not too Irish, not too Catholic.[70] The first Irish Brahmin.

John Kennedy campaigned as a liberal New Dealer with an especially strong anticommunist stance that fit well with his Catholic, working-class constituency. By this time his father was "vociferously conservative," isolationist, and militantly anti–New Deal.[71] But then and subsequently he accepted his son's "tactical liberalism" as the price one had to pay to advance in national Democratic Party politics.[72]

John Kennedy was bored in the House, seeing it as a mere stepping stone to higher office—the Senate or governor of Massachusetts and then the presidency. Frequently absent and dilatory in his work, after one term he began planning to run for the Senate. In 1952, he challenged Henry Cabot Lodge Jr., the patrician grandson of the former senator who had defeated Honey Fitz for the Senate in 1916.

Once again all the elements of the Kennedy family machine were brought to bear, and Kennedy won a stunning upset, defeating Lodge by a margin of 70,000 votes, while Democrats in Massachusetts and across the country were being defeated in the Eisenhower landslide. Indistinguishable from each other in backgrounds and on the issues, Kennedy and Lodge were both wealthy, Harvard-educated patrician war heroes. Except one was Anglo-Saxon, the other Catholic Irish, symbolizing the decline of one ethnic group and the rise of the other. Rose Kennedy said after the election, "At last the Fitzgeralds have evened the score with the Lodges."[73]

Although he found the Senate less boring than the House, he saw it, too, as a stepping stone and began plotting for the presidency shortly after he was elected.

The Catholic Irish and the African Americans in Chicago

In their relationship to African Americans, the Catholic Irish in Chicago played a role akin to that which the Anglo-Saxons played in their relationship to the Catholic Irish in Boston. African Americans and Irish Catholics settled in Chicago in relatively large numbers beginning in the 1840s, although the African American presence in the city can be traced to its founding.

During the antebellum era, the "Land of Lincoln" and its largest city were like most northern places, dominated by racism and the ideology of white supremacy. Lincoln, despite his unwavering opposition to slavery, was a racist and white supremacist. He argued that Africans were "inferior in color and perhaps moral and intellectual endowment," and in one of his debates with Stephen Douglass, he unequivocally declared about his racism, "I am not now nor have I ever been in favor of the social and political equality of the white and black races; I am not in favor of making voters of the free Negroes, or jurors, or qualifying them to hold office or having them to marry with white people. . . . As much as any other man I am in favor of the superior position being assigned to the white man."[74]

Elsewhere in Illinois, inferior positions were assigned to Africans and superior ones to white men, including Catholic Irish men. Throughout Lincoln's career in Illinois politics and after, blacks in the state were denied the right to vote, denied the right to intermarry, and were discriminated against in employment, schools, housing, and public accommodations.[75]

In the 1870s civil rights laws were enacted prohibiting discrimination in public places, the franchise was granted, and schools were desegregated. By the late nineteenth century blacks, like most of Chicago's ethnically distinct groups, not only lived in ethnic enclaves, but they also lived interspersed among whites as well.[76] But as their numbers increased, whites in the city decided to confine the black population to ghettos. Segregated, impoverished, and criminalized, these twentieth-century slums were maintained by law, custom, and mob violence.[77] The 1919 Chicago riot was emblematic of this mob enforced ghettoization, as it was touched off when a black youngster swam past an imaginary line that separated the "white" from the "black" part of a Lake Michigan beach.

Thus, in Chicago, as Alan Spear painstakingly documents, the black ghetto in Chicago was not a product of poverty or ethnic choice on the part of African Americans. It was rather "primarily the product of white hostility," which law and the mob enforced.[78] In this regard Chicago was not unique. Whites created black ghettos in cities throughout the United States.

In spite of this racist cultural division of labor and residence, to the more brutally oppressed southern peasantry and proletariat Chicago became, in the words of an old Negro spiritual, the "city called heaven."[79] The *Chicago Defender*, at one time the nation's most influential black newspaper and widely distributed throughout the South, published year after year scores of articles urging blacks to abandon the South for the "promised land" of the metropolis of the Midwest.

Although one does not wish to make too much of distinctions of this sort—given the overwhelming sameness of the oppression throughout the North—Chicago may have been in the early twentieth century the best big city for black people in the United States. Although Harlem was the intellectual and artistic capital of black America, Chicago was where "its political and economic manifestations were probably greatest."[80] Chicago was also the birthplace of the urban blues and a "purer," "real" form of jazz.[81] The migrants from Mississippi, Louisiana, and Texas also brought with them a purer form of black religiosity and established a thriving, diverse religious community. Although many black churches became "plantation churches" in the Chicago political machine, others played a leading role in "advancing the race as 'protest institutions' in a hostile white world."[82]

Overtime blacks in Chicago developed a strong sense of race identity, consciousness, and solidarity, stronger, Gosnell contends, than any other ethnic group in the city including the Catholic Irish and Jews.[83] This heightened sense of race consciousness and solidarity of course is partly a reaction to pervasive racial oppression. But Richard Wright, who migrated to the city from Mississippi and made Chicago the setting for his acclaimed novel, observed, "Chicago is the city from which the most incisive and radical Negro thought has come."[84] The city has an old and enduring tradition of Black Nationalism. In 1934, Elijah Muhammad moved the headquarters of the Nation of Islam from Detroit to Chicago, and the Nation and its leader Louis Farrakhan, and the philosophy of Black Nationalism remained influential forces in the city when Baraka Obama arrived. (Additionally, for a brief time during the late 1960s the city was home to one of the most active chapters of the Black Panther Party.) Martin Luther King Jr. made Chicago the target city for his first effort to tackle the problems of urban oppression.[85] And, as discussed later in this chapter, Jesse Jackson made the city his base of operation to carry on Dr. King's legacy and work.

Finally, Chicago and politics are near synonymous. A thoroughly politicized city, it was the site of the nation's most enduring Catholic Irish dominated political machine. It is also the place where African Americans made their earliest political breakthroughs in the aftermath of Reconstruction. As early as 1876 Chicago sent an African American to the state legislature (elected from a majority white district). The first Chicago alderman was elected in 1905, and in 1928 the first African American from a northern state (and the first since Reconstruction) was elected to Congress. In 1992, Illinois became the second state after Massachusetts to elect a black person to the U.S. Senate, and in 2004 it became the only state to twice elect a black to that prestigious position. Overall, then, in Illinois blacks achieved the earliest degree of political incorporation and perhaps the greatest as well since the state has probably elected more blacks to statewide office than any other.[86]

Yet, in Chicago in their quest for full economic and political incorporation, African Americans faced the most formidable foe that they would encounter in any big city in the country—the legendary Catholic Irish machine of "Boss" Richard J. Daley, the last of the big-city machines. In its waning days one scholar of the Chicago machine wrote that as black demands escalated in the late 1960s, "the machine increasingly took on the retrograde character of a southern white supremacist Democratic Party."[87]

Daley's Catholic Irish Machine and the Subordination of African Americans

Although the Catholic Irish immigrants initially faced discrimination from Chicago's Anglo-Saxon Republican establishment and the Illinois Know-Nothings, by the 1870s, their political incorporation was well under way.[88] By the 1890s, they dominated the city council, and in 1905, Edward Dunne, the first Irish Catholic mayor, was elected.[89] In 1933, Edward Kelly was elected from the Catholic enclave of Bridgeport. Thereafter this part of Chicago became known as the "mother of mayors," sending three mayors to city hall, including Richard Daley and subsequently a fourth, Daley's son Richard M. Daley.

At the beginning of Daley's term in 1955, the Catholic Irish population constituted less than 10 percent of the city's population (an estimated 350,000) far less than the Polish population of 600,000. Yet they dominated the city's politics, controlling not only the mayor's office but one-third of the city council seats.[90] Catholic Irish dominance of the city's politics may be attributed to the predominance of Catholicism (the Chicago Archdiocese was for a time the largest in North America), Irish political consciousness, sophistication, and the role of Irish saloons as centers of political organizing.[91] Unlike the second-generation Kennedys and Fitzgeralds of Boston, the Daleys of Chicago remained "Catholic to the Core."[92] Lifelong residents of working-class Bridgeport, the Daleys sent their children to parochial schools and local Catholic universities and maintained ties to the church and Irish traditions. A "devout Roman Catholic," Rakove describes Daley as "fiercely Irish, Gaelic in temperament, and Hibernian in behavior. Practically all of his close friends are Irish. Most of the people he surrounds himself with in government and politics are Irish."[93] Even from the overwhelming Protestant black community, Daley frequently selected Catholics as ward committeemen isolating them from the black community while at the same time binding them to the machine's Catholic hierarchy.[94]

On these ethnic cultural attributes Daley built the most enduring and racially oppressive urban regime in U.S. history.[95] By the 1960s, Grimshaw writes, the "Daley machine acquired a new electoral stranglehold in the working class and middle class white ethnic words . . . and abandon[ed] virtually all pretense of being a liberal Democratic New Deal party. . . . [It] increasingly took on the character of the old Deep South, openly supporting a range of conservative and racist policies and practices."[96]

A political machine is a predominantly material-based rather than an interest or ideological political organization, exchanging the votes of poor people for things (jobs, housing, food, and so forth).[97] Pinderhughes describes the Chicago machine in the 1970s as a "static hierarchy ruled by the Irish, managed at intermediate levels by loyal but restive European ethnics such as Poles, Germans and other eastern Europeans. At the bottom of the hierarchy blacks controlled black areas but competed for leadership in other neighborhoods of the city."[98]

The black areas until the late 1970s were controlled by a "black submachine," which Congressman William Dawson dominated. Dawson was a ruthless "organization man" who rarely spoke out on race issues, instead focusing his energies on patronage and its use in building and maintaining an efficient organization that could deliver the black vote to Daley. Even during the civil rights movement and Dr. King's Chicago campaign, Dawson remained silent, even voting against legislation prohibiting racism in the distribution of federal funds that Adam Clayton Powell, his Harlem colleague, introduced.

European ethnic groups—especially the large population of Polish Americans—were disenchanted with domination of the city's politics by the entrenched Irish minority. But they were unsuccessful in several attempts to wrest power from Daley largely because of the relative lightness of their subordination and the resulting failure to develop a high degree of ethnic solidarity.[99] Thus, the burden of unraveling the power of the nation's last big-city political machine fell to African Americans—the city's most oppressed ethnic group.

The fall of Chicago's machine was inevitable. Economic incorporation of white ethnic groups as they acquired stable working- and middle-class employment, and their increasing levels of education and suburbanization contributed to the withering of machine politics. The institutionalization of the New Deal welfare programs also played a part. Finally, in Chicago in 1972 in *Shakman v. Democratic Organization of Cook County*, the courts ruled that city employees could not be fired on political grounds and subsequently that politics could not be a basis of hiring. These decisions threatened to destroy over time the ward-based patronage system on which the machine was able to reliably generate votes.

Meanwhile the African American community was becoming increasingly restive. First, the ethos of the civil rights and black power movements began to impact political thinking and behavior even in the city's impoverished "plantation wards." Second, in 1966 Martin Luther King Jr. selected Chicago as the site for his first campaign against northern racism and poverty. Although King's efforts resulted in little more than symbolic concessions from Daley's machine, it contributed to a sense of militancy in parts of the black community. Third, new leadership emerged in the person of Rev. Jesse Jackson.

Ironically, when Jackson moved to Chicago in 1964 to attend seminary he first interviewed for employment with Mayor Daley (on the basis of a letter of recommendation from North Carolina Governor Terry Sanford). When Daley offered him a job as a toll collector, an angry Jackson rejected the position and became a community organizer for the Coordinating Council of Community Organizations, a coalition of the city's civic and civil rights organizations.[100] Six months later he organized a pilgrimage to Selma, Alabama, to participate in the demonstrations after the televised beating of protesters by the state police. While there he so impressed Dr. King's Southern Christian Leadership Conference (SCLC) staff that he was named an informal SCLC aide based in Chicago.[101]

In 1967 he was appointed national director of Operation Breadbasket, SCLC's northern arm. Under Jackson's leadership, Operation Breadbasket (and subsequently operation People United to Save Humanity [PUSH], when Jackson broke with SCLC after King's death) became a major force in Chicago politics, leading highly visible protests and boycotts that sometimes resulted in employment opportunities for black workers and contracts for black businesses. The Saturday radio broadcasts of Operation Breadbasket/PUSH rallies transformed Jackson into a well-known, charismatic leader of Chicago's black community, who was eager to challenge Daley's machine. Jackson's biographer concludes that he was the first civil rights leader to establish an urban "power base" and that this base "may have been the decisive organizational brawn in the election of Chicago's first black mayor."[102]

The proverbial straw that cracked the back of the Daley machine's subordination of the black community occurred in 1972 when Chicago police beat up two black men. The police in Chicago routinely brutalized blacks (in 1968 during the riots following the murder of Dr. King, Daley famously ordered the police to shoot to kill), but the men beaten this time were prominent dentists and friends of Congressman Ralph Metcalf.

Daley selected Metcalf, Catholic and a loyal organization man, to succeed the deceased Dawson. When Metcalf requested a meeting with the mayor in his—Metcalf's—office to discuss the beatings, Daley refused. Metcalf then openly broke with the machine. Explaining the break to *NBC News* he said, "I just got tired of not being my own man, sometimes voting against my own conscience. . . . So, I just wanted to get off the plantation."[103]

Thus, when the aging, autocratic, arrogant Daley died in 1976, his machine—due to the inevitabilities and a unique set of circumstances in Chicago's black community—began to die with him. Its death was brought about by the extraordinary Harold Washington mayoral campaign.

Harold Washington and the Making of Obama's Chicago

Harold Washington, like most successful Chicago politicians, began his career as a cog in Daley's machine. After working for Congressman Metcalf in 1965 he was elected to the Illinois House and to the state Senate in 1976. In the Senate, Washington broke with the machine on several issues. He first took the lead in organizing an independent black legislative caucus. Later, he defied the machine by supporting legislation to create a civilian review board for the Chicago police. Then, he joined with liberal reformers to defeat the machine's candidate for Senate president.[104] Although Daley was angered, Washington's support was so strong, the machine could not oust him.

When Daley died, the city council bypassed the African American president *pro tempore* and selected Michael Bilandic interim mayor. Although Bilandic had promised not to seek election to the office, he contested the special election and won. Washington, however, mounted an insurgent campaign and carried several black middle-class wards. In 1978 Congressman Metcalf died, and the machine selected a "notorious machine hack"—Bennett Stewart—to replace him. In the 1980 primary Washington easily defeated Stewart, winning nearly half the vote in a four-candidate race with Stewart getting only 17 percent.

In the 1979 mayoral election Jane Byrne, Daley's long-time director of consumer affairs, challenged Bilandic. After Bilandic fired her, she defeated him in the next election drawing on the support of African Americans and liberal reform factions. Once in office, however, she distanced herself from blacks while openly favoring the city's white ethnic minorities who constituted a majority of the city's voters.

Byrne may have distanced herself from blacks in anticipation of a challenge from the late mayor's son, Richard M. Daley. What she did not anticipate was a challenge—at least an effective one—by Washington. But in Grimshaw's words, "between the City's two Irish titans," Washington—the "black messiah"—won.[105] Washington did not run as a black messiah. Indeed, Chicago's influential Black Nationalist community was somewhat wary because Washington ran a broad, multiracial "rainbow" campaign.[106] At the outset of the campaign most observers assumed that Byrne and Daley would split the white ethnic vote and that the machine would deliver enough of the black vote to make Daley the winner. As one longtime observer scoffed, "The organization owns a lock on 20 percent of the black vote. This is a vote the machine would deliver for George Wallace—against Martin Luther King."[107]

The entire black community, including the so-called plantation wards, however, came out in unprecedented numbers for Washington. Even the leaders of the plantation wards embraced Washington in the largest mobilization against the machine ever. African Americans—one-third of the city's population—gave more than 90 percent of their vote to Washington and with significant support by liberal whites (largely Jewish) and Latinos, Washington garnered 37 percent of the primary vote to Byrne's 33 percent and Daley's 30 percent.

In Chicago, winning a Democratic nomination is tantamount to election. In Washington's case, however, the retrograde racism of the decaying machine turned against the black Democratic nominee. Led by the Polish American chairman of the Cook County Democratic Party, most of the white ward committeemen supported Bernard Epton, the obscure Jewish Republican nominee. In what was probably the most racist and racially rancorous mayoral election in U.S. history, Epton almost defeated Washington. The Democratic nominee in one of the most reliably Democratic cities in the nation won the election by a mere 51.7 percent of the vote.[108]

Throughout his first term Washington was involved in racially rancorous disputes with remnants of the machine on the city council. He did not consolidate power on the council and the city until after his reelection four years later. Shortly thereafter Washington died in December 1987. The hapless Eugene Sawyer, an African American councilman was named as Washington's interim replacement. He was easily defeated by Richard M. Daley in the 1989 election (Daley received 9 percent of the black vote). Since then—advised by David Axelrod, Obama's top campaign strategist—Daley was consistently reelected and eventually came to be viewed as a racially moderate, reasonably competent, and effective mayor.[109]

In 2010 the son of the boss declined to seek reelection, having surpassed his father as the longest serving mayor in Chicago history. Between the two of them they had held the office for forty-two of the last fifty-five years, and persons of Catholic Irish descent for sixty of the last seventy-five years.

This is the city that Obama returned to in 1992 to start his political career. A city of partial political incorporation, where "blacks once again were back in the peculiar position that had been their lot for so many years. Politics had little to offer but bitter fruit."[110]

Economic incorporation was even more limited, as the data in Table 4.1 show. On measures of economic incorporation from the bottom to the top, one observes a deep cultural division of labor. African Americans are heavily concentrated among the low income and those in "deep poverty" and are hardly to be found at all among the corporate and legal elites. Of Chicago's fifteen poorest neighborhoods—with rates of poverty from 55 percent to 71 percent—all but one was at least 94 percent black.[111] Meanwhile, in the prestigious law firms where the Harvard-educated Barack and Michelle Obama might have practiced, blacks constituted only 0.7 percent of 2,950 partners.

In his memoir, Obama recalls an encounter with Mayor Washington at an event Obama organized. The black low-income Chicagoans were giddy and inspired by the Mayor's visit. After he left Obama reflected on the constraints of black mayoral power. Noting the "radiance" of Washington's victory, he lamented that in the projects he was organizing "nothing seemed to change."[112]

Table 4.1. Black Economic Incorporation in Chicago, 2000

Family Income and Poverty Status, Percent Corporate Officers/Directors and Law Partners	Black	White
Median family income	$36,298	$61,952
Percent income above $100,000	7.5%	20%
Percent below official poverty level	20	5.6
Percent children in poverty	35	5
Percent African American corporate officers	2.6	—
Percent African American corporate directors	7	—
Percent Black Partners major law firms	0.7	—

Source: Martin Dupuis and Keith Bockelman, *Barack Obama and the New Face of American Politics* (Westport, CT: Praeger, 2008).

Robert Starks, a leader of Chicago's black nationalist community as well as a leading scholar of Chicago politics, assessed the Washington mayoralty thusly: "he was able to revolutionize the thinking and broaden the horizons of the black masses and command the respect, if only grudgingly, of the white community. . . . It is clear that regardless of what changes may occur from this point on, black voters will never allow themselves to be subjected to political subordination again."[113]

In the end, the Obama and Stark evaluations of Washington might be codas for the radiance of Obama's election and the fate of his presidency. But these are matters for later chapters. For now a prolegomenon to the next chapter: Jesse Jackson told *Playboy* that the 1983 Chicago mayoral election was a major factor in his decision to run for president the following year. "Before the election, Walter Mondale came to town to support Richard Daley's son while Ted Kennedy came to support then-Mayor Jane Byrne. In other words, the progressive wing of the Democratic Party was moving to the right. What could we do? Most people got upset. I said we've got to figure a way out of this."[114] Jackson's way out was to seek the Democratic presidential nomination to make sure "blacks will never be taken for granted again." Jackson's campaigns became a template for assessing Obama's campaign twenty-five years later. The next chapter examines the Jackson campaigns, but first a study of the beginnings of Obama's career in Chicago politics.

Obama's Career in Chicago Politics

Unlike when John Kennedy started his career in Boston, Obama did not have a famous family name; his father-in-law had not been a popular mayor and congressman; he did not have a famous, wealthy, well-connected, media-savvy father; he did not have unlimited money to mount a well-staffed, sophisticated campaign; he was neither a well-publicized war hero, nor the scion of black Brahmins. Rather, when Obama entered politics he had only his character, ambition, intelligence, and what has been described as a "special and rare charisma."[115] These attributes alone were not enough to propel him a dozen years later from obscurity to the presidency. Instead, Obama's career has been marked by a "series of fortunate events."[116]

After graduating from Columbia University, Obama arrived in Chicago at age twenty-three to work as a community organizer for the Calumet Community Religious Conference. Obama acknowledges that his work as an organizer brought about only modest changes (getting toilets fixed, windows repaired, and the heaters working) in the lives of the people of the Altgeld Project or elsewhere.[117] But in a first fortunate event, "as the organization's stock had grown, so had my own. I began receiving invitations to sit on panels and conduct workshops, local politicians knew my name, even if they couldn't pronounce it."[118] Thus, by the time he left Chicago to attend Harvard Law School, he had already established a modest political base for the political career he had decided to pursue.

When he arrived at Harvard in 1988 Obama had already decided to return to Chicago and enter politics, with an eye on the mayor's office.[119] Another fortunate event occurred at Harvard—he was elected the first black president of the Law Review. His election received national media attention, leading to an invitation to write a book. Although he initially had planned to write a scholarly treatise on civil rights litigation, his memoir, *Dreams of My Father*, turned out to be a meditation on blackness and a useful way to establish his blackness or racial authenticity, while validating his subsequent claim that his multiethnic background uniquely allowed him to transcend race.

In 1992 Obama returned to Chicago and in another fortunate event married Michelle Robinson, a dark-skinned, Ivy League–educated African American woman who was a native of the city. This was fortunate because it integrated him into a "budding network of Chicago's community of successful white collar African Americans."[120] This network also included important black churches and the Jesse Jackson family.

Instead of taking a job at one of the city's prestigious downtown law firms, Obama joined a firm specializing in civil rights law and whose senior partner had been Harold Washington's corporation counsel. This, too, was fortunate because it furthered his integration into the city's black establishment.

In his first year back in the city Obama became director of Illinois Vote Project, which registered thousands of blacks for the 1992 elections. In 1992 he joined the faculty of the University of Chicago Law School and was appointed to a couple of civic boards, integrating him into the elite, white, liberal intellectual circles of Hyde Park.

All the time Obama was searching for a political opening that would launch his political career. Fortunately, a vacancy occurred in the state Senate when the incumbent—Alice Palmer—decided to run for a seat in the U.S. House left vacant when Congressman Mel Reynolds was forced to resign in the wake of a sex scandal. Obama seized the opportunity to run for Palmer's seat. Palmer, however, soon withdrew from the House contest (which was eventually won by Jesse Jackson Jr.) and asked Obama to drop his candidacy so that she might continue in the Senate. Obama refused and eventually was able to identify enough irregularities in the signatures Palmer and his other opponents had gathered to disqualify them, allowing him in effect to run unopposed. This was indeed fortunate.

In the state Senate Obama compiled a liberal record on civil rights and civil liberties, but a somewhat more conservative record on business and economic issues.[121] Obama's state Senate career was also characterized by a politics of ethnic avoidance, emanating from his ambition for higher office and his "crossover dreams" of a biracial constituency.[122]

In what he later described as an "ill conceived" decision fueled by a sense of "chronic restlessness," Obama in 2000 challenged incumbent African American Congressman Bobby Rush.[123] Rush, the former head of the Illinois Black Panther Party had served in Congress for almost a decade and in 1999 had run unsuccessfully for mayor. Although Rush easily defeated Obama, this too may have been fortunate. First, representing an overwhelmingly black congressional district may have limited his capacity to transcend race and seek statewide office.[124] Also, in this race between "the Panther and the Professor," Obama for the first time was required to deal with questions about his blackness.

Although his biracial heritage, Ivy League pedigree, presidency of the Harvard Law Review, and teaching position at the elite University of Chicago Law School made him at ease with and acceptable to Hyde

Park white liberals and the editorial writers of the *Chicago Tribune*, to some Chicago blacks it suggested that he might be "dicty," "hincty," or an "Oreo." Some Black Nationalists contended that he was too much under the influence of—if not the control of—white interests. Like the Catholic Irish in Boston who worried about the loyalties of their lace-curtain, Harvard-educated leaders, Bobby Rush said of Obama that he "went to Harvard and became an educated fool. We're not impressed by these folks with those eastern elite degrees. . . . Barack is a person who read about the civil rights protests and thinks he knows about it."[125]

Chapter 7 studies the question of Obama's blackness, comparing it to questions about how Irish and Catholic John Kennedy was, but in the Rush campaign he was fortunate that he was forced to deal with the question early on, thereby preparing him for the ordeal of the presidential campaign.

From reading and listening to the speeches of Martin Luther King Jr. and Malcolm X, Obama was made keenly aware of the importance of oratory in the black culture. In his campaign against Rush and earlier as a community organizer, he "spent countless hours in Chicago's African American churches digesting the cadence of preachers that stoke at the heart of an African American audience . . . peppered with hints of the Bible and . . . phrases from Martin Luther King [Jr.]."[126] As Michael Eric Dyson later writes, "his rhetoric is firmly rooted in black soil . . . in the tradition known as signifying."[127]

His marriage also helped authenticate his blackness during the Rush campaign as it would during the presidential campaign. As one of the office managers in the congressional campaign said, "[I] would be constantly asked if he had married a black or white woman: It was the first question I would get—and I would get it a lot. When [I] answered that he had married a black woman the wariness would subside."[128]

It was fortunate when Obama decided to run for the U.S. Senate in 2004 that Carol Moseley-Braun decided to run a quixotic campaign for the presidency instead of trying to reclaim her Senate seat.[129] Moseley-Braun apparently did not like Obama, viewing him as a "young whippersnapper, a pretender, a cheat . . . messing in her territory."[130] If she had elected to run, Obama perhaps would not have, telling Axelrod, "I am not going to run against a black woman."[131] Not wishing to run against a black woman may have been a factor, but it was also clear that he would have had little chance of defeating Moseley-Braun in the Democratic primary.

Obama's campaign for the U.S. Senate was marked by multiple fortunate events. First, his principal opponent in the Democratic primary—Blair Hull—was tarnished when his former wife accused him of physical abuse.[132] Second, his Republican opponent in the general election—Jack Ryan—was forced to withdraw in the midst of a sex scandal. Third, as Ryan's replacement, Alan Keyes—the bombastic, ultra conservative, chronic candidate from Maryland—was selected.[133] Keyes's selection marked the first time that both major parties had selected African Americans as senate nominees. But the election was no contest; indeed it is remarkable that Keyes was able to win 30 percent of the vote.[134]

In effect, Obama ran unopposed for the U.S. Senate, just as he had done earlier for the Illinois Senate. With his main rivals doing themselves in, Obama was never required to launch an attack ad, and he never had a major negative attack launched against him.[135]

The final fortunate event in the series was John Kerry's decision to ask Obama to give the keynote address at the 2004 Democratic Convention.[136] At the Democratic Convention four years earlier, Obama had taken a cheap Southwestern flight; the rental car agency rejected his credit card, and he could not get a pass to get on the floor.[137] In 2008 he delivered a history-making address that overnight made him a John Kennedy–like celebrity, the new superstar of American politics. Michael Barone, the conservative commentator, wrote in *The Almanac of American Politics* that after the speech, "immediately, and not without justification, commentators were hailing this state senator from Hyde Park as a national leader and a possible future president."[138]

After his election to the Senate, the national media coverage was idolatrous, hailing Obama as a political leader whose kind had not been seen since John Kennedy or his brother Robert. John Kennedy had always been an Obama role model,[139] and as soon as he got to the Senate, Axelrod and other Obama staffers started "scheming for the presidency."[140]

The relatively high degrees of subordination of the Catholic Irish by the Anglo-Saxons in Boston and of the blacks by the Catholic Irish in Chicago gave rise to relatively high degrees of ethnic identity, consciousness, and solidarity in Boston's Catholic Irish community and in Chicago's African American community. When John Kennedy ran for office for the first time in Boston, the Catholic Irish had been fully incorporated politically, allowing him to run a deethnicized campaign. Obama also ran a deethnicized campaign in his first bid for office, although African Americans in Chicago were only semi-incorporated politically. The political status of their respective ethnic groups in Boston and Chicago at the time of their elections did little, however, to shape how they conducted their campaigns for the presidency. In a sense, both Kennedy and Obama stood apart from their cities' tumultuous ethnic histories and cultures. Obama was a newcomer to Chicago, having spent most his life in the racially tolerant climate of Hawaii and the cosmopolitan environs of Columbia and Harvard. When John Kennedy returned to Boston to run for Congress, he was a stranger to the city, having spent most of his life in exclusive Protestant prep schools; at Harvard; and in the cosmopolitan environs of Bronxville, Miami, London, and Washington. This allowed both men to identify symbolically with their city's ethnic history while at the same time not being a part of it. In other words, both Kennedy and Obama in their backgrounds embodied both the politics of ethnic identity and the politics of ethnic avoidance.

5

Ethnic Men

The Al Smith and Jesse Jackson Campaigns

Al Smith was the first Catholic Irish political leader with a national following. Jesse Jackson was the first African American leader with a national electoral power base. When Smith ran for president in 1928 he was the four-time governor of the nation's most populous state. When Jackson ran in 1984 he had never held elective office and was attempting to make a transition from protester to political leader. Smith's campaign emerged from the mainstream of Democratic Party politics and was marginal to ethnic Catholic Irish politics. Jackson's campaigns were anchored in the mainstream of ethnic black politics but were marginal to Democratic Party politics. Although Smith probably had little chance of winning the presidency in 1928, his nomination was almost inevitable. Jackson had no chance to win the nomination or presidency in 1984 or 1998. His was a protest candidacy designed to empower the black electorate in national politics by exercising "independent leverage" within the Democratic Party.[1]

In 1928 Catholics generally and the Catholic Irish specifically were not fully incorporated economically, socially, culturally, or politically, living for the most part in distinctive ethnic enclaves and facing discrimination from the Protestant majority. When Jackson ran, African Americans were barely one generation removed from legalized subordination; they were still ghettoized, impoverished, and stigmatized. Finally, Jackson and Smith were both ethnic men trying to be mainstream. Both men sought to appeal to the broader Protestant and white electorates. But, what James MacGregor Burns and Oscar Handlin wrote of Smith in 1928 could have been written of Jackson in the 1980s. Burns wrote, ". . . Mr. Smith was proud of his background. Even in 1928 when as a presidential candidate he had good reason to broaden his appeal, he refused to compromise his urban, immigrant Catholic background."[2]

Handlin wrote, "It was as if he feared that in concealing the accents of the Bowery he would be turning his back upon the people among whom he had grown up, be untrue to himself. He would campaign as Al Smith and as nothing more."[3] Jesse Jackson would campaign as Jesse Jackson—a cultural and political African American—and nothing more.

Thirty-two years separate Smith's unsuccessful run as the first Catholic candidate and John Kennedy's triumph. Twenty-four years separate Jackson's first run and Obama's election. In the years separating Smith and Kennedy, the Catholic Irish were fully incorporated—integrated—into American society. In the years separating Jackson and Obama, with the exception to some extent of cultural incorporation, little had changed; blacks remained semi-incorporated.

Comparing the Smith and Jackson campaigns shows how continuities and change in the roles of race and religion in U.S. politics as structural factors were transformed in one case and remained the same in the other. Comparing the Smith–Kennedy and Jackson–Obama campaigns will also show how ethnic men transcend their ethnicity in order to be accepted by the larger society. As the stories unfold we will see how—ironically—it was easier for Obama in 2008 to transcend his blackness than it was for Kennedy in 1960 to transcend his Catholicism.

The Making of the First Ethnic Candidate for President: Al Smith's Campaigns

Alfred Emanuel Smith was the first non–Anglo-Saxon Protestant to be viewed as a credible candidate for president. The grandson of immigrants, he was born in 1873. His paternal grandparents were German, but Smith always identified with the Catholic Irish heritage of his mother's parents. His parents were not impoverished, but Smith had to drop out of school at age twelve when his father died. As a young man, he worked for a time at New York's famed Fulton Fish Market before entering politics as a functionary in Tammany Hall, the most famous Catholic Irish machine of them all. A devout Catholic, Smith's earliest mentors in the machine—Paddy Diver and Charles Murphy—owned saloons (Murphy owned two). Smith began his career as a Manhattan commissioner of jurors. In 1903 he was elected to the state Assembly, in 1913 he was elected speaker, in 1915 Manhattan sheriff, in 1917 president of the New York City alderman, and in 1918 governor of New York. In 1920 he was defeated in Warren Harding's landslide presidential election, but he returned to the governor's chair in 1922 and subsequently was reelected to an unprecedented fourth two-year term.

A progressive, by all accounts Smith was a competent governor with one scholar describing his tenure as "brilliant."[4] Although Smith championed the cause of urban, working-class Catholic immigrants who viewed him as a fulfillment of their wish for recognition and incorporation, he saw himself and indeed was more than an ethnic politician. In the 1920s he was, Finan writes, "the most powerful spokesman for liberalism in the United States."[5]

The United States, however, was far from being a liberal nation in the 1920s. The fundamentalist Protestant areas of the country exercised disproportionate influence culturally and politically, and they continued to disparage urban America—especially New York City—with its mass of "alien," "foreign" adherents of "rum and Romanism." As indicated in chapter 2, the Klan had revitalized itself as a militant Anglo-Saxon Protestant formation opposed to "Niggers, Jews and Catholics."[6] By the early 1920s, its estimated one million members were an important force in national politics.[7] Lastly, the conservative, laissez-faire, antiliberal business ethos had been ascendant since the 1890s, interrupted only briefly by the progressive tendencies of Theodore Roosevelt and Woodrow Wilson.

A major manifestation of this conservative, Protestant fundamentalist climate was the ratification in 1920 of the Eighteenth Amendment, prohibiting the manufacture or sale of alcohol anywhere in the United States. Although the adoption of this moral police state had many sources, nativist, fundamentalist Protestant bigotry against Catholic immigrants was an important one.[8] This was, however, more than just religious and cultural prejudices because "at the time when many of the immigrant leaders were also saloon keepers attacking alcohol was also striking a blow at the emerging political machines."[9]

At least since the Civil War, governors of New York were always on the short list of those mentioned for the presidency. After his landslide reelection to a third term in 1922, ethnicity was the major barrier to Smith winning the Democratic nomination in 1924. The 1924 Democratic Convention was the longest and most rancorous in history. After an angry debate a platform plank condemning the Klan was defeated $542^{3}/_{20}$ percent to $541^{3}/_{20}$ percent. Although Smith had condemned the Klan, in deference to the southerners he would need to win the nomination and the presidency, his support for the anti-Klan resolution was tepid.[10]

Nevertheless, the nomination went to John Davis, the distinguished lawyer and diplomat from West Virginia. A deeply divided convention overlooked the obvious choice of Smith because the grand old man of the party—William Jennings Bryan—was trying to make one last fight for the presidency. On the 103rd ballot Davis became the compromise choice. Viewed as a moderate conservative and under pressure from liberals, Davis had denounced the Klan and anti-Catholic bigotry. He was defeated overwhelmingly by Calvin Coolidge. After Davis's defeat, Smith knew he was the inevitable 1928 nominee. Having denied him once, the party simply could not take the risk of denying him a second time and further alienating its growing urban, immigrant constituency to which Smith was a hero.

The party establishment in desperation searched for an alternative, a Catholic alternative, and found him in Montana Senator Thomas Walsh. Walsh was the Catholic anti-Smith, rural rather than urban, conservative not liberal, dry not wet, Catholic but not too Catholic; he was not associated with New York City and its machine politics. The establishment's transparent ploy to substitute Walsh the good Catholic for Smith the bad Catholic failed. Walsh received little Catholic support and much abuse and disparagement.[11] As a Los Angeles Catholic newspaper observed, "now we have two candidates who are Catholic or rather one candidate and a decoy."[12]

Smith was an ethnic man, proud and unwilling to downplay his heritage. He was determined, as Rose Kennedy might have said, to "Be Catholic, Be Irish." He openly scorned prohibition and emphasized his working-class origins as a big-city boy out of the slums. Lichtman describes him as a "a true New York provincial . . . he flaunted the dress and manners of his city. The derby hat, set at a slightly rakish angle, the flashy suits, the big cigar, the slight swagger, the striking pronunciations."[13] A devoted Catholic,[14] Smith refused to distance himself from his faith going so far in one controversial incident to kiss a Cardinal's ring upon being introduced. This incident led one New York bishop to exclaim, "No governor can kiss the papal ring and get within gunshot of the White House."[15] Smith apparently did not care. Joe Kennedy did care. He voted for Hoover in 1928 because of his "belief that Catholic politicians needed to work within the protestant system to succeed at the national level . . . [and] refuse[d] to challenge the rules of a protestant dominated world. . . ."[16]

It was not merely Smith's Catholicism that disturbed the would-be Irish Brahmin Joe Kennedy. It was Smith's working-class, near shanty Irish lack of refinement. During the course of the campaign Smith discarded his "Dapper Dan" wardrobe in favor of the "somber grays" of the statesman, but he could not hide his lack of learning and lace-curtain refinement.[17] Smith sometimes joked about having never read a book, but it was not a laughing matter to many Americans who already looked down on Smith because of his ethnicity and who had come to view a college education as a requirement for the presidency.[18] The last Democratic president, after all had held a Ph.D. and was former president of Princeton, and Herbert Hoover was a distinguished graduate of Stanford. Thus, Smith ignored at his peril doubts about whether he had the "heft" to handle the presidency. In addition, commentators disparaged Smith's wife. Unlike the elegant, French-speaking Jacqueline Kennedy, Catherine Dunn, Smith's wife, was too Catholic and too common in her language, dress, and manners.[19] In other words, the Smith family was too immigrant, too urban, too Catholic, too lower class to occupy the White House.

Smith was also perhaps too liberal, too progressive. During the campaign, he did not retreat from liberalism, embracing positions such as public water power, federal aid for social welfare, protective legislation for women and children, and agricultural price supports.[20] However, he did try to appeal to more conservative and southern elements; like John Kennedy, he selected an influential southern senator—Joseph Robinson of Arkansas—as his running mate (Robinson also supported prohibition). Smith's most dramatic move to attract conservative, business support was the selection of Jacob Raskob as chair of the Democratic National Committee. Catholic and antiprohibition, Raskob was vice president of General Motors and a leading spokesman for business interests. None of this, however, prevented Hoover from alleging that Smith was espousing radical, un-American ideas that sounded like "state socialism."[21]

For a short time, Smith calculated that the black vote in several northern states might counterbalance the expected anti-Catholic vote. Blacks at this time were firmly anchored in the Republican Party; nevertheless the Smith campaign thought that his progressive record as governor and his ethnic minority background might be attractive to some black voters. Smith asked Walter White of the NAACP to lead an effort to organize black voter support. Although White declined to join the campaign formally, as an informal advisor he prepared a memorandum showing how the black vote might tip the balance of power in several closely divided states.[22] In the end, however, Smith concluded that any outreach to blacks would put at risk the party's white racist core southern constituency.

The 1928 election has been described as "the dirtiest campaign in American presidential history."[23] Meanwhile, Hoover was pursuing an early version of the Republican "southern strategy" by linking Catholicism, prohibition, and racism.[24] The Catholic Church's opposition to segregation was highlighted in Republican and Klan propaganda, leading some black leaders and newspapers to endorse Smith. Most blacks, however, voted for Hoover because Smith stood by the party's traditional antiblack postures (at the 1928 Democratic Convention,

Smith acquiesced in the segregation of blacks behind a chicken wire barrier). Hoover's southern strategy was successful; he carried four southern states (Texas, North Carolina, Virginia, and Florida)—the first Republican nominee to do so. *The Crisis*, the NAACP's magazine, reflecting on both the Hoover and Smith campaigns described the 1928 election as "the most anti-Black since the Civil War."[25]

The main issue in the election, however, was religion, not race. In many ways prohibition was a surrogate for Catholicism, but the Klan, the president of the Southern Baptist Convention, and Alabama Senator Thomas Heflin openly opposed Smith because of his religion. In addition, there was a "profusion of anonymously published, . . . scurrilous propaganda" filled with religious bigotry distributed covertly by the Republican Party.[26] Liberal journals such as the *Nation* and the *Atlantic* opposed Smith because of what they said were the contradiction between his constitutional oath and his supposed loyalty to the "Two Powers" theory of the church.[27] Throughout the campaign historians agree that "Hoover reluctantly and rarely made public statements condemning anti-Catholic activities."[28] And Lichtman concludes Catholics "did not dare launch a counteroffensive" to the anti-Catholic propaganda because "they would have added credibility to [their] arguments and jeopardized the future prospects of Catholic aspirants."[29]

Smith's major response came on September 20 in an Oklahoma City speech. He spoke to an audience that included the head of the national anti-Catholic fundamentalist Protestant movement and in which rumors of possible violence were widespread. The speech anticipates the one John Kennedy would deliver in Houston thirty-two years later before Protestant ministers, although no evidence exists that Kennedy's staff consulted it in preparation for his address. Smith's address was eloquent. In part, he said:

> I here emphatically declare that I do not wish any member of my faith in any part of the United States to vote for me on religious grounds. I want them to vote for me only when in their hearts and consciences they become convinced that my election will promote the best interests of the country. By the same token, I cannot refrain from saying that any person who votes against me simply because of my religion is not, to my way of thinking, a good citizen. Let me remind the Democrats of the country that we belong to the party of Thomas Jefferson, whose proudest boast was that he was the author of the Virginia statute for religious freedom. . . . The absolute separation of state and church is part of the

> fundamental basis of our Constitution. I believe in that separation and in all that it implies. That belief must be a part of the fundamental faith of every American. Let the people of this country decide this election upon the great and real issues of the campaign and nothing else.[30]

Like Kennedy's speech, Smith's speech was well received by the national press, but it apparently had little impact on the course of the campaign.[31]

Smith was reluctant and ambivalent in dealing with the religious issue, but he was forthright and courageous in addressing prohibition and probably more than any other person paved the way for its repeal four years later.[32] In his famous "wet telegram" to the convention Smith said he favored modifications in enforcement that would allow the states to permit the sale of beer and wine. This inevitably allowed his opponents to make prohibition the centerpiece of their attacks on him. Mabel Walker Willebrandt, the assistant attorney general in charge of prohibition enforcement, lead the charge in the attacks on Smith. Campaigning as a surrogate for Hoover, she repeatedly assailed Smith for his "wetness," linking alcohol consumption to the corruption of New York City and its Catholic Irish dominated machine.[33] Others linked Smith's antiprohibition stance with other "sins," suggesting that he supported gambling and prostitution.[34] Finally, the stereotype of the drunkard Irishman was deployed, with rumors that "(Al)cohol" Smith was drunk during campaign appearances.[35] There is no credible evidence that he was ever intoxicated at campaign events, however, he acknowledged breaking the law by drinking, and he was a "heavy, perhaps compulsive" drinker.[36] Finan concludes, "It is not possible to draw conclusions about how deep an imprint this had on him, his family or career."[37]

While Smith's drinking and stance on prohibition may have upset Protestant fundamentalists, it endeared him to his core constituency of urban, immigrant Catholics. It showed he was one of them, an ethnic man, true to his roots, with a chance nevertheless to become president. Throughout the campaign in the Northeast cities he drew large, enthusiastic, and sometimes emotional crowds. This enthusiasm was particularly pronounced among the Catholic Irish who saw Smith as a "fellow Hibernian, the first American of Irish descent with a real chance to win the nation's highest office."[38]

Smith lost the election decisively. Hoover won by a popular vote margin of 58 percent to 41 percent and in the Electoral College 444–87. Smith carried only the heavily Catholic states of Rhode Island and Massachusetts and the several Deep South traditional Democratic strongholds. Hoover even won Smith's home state of New York. All students of the 1928 election conclude that no Democrat—not even Franklin Roosevelt—could have won in 1928, given the prosperous state of the economy. Experts also conclude that given the rapidly changing state of opinion on prohibition it was not decisive in Hoover's landslide. In the most detailed study of the election data, Lichtman concludes the "available evidence suggests that opposition to Smith's prohibition policy served as a cloak for opposition to his Catholicism."[39] In other words, the election was about the economy and religion. The former was decisive, but Smith's religion almost certainly contributed to the scale of his defeat. Lichtman avers that Catholics and Protestants voted their religion in 1928. Approximately 15 percent of the electorate, the Catholic vote for Smith increased by 28 percent compared to the 1924 Democratic vote and the Protestant vote declined by about 11 percent.[40]

Yet more so than any other Democratic nominee, Smith mobilized poor, urban Catholic immigrants, paving the way for the establishment of the New Deal Coalition four years later.[41] Turnout in 1928 increased by almost 8 million more than in 1924, and Smith's vote exceeded the 1924 Democratic nominee by more than 6 million.[42] Overall, Smith's 41 percent of the two-party vote was greater than any other Democratic candidate since the Civil War, except for Woodrow Wilson in 1916 and Grover Cleveland in his two victories. And if he had been renominated in 1932—given the shift of opinion on prohibition but especially the collapse of the economy—he might have defeated Hoover.

The 1932 nomination instead went to Franklin Roosevelt, Smith's protégé and handpicked successor as New York governor (Roosevelt had nominated Smith in 1928 famously describing him as the "Happy Warrior"). The nomination went to the Anglo-Saxon patrician from Hyde Park partly because it was becoming conventional wisdom that Smith's landslide loss demonstrated that a Catholic could not be elected president.

The evidence, however, does not support this wisdom, and Joe Kennedy certainly did not believe it because he thought about running himself in 1940 until his controversial tenure as ambassador destroyed any chance he might have had. He then transferred his ambitions to his son, assuming that a Catholic could win the presidency if he was not too Catholic, not too ethnic—and not a high school dropout, wearing a brown derby, drinking whiskey, and kissing ecclesiastical rings, but instead a Harvard man, war hero, and best-selling author who never wore hats and was rarely even photographed with priests or nuns.

Smith may have been bitter about the anti-Catholicism that characterized the 1928 election, but he never openly expressed it and left few personal papers from which historians might gain an understanding.[43]

His legacy, however, as the happy warrior in the cause of ethnic incorporation and liberalism was tarnished by his post political career. After his defeat he entered business (becoming president of the Empire State building) and became a wealthy "resident of swank Fifth Avenue, and a man seldom seen in his old haunts unless his chauffeur-driven limousine happened to flash by."[44]

More important, the liberal hero of the urban, immigrant working class whom Hoover had called a socialist in the late 1930s became a tribune of the most reactionary, antiliberal forces in the country. In 1936 he completely broke with Franklin Roosevelt and New Deal liberalism, accusing Roosevelt of socialism or perhaps even communism, exclaiming in a speech, "It is all right with me if they want to disguise themselves as Karl Marx or Lenin or any of the rest of that bunch, but I won't stand for their allowing them to march under the banner of Jackson or Cleveland. Let me give this solemn warning: There can be only one capital, Washington or Moscow."[45]

Undoubtedly, Smith was disappointed that Roosevelt took the nomination away from him in 1932, but it was probably more than that that led him to such vituperations.[46] Perhaps it was the allure of wealth, status, and acceptance in the Anglo-Saxon establishment; after all, Joe Kennedy also became a harsh critic of New Deal liberalism. Smith and Roosevelt later reconciled, but his betrayal of liberalism tarnished his legacy as well as the legacy of his historic campaign as the first major party ethnic nominee for the presidency.[47]

Historians have largely ignored Smith and the 1928 campaign, and John Kennedy paid little attention to Smith and 1928 in his quest for the presidency thirty-two years later. Indeed, in virtually every way, the second Catholic Irish campaign for the presidency was the exact opposite of the first. In all the books and articles on Kennedy and the 1960 election, Al Smith is an invisible man, an embarrassment, too crude, too Irish, too Catholic, and perhaps even too liberal.

The Making of the Second Ethnic Candidate for President: Jesse Jackson's Campaigns

Jesse Jackson in his long career is the embodiment of the central tendencies in African American politics from the civil rights protest era of the 1950s and 1960s to the present. Jackson began his activism at age sixteen when, like Rosa Parks in Montgomery, he sat at the front of a bus in segregated Greenville, North Carolina. At the historically black North Carolina A & T University he was leader of the campus chapter of the Congress on Racial Equality (CORE), a leading civil rights protest organization. Later, he led demonstrations protesting segregation at Greensboro's lunch counters and helped to organize a student civil rights group, the North Carolina Intercollegiate Council on Human Rights. Enamored of Dr. King from first hearing of him, Jackson attended the 1963 March on Washington and, determined to follow Dr. King's path, in 1965 he enrolled in seminary. (Chapter 4 discusses Jackson's perspicacity in becoming a part of King's SCLC staff and emergence as a leader of Chicago's African American community.)

Jackson was with King when he was murdered and in a much-disputed account claimed to have cradled the dying leader on the balcony of the Lorraine Motel.[48] At the time of his death King was planning the poor people's campaign. In internal SCLC deliberations, Jackson had opposed the campaign, but through the force of his personality and media savvy, he emerged as the de facto leader of the campaign's Washington demonstrations after King's death.[49]

Although a charismatic and strong-willed leader, King surrounded himself with several talented associates, including Ralph Abernathy, Hosea Williams, Andrew Young, and Wyatt Walker. Jackson, however, clearly believed he was better equipped to succeed King than any of them. By the 1980s, Jackson had accomplished this aspiration, winning recognition in the media and public opinion as the preeminent African American leader.[50] The peripatetic Jackson (Chicago columnist Mike Royko labeled him "Jetstream Jesse" because of his consistent failure to follow through on the multiple issues he would launch with great media fanfare) for a time traveled the country as the self-styled "country preacher." Dressed in the fashions of the moment (a huge Afro, bell-bottoms, dashikis, medallions, and leather vests), Jackson, like Booker T. Washington and Elijah Muhammad, preached the gospel of self-help, education, entrepreneurship, and personal responsibility. Subsequently, with financial support from the federal government he established PUSH–Excel to convey this message to black schoolchildren.

In the spring of 1972, Jackson joined at the National Black Political Convention with the radical and Black Nationalist forces in calling for the formation of a black political party. Taking on the established black leadership of elected officials and civil rights leaders, Jackson declared, "It's nation time." With this popular Black Nationalist refrain Jackson said, "Gary[, Indiana, the site of the convention,] is the birth of a new black political party. We can no longer afford to be boys in any major party. We must start believing in ourselves. . . . Damn both white parties. . . . I am a black man. I want a black party. I don't trust white Republicans or white Democrats."[51]

Several months later he took on Mayor Richard J. Daley and the Democratic Party establishment, cochairing an alternate Illinois delegation to the 1972 Democratic Convention. Charging that the regular delegation Daley headed had excluded minorities and women, Jackson played a pivotal role in persuading the convention to oust the Daley delegation and replace it with one he cochaired. A dozen years later he played an important role in mobilizing the black vote in Chicago that elected the city's first black mayor. All along he was engaging in "citizen diplomacy" abroad,[52] while continuing to lead marches and rallies for civil rights, workers' rights, women's rights, the environment, and nuclear disarmament. Thus, when he sought the presidency in 1984 he was one of the best-known political leaders in the United States.[53]

Jackson held this preeminence when Obama in 2008 became the second credible black candidate for the Democratic nomination. However, his stature had been diminished as a result of revelations in 2001 that he fathered a child with a young member of his staff. A survey by the Joint Center for Political and Economic Studies found that between 2000 and 2002 Jackson's favorability rating among blacks declined from 83 percent to 60 percent and his unfavorability increased from 9 percent to 26 percent.

Yet his blackness was never in doubt. Unlike Obama who, as Bobby Rush suggested, had to acquire his blackness by reading books, listening to music, and playing basketball, Jackson was in a sense "born" black. Born to a single teen mother amidst "the pervasive degradation of Greenville's small town system of apartheid," Jackson recalled that "given the scars on our souls, . . . it's amazing that there're so few blacks now who are openly and verbally hostile to whites."[54] Jackson's time and place, like that of Rev. Jeremiah Wright, Obama's former pastor, is a sharp contrast to Obama's growing up in Hawaii, perhaps the least apartheid-like state in the union.

Jackson, the star high school quarterback, believes that racism and white supremacy were factors in his being denied the opportunity to play that position at the University of Illinois, causing him to return to study and play that position at an all-black institution. These scars on Jackson's soul, he recalled, as a young man led him to spit in the soup of whites while working as a waiter in all white restaurants. "Hardly call it even though," he said, "spit in their soup while they burn our churches."[55] Jackson later claimed that he never did the spitting, but as Frady writes, the mere telling of the story is "testimony to his submerged fury" as a black man and his continuing need to "identify passionately with the pains of the black past in America."[56]

Jackson's blackness is reflected in his life of activism in the struggle for the liberation of black peoples throughout the world. His politics (including his presidential campaigns) are deeply rooted in African American culture—in the church and its religiosity, in its oratorical tradition, its music, and its ethos.[57] Like Al Smith, Jackson understood that to be credible as a presidential candidate he had to deethinicize, to be less black. In the course of the campaigns he attempted to become less ethnic and reach out to all the colors in his rainbow. Like Smith, he abandoned the dashikis and Afro for a close haircut and somber, gray pinstripes. And, like Smith, he never attempted to "whiten" his enunciation into the reassuring, colorless precisions of, for example, a Colin Powell. Nor did he in reaching out to whites abandon the cause of the black poor. In 1988, when his campaign deliberately became less an insurgency and more incorporationist he did emphasize "valence" issues (described in the following), but as Frady writes, even then "he seemed unable to disenthrall himself from the racial pains of his own past, and reluctant to risk any disenchantment among the black constituency that was his one great asset, to stretch himself enough to truly embrace the wider popular coalition he helped to form."[58]

One thing, then, is clear in Jackson's case: the question of his blackness was not a question. However, it was a problem because for too many nonblack Americans it was equally clear that there is no black at the end of the rainbow.

As chapter 4 indicates, Jackson said he was prompted to run for president in 1984 because when Walter Mondale and Edward Kennedy came to Chicago, they endorsed the two Catholic Irish mayoral candidates rather than the African American candidate. However, as Ronald Walters and Lucius Barker indicate, the "general black consensus" was that a black person should run for president in 1984. This consensus emerged out of disenchantment with the conservative policies of the Reagan administration and increasing alienation from the Democratic Party. As Barker puts it, "Another spur to a black candidacy was the increasing disenchantment of blacks with the policies of the Democratic party. While the Republicans were openly hostile and had all but written off black interests, Democrats too were becoming increasingly more inattentive and uncaring of their interests and concerns."[59] Thus Walters, an influential advisor to the black establishment and subsequently deputy campaign manager in Jackson's 1984 campaign, argued that the black ethnic group should develop a strategy of "independent leverage" within the Democratic Party.[60] This strategy, akin to what George Wallace accomplished in his multiple presidential campaigns, would establish the black community as an independent constituency of which Democratic Party elites would have to take account.

From the outset, therefore, Jackson's campaigns included a powerful ethnic nationalist strain, envisioned as an effort to empower the black community and compel the political system to address its ethnic group interests. Although elements from the Black Nationalist community (including Louis Farrakhan's Nation of Islam) were included in the 1984 campaign, from the outset Jackson had a broader vision of a populist Rainbow Coalition that would include feminists, homosexuals, workers, environmentalists and other peoples of color in a "struggle against the economic aristocracy."[61] As he told the 1984 Democratic Convention, "My constituency is the desperate, the damned, the disinherited, the disrespected and the despised."[62] The excesses of political oratory aside, the Jackson campaign clearly was not designed to represent middle-class, mainstream American politics.

In addition to the nationalist and populist strains, however, in 1988 a third, incorporationist one was also included. The 1984 campaign was more of a movement-style insurgency than a typical presidential campaign.[63] In spite of the general black consensus that an African American should run for president in 1984, virtually the entire black leadership establishment opposed Jackson's campaign. Seeing the support Jackson gained from blacks in 1984, in 1988 black establishment leaders joined in and helped to shift the campaign from insurgency toward incorporation.[64] Not only did black establishment figures join the 1988 campaign, but so did white Democratic Party insiders.[65] The inevitable tensions between these three elements—ethnic nationalism, rainbow populism, and establishment incorporation—ultimately were resolved in favor of the incorporation. This transformation from insurgency in 1984 to incorporation in 1988 was fueled, according to Richard Hatcher, the general campaign manager in 1984, by the Jackson "fantasy" that "he might somehow become the vice presidential nominee."[66]

In 1988, Jackson continued to espouse a populist, left-of-center domestic and foreign policy agenda, but he downplayed issues of special concern to blacks while highlighting what political scientists call "valence" issues, those issues on which candidates compete by claiming to stand for some universally desired values. These issues do not divide voters, but if well-articulated they may have powerful effects on voter support. Such was the case for Jackson on two issues in 1988, drug use and personal responsibility of the young for sex and pregnancy. Jackson was almost universally acclaimed by the media and his opponents (in both parties) as the most effective advocate on these issues. While this valence advocacy probably did not attract many voters, it did somewhat position Jackson in the mainstream of U.S. politics.

The turn toward incorporation disillusioned the ethnic nationalists in the coalition. Robert Starks lamented, ". . . he should have organized a solid force to regenerate the Democratic Party or formed his own party. . . . [But because of his abiding wistfulness, despite everything to come in from the outside, to be admitted into the Party's inner pavilions of importance,] none of this happened. And the window of opportunity was gone. Eighty-four was a missed opportunity."[67]

But the transformation from insurgency to establishment, from ethnic nationalism to incorporation, is inevitable for any credible presidential candidate. George Wallace's successive white nationalist campaigns became less racist, less nationalist, and more establishment and incorporationist.[68] This is partly because even ethnic men, committed to the interest of their group necessarily wish to broaden their appeal in order to attract the broadest possible configuration of support. This is not to suggest that Jackson abandoned his solidarity roots or his blackness. Rather, it is to say that between 1984 and 1988 as the credibility of his candidacy increased, he became somewhat less ethnic.

The idea of a progressive Rainbow Coalition of voters that might become an influential faction in the Democratic Party was based on two distinct but interrelated assumptions. The first was the mobilization of the black vote. Since 1972 blacks have constituted roughly 20 percent of the Democratic Party voter coalition, and they are homogeneously liberal; thus, if they could be mobilized in significant numbers, they could become a core or base in the progressive Rainbow Coalition. The second assumption was that enough nonblacks (whites, Hispanics, and Asian Americans) could be mobilized in a coalition with blacks to form a rainbow majority.

Data from the 1984 campaign from a variety of sources indicate a significant increase in black registration and turnout during the primary and caucuses. Indeed, for the first time in the history of the Democratic Party's nomination process, black Americans probably voted in the primaries at a greater rate than whites. An analysis by the Joint Center for Political Studies of turnout in twelve Democratic primary states showed that in every state voting was greater in "black areas" than in the state as a whole. Increased black turnout from 1980 to 1984 ranged from 14 percent in Georgia to 127 percent in New York state.[69] This compares to an overall increase in Democratic primary voting of 4 percent between 1980 and 1984.

This massive increase in black participation in the 1984 primaries was attributable in large measure to the enthusiasm Jackson's campaign generated. Blacks comprised 18 percent of Democratic primary voters in 1984. Black turnout in Democratic primaries in 1988 increased to 21 percent.[70]

In 1984, exit poll data showed that Jackson carried about 85 percent of the black vote overall. In the early primaries in Alabama and Georgia, Jackson received 50 percent and 60 percent of the black vote, respectively, with Walter Mondale receiving the vast majority of the remaining. However, as the primary season developed, Jackson's percentage of the black vote steadily increased until he was receiving between 85 percent and 90 percent of the total. Jackson's support in the black community cut across all demographic categories. In the early southern primaries, young and rural blacks were slightly more favorable to Jackson than older and urban blacks. However, by the end of the primary season Jackson was receiving about the same level of support from all strata of the black community. In 1988, Jackson increased his percentage of the black vote from 80–85 percent in 1984 to 90–95 percent. Thus, in 1988 black voter support of the Rainbow Coalition was virtually complete. Indeed, unlike in 1984, all his opponents in 1988 conceded the black vote to Jackson. At the Congressional Black Caucus's annual meeting in 1987, for example, Michael Dukakis asked plaintively, "Let me be your second choice." The campaigns, therefore, were highly successful in both elections in mobilizing their core constituency.

In 1984, Jackson received about 10 percent of the white primary vote (about 20 percent of his total). Among Hispanics, Jackson got 33 percent of the Puerto Rican vote and 17 percent of the Mexican American vote. Among Asian Americans, experts estimate that he got 35 percent of the vote in New Jersey and 20 percent in California; Arab Americans voted for Jackson overwhelmingly, but he received only 5 percent of the Jewish vote in New York and 8 percent in California. Except perhaps for the relatively small Arab American population, Jackson received majority support in 1984 from no nonblack ethnic group, doing best among Puerto Ricans, where he got about one-third of the vote. Jackson's white vote in 1984 was too small to draw inferences about its class basis. Still, as Lorenzo Morris and Linda Williams observe, the white vote was apparently not lower class.[71]

In 1988, Jackson significantly increased his support among whites and Hispanics, winning about 20 percent of the white vote overall, ranging from 10 percent in the southern Super Tuesday states to about 25 percent in Wisconsin and Connecticut. The size of the 1988 white vote was large enough to draw statistically significant inferences about its class composition. *New York Times–CBS News* exit poll data from all the states where Jackson received important white support show it came overwhelmingly from liberal, well-educated, affluent voters rather than the poor and working-class voters. This in spite of the objective similarities in the material conditions of blacks and low-income whites and Jackson's frequent and eloquent appeals for their support. Apparently Jackson's campaign appeal could not overcome the racism and conservatism of the white working class.

Jackson also increased his Hispanic vote in 1988. In New York he won the Puerto Rican vote (61 percent), but in Texas he lost the Mexican American vote to Dukakis (50 percent to 21 percent). Although blacks and Mexican Americans share similar material conditions and exhibit similar liberal policy preferences, considerable social distance exists between the groups, which makes black–Mexican American voter coalitions problematic. Puerto Ricans, on the other hand, not only share similar material conditions and issue preferences, but there is also less social distance between the groups as well as more consciousness of common ethnic group interests.

Apart from the absence of white working-class support, the most unusual aspect of Jackson's campaigns in 1984 and 1988 was the disaffection of American Jews. Although recent years have seen a little movement in a conservative direction, American Jews still score disproportionately high on measures of liberalism. Also, in big-city elections, Jews among whites have been disproportionate supporters of blacks, as in Chicago in 1983 when the opposing candidate was Jewish.

Jews, therefore, should have been a natural constituency in the Rainbow Coalition. However, in 1988, when Jackson was receiving about 20 percent of the white vote, he got only 7 percent of the Jewish vote. A part of this dissatisfaction had to do with Jackson's controversial past—his alleged anti-Semitic remarks and relationships with Palestine Liberation Organization (PLO) leader Yasser Arafat and the Nation of Islam's Louis Farrakhan. However, the root of the problem was Jackson's position on the Middle East conflict, specifically support of the Palestinian quest for self-determination.

In 1984 Jackson won primaries or caucuses in three states (Louisiana, Virginia, and South Carolina) and the District of Columbia, ending the campaign in third place with 18 percent of the vote and 9 percent of the delegates. Jackson substantially improved on this performance in 1988, winning the District of Columbia and five southern states (Alabama, Louisiana, Georgia, Mississippi, and Virginia), and five diverse caucuses (Alaska, Delaware, South Carolina, Puerto Rico, and Michigan). By the time the Democratic Convention convened Jackson had amassed 29 percent of the vote (compared to Dukakis's 43 percent) and a projected 1,105 delegates compared to Dukakis's 2,309. Placing second in a field of eight established Democratic leaders demonstrates that in 1988 the Jackson campaign became more inclusive with a broader and more diverse base of support.

When Jackson ran for president 20 percent of whites told pollsters they would not vote for a qualified black candidate for president.[72] When Obama ran twenty years later, that figure had declined to 5 percent. The Jackson campaigns must be given some credit for this change. As Frady writes, ". . . there is little question that Jackson himself made the initial breach through that old barrier in the general mind to any serious consideration of a presidential candidacy by a black—leaving open the possibility through which, it appeared for a while in 1985, Colin Powell could well pass."[73]

Jackson's campaigns were not successful in halting the Democratic Party's drift to the right on issues of concern to blacks and poor people. To the contrary, Bill Clinton in his campaigns used symbolic attacks on Jackson as a means to distance the party from African Americans, move the party to the right on race in an appeal to Reagan Democrats.[74] But Jackson's campaigns did facilitate the near full incorporation of blacks into the Democratic Party, including the appointment of his protégé Ron Brown as the first black chair of the Democratic Party. (Al Smith's campaign resulted in the appointment of the first Catholic chair of the party.)

Jackson's campaigns also resulted in changes in the formula for allocating delegates that made possible Obama's narrow win of the primaries and caucuses. When he ran in 1984 he won 18 percent of the Democratic primary vote but was allocated only 8 percent of the delegates. Jackson argued this was undemocratic and pressed for changes in the rules. As a result the 1984 convention appointed a Fairness Commission, which revised the delegate allocation rules so that they would more closely reflect the wishes of the voters. Without these reforms in the nominating process, Obama could not have won the nomination in 2008.

Jackson also established the Rainbow Coalition parameters that would elect the first black president. Jackson's rainbow was anchored by winning 90 percent of the 20 percent of the Democratic primary vote blacks constituted. Obama duplicated this in 2008. Among whites Jackson's supporters were disproportionately the young, the well-educated, and the upper income. With the addition of Jews, these were the same groups (in much larger numbers for sure) that propelled Obama to the presidency.

Jackson's candidacy underscored the need for a successful black candidate not to be too ethnic or too black and to run a deracialized campaign. As Williams wrote after the 1988 election, in order to be successful a black candidate "must increasingly articulate political methods, goals, rhetoric and symbols that are ***unmistakably inclusive*** and not viewed as the special province of any particular interest group."[75] After the 1988 election Jackson campaign manager Richard Hatcher suggested that Jackson was like Moses, who would never get to the promised land of the presidency. Who, Hatcher mused, might be the Joshua who would get there:

> Ironically, that could be some person very different from Jesse, who in what he represents and wants to do, will irritate fewer whites, will be more acceptable to them, because they will see him as more like themselves. . . . What difference does it make that the color of their skin happens to be like mine if, in fact, they are not sensitive to the problems African Americans face in this country, if they have in fact spent their careers and will spend their entire tenure running away from that.[76]

On March 4, 2007, in one of his rare speeches on race, Obama embraced this Moses-Joshua analogy. He spoke in the presence of Jackson and other veterans of the civil rights movement at Selma, Alabama's historic Brown African Methodist Episcopal Church; the church from which civil rights marchers in 1965 confronted George Wallace's troopers on Bloody Sunday. In the speech, he declared that Jackson and the Moses generation had brought blacks 90 percent of the way to the Promised Land, and it was the duty of his, the Joshua generation, to take the race the last 10 percent of the way.[77] These things, of course, cannot be measured with exacting precision, but as the analysis in chapter 6 shows, blacks are not—not even close—to 90 percent incorporation into the Promised Land. That the always-careful Obama—especially so when talking about race—would so grossly exaggerate the extent of African American incorporation suggests he was addressing not only the Moses generation but Pharaoh and his followers as well.

6

The Incorporation of the Catholic Irish and the Semi-Incorporation of African Americans

Writing in 1972 Andrew Greeley observed:

> Practically every accusation that has been made against blacks has also been made against the Irish: their family life was inferior, they had no ambition, they did not keep up their homes, they drank too much, they were not responsible, they had no morals, it was not safe to walk through their neighborhoods at night, they voted the way crooked politicians told them to vote, they were not willing to pull themselves up by their bootstraps, they were not capable of education, they could not think for themselves and they would always remain social problems for the rest of the country.[1]

We do not have survey data but perhaps as early as the 1930s these negative, invidious stereotypes about the Catholic Irish were being replaced by more benign ones. I was not able to locate data on Catholic or Irish Catholic stereotypes at the time of Kennedy's election, but more recent studies suggest where things might have been or might have been headed in 1960. Of course, Kennedy's election, martyrdom, and the Camelot myth no doubt contributed to and perhaps accelerated the decline of the negative stereotypes.

In 1994 the National Conference on Inter-Group Relations (formerly the National Conference of Christians and Jews) commissioned Louis Harris to conduct a survey to gauge the level of adherence to ethnic stereotypes. Respondents were asked to list both positive attributes and negative beliefs about selected ethnic groups, including blacks, Latinos, Asians, Jews, Catholics, Muslims, and whites.[2]

With respect to positive attributes, 74 percent of non-Catholics agreed Catholics "have made significant contributions to American life," 67 percent believed that they are "compassionate and care about the poor," and 57 percent thought that they are "devout."[3] On the negative side, 55 percent of non-Catholics share the view that Catholics "want to impose their views of morality on the larger society," 32 percent accept the idea that they are "narrow-minded and controlled by their church," and 25 percent agreed that Catholics "are highly biased against people of other races and ethnic groups." Finally, an overwhelming majority believed that Catholics faced little discrimination in American society.[4]

Regarding positive attributes of African Americans, 80 percent of nonblacks believe blacks have made "valuable contributions to American society," 62 percent said that they "believe strongly in the American dream and ideals," and 52 percent thought they are "deeply religious."[5] On the negative side 46 percent of nonblacks adhere to the view that blacks "are more likely to commit crimes and violence," 40 percent thought that they have "less family unity," and 22 percent accept the view that they "want to live on welfare."[6] Additionally, 63 percent agreed that blacks "suffer from a lot of discrimination."[7]

Regarding the Catholic Irish specifically, in the mid-1980s Richard Alba employed a random sample to study ethnic consciousness and identity among European ethnic groups (Irish Catholics, Italians, Jews, French Canadians, Scotch-Irish, and Dutch) in the Albany metropolitan region of New York. He found that of all the groups the Catholic Irish evoked (after the Italians) the most distinct ethnic stereotypes. The non–Catholic Irish stereotyped the group as "good with words," as politicians, heavy drinkers, policemen, and the plight of the "long suffering Irish woman."[8] Except for the drinking and the plight of women, none of these stereotypes are negative or invidious. Certainly none of them are of the slanderous character Greeley alludes to at the outset of this chapter.

In its 1991 General Social Survey, the University of Chicago found that white attitudes toward blacks corresponded near precisely to those Greeley wrote were formally used to stereotype Irish Catholics: 47 percent of whites said that blacks tend to be lazy, 59 percent said they prefer welfare to work, 54 percent said that they were prone to violence, and 31 percent said they were less intelligent.[9] During the 2008 presidential election, major news organizations reported similar results and speculated about how these negative stereotypes might affect Obama's prospects for election.[10]

Although we do not have survey data on stereotypes about Irish Catholics when Kennedy ran for president in 1960, he almost certainly did not confront an Anglo-Saxon electorate with the kind of hostility toward his ethnic group that Obama faced in 2008. In 1960 the Catholic Irish had been fully incorporated—culturally, economically, and politically—while black incorporation when Obama was elected was token in each of these arenas, except perhaps the cultural. This chapter compares the long road of Catholic Irish full incorporation from the 1840s to the 1930s–1950s to the even longer road of African American partial or incipient incorporation from the 1780s to the 1960s–2008. The impact of these differential patterns of incorporation on the campaigns and presidencies of Kennedy and Obama are principal theoretical concerns of this book.

This chapter uses Hechter's three analytical black boxes discussed in chapter 2, beginning with the cultural, followed by the economic, and then the political. The cultural is divided in two categories. The first category is the popular culture, the extent to which the group is incorporated and fairly represented in sports, movies, literature, and the arts. The second category is the culture more generally, especially the extent to which mass media display negative stereotypical images of the groups. This is important in the larger processes of incorporation because popular culture reflects the "aspirations and values" of the society and is often a precursor to and an affirmation of cultural incorporation more generally. As Curran, writing of the Irish Catholics and the movies, observes, ". . . by reflecting and sometimes influencing their audience's changing perception of the Irish, motion pictures facilitated their assimilation into American society."[11]

Catholic Irish Incorporation

Every subordinate ethnic group is usually caricatured in the media of the dominant group. These caricatures usually take some real or imagined attributes of the group and exaggerate them for purposes of entertaining the dominant group and disparaging the subordinate one. This has always been an effective and efficient means of maintaining relationships of ethnic domination. Subordinate ethnic group leaders have always understood this, and as they develop a voice in the society—which is usually associated with the development of a middle class of some size—they mount protests against the negative portrayal of the group in the mass media. Within the subordinate ethnic group this often gives rise to centrifugalism or class tension, with the emergent middle class wishing to disassociate itself from a lower class that it views as stigmatizing them and hindering their quest for respectability. Representatives of the lower class, however, may view some of these portrayals as expressions of the authentic culture or traditions of the group. Middle-class persons, then, are viewed as dicty, as turning their backs on their heritage in an effort to win acceptance in the mainstream. These tendencies and tensions characterize both the African American and Catholic Irish experiences in the United States.[12]

"The stage Irishman" must go, inveighed the *Boston Pilot* in the 1860s.[13] Representing the pretensions and aspirations of the lace-curtain, the *Boston Pilot* was offended by the shanty Irish image of the stage Irishman:

> Here was the "stage Irishman" in perfect stereotype, dressed in frieze clothes, battered caubeen, and heavy brogans, swinging his shillelagh in a fight at a fair, smoking a foreshortened clay pipe, a heavy drinker, a jollier of the ladies, a believer in the little people, improvident, happy-go-lucky, a buffoon, lacking nothing but a pig tied to a string.[14]

In the late 1890s the Ancient Order of the Hibernians and other Catholic Irish groups began a concerted campaign to eliminate these images from the stage, newspapers, and magazines. Using boycotts and other forms of protest, by the time of the arrival of the motion picture after World War I the stage Irishman was largely a relic.[15] The disappearance of the stage Irishman reflected both the acculturation and incorporation of the group. These processes are reflected in the gradual transformation of St. Patrick's Day into an American as well as an ethnic celebration, with Anglo-Saxons joining the Catholic Irish in celebrating the patron saint of Ireland by "wearing of the green" and perhaps partaking of some corned beef and cabbage.

Although the movie industry from its inception in the United States was dominated by Jews, some persons of Catholic Irish origins made their mark in production and management as the industry grew, including Joseph P. Kennedy.[16] And while the stage Irishman was rarely seen in the movies, the stereotypical Irish cop, priest, and politician were standard fare. In the 1930s James Cagney, "the quintessential Irish American," became perhaps the first Catholic Irish movie star with a national following.[17] Then there was *Gone with the Wind* "where the most famous Irish screen family of the 1930s appeared in the greatest movie of the decade and perhaps of all time."[18] In 1938 Spencer Tracy won an Oscar for his role in *Boys Town*, and thereafter Irish Catholics were ubiquitous on the American screen. By the time of Kennedy's election Catholic Irish integration into the movies was complete, symbolized by the "Kellys"—Grace, "the national symbol of beauty and class," who married a prince, and Gene, who "often played in Irish American movies, but . . . was always an all American."[19] Earlier in music, George M. Cohan won the acclaim of the nation with his "super patriotic, flag waving songs." Cohan's career, Curran writes, "represents a landmark in the history of Irish Americans, both because he combined their patriotic spirit and because in him they reached the peak of success as entertainers on the American stage."[20]

In literature, F. Scott Fitzgerald became the first major Irish Catholic novelist in the United States. Although Irish Catholic references appear throughout Fitzgerald's writings, he, like Ralph Ellison, played down his ethnicity, "work[ing] to win acceptance as an artist in his own right, unconnected with any disturbing association with Pat-and-Mike jokes, the Irish brogue . . . and the church."[21] Eugene O'Neill, perhaps the nation's greatest dramatist, reflects the centrifugal tendency that often accompanies seminal ethnic literature, observed later in this chapter in the discussion of the Harlem Renaissance. Throughout his career some accused O'Neill of being anti-Irish, anti-Catholic, of "exposing the failings of Irish life."[22] Like W. E. B. Du Bois's criticisms of Langston Hughes and other "primitivism" writers of the Harlem Renaissance, critics disparaged Fitzgerald's work as "nasty, dirty, as putting too much emphasis on sex and four letter words, and as not giving a true, balanced account of the American Irish."[23] These criticisms of Fitzgerald, however, most likely made him more acceptable to the literary establishment because they demonstrated that he was an artist able to use ethnic material to transcend ethnic boundaries.

In the United States and other places as well, sports are often more than spectacle for the masses or forms of recreation or leisure. Often they are also an expression of nationalism and a means to inoculate and sustain system values and patriotism. In the United States progressive reformers viewed athletics as means to transform Catholic immigrants into good Americans. Viewing their traditional games (racetracks, gambling, boxing, and pool) as "barbaric and destructive," "legitimate sport" was seen as a "means to assimilate immigrants, spark nationalism, smooth class tensions and ameliorate racial divisions."[24] But the leaders of the immigrant communities—especially the Irish—unwilling to abandon their traditions and culture, sought to use sports as a means to show that one could be both Irish Catholic and American.[25]

In 1897 Irish Catholics established the Irish American Athletic Club in order to encourage participation on the U.S. Olympic team. At the 1908 games held in London, Irish Americans dominated. President Theodore Roosevelt had appointed James Sullivan, the son of Irish immigrants, president of the American Olympic Association, and "Mike" Murphy, who also was of Irish descent, coached the team.[26] Americans won thirteen of twenty-three track and field events and of this number members of the Irish American Athletic Club were responsible for more than half. John Hayes, an eighteen-year-old club member, was the star of the 1908 games, defeating the British in the marathon. Celebrated in newspapers throughout the country, Hayes's victory was "proof that Irish Americans could gain a place within the mainstream without sacrificing their ethnic identity. He showed that Irish Americans could gain acceptance by achieving success for America."[27]

The achievements of the Irish at the 1908 Olympics inaugurated a long period of Irish dominance of American sport.[28] The Catholic and Irish presence in boxing, baseball, and football was by the 1950s so commonplace that it was taken for granted.[29] Undermining old stereotypes, Catholic Irish participation in sport, like their presence in movies, legitimatized the group in the eyes of the Protestant public and the Anglo-Saxon establishment. After all who could think Knute Rockne and the "Fighting Irish" at Notre Dame "were conspiring to anything more subversive than a victory over Army."[30]

At the same time their success in sports contributed to a sense of ethnic pride, as well as a sense that being Catholic and Irish was not apart from being American. Playing baseball, then, was partly how the Irish became American, as well as a precursor to cultural incorporation more generally and to incorporation into the economy and polity.

The principal evidence of the acculturation and cultural incorporation of any ethnic group is the disappearance of ethnic-specific ghettos. Another important indicator is widespread interethnic marriage, especially with members of the dominant group. Another important piece of evidence is the decline of ethnic consciousness and identity, a withering away of the memory of the bond of "bearing one common wrong." By each of these indicators, Catholic Irish cultural incorporation was near complete by 1960.

Although distinctive Catholic Irish residential enclaves can be found even today in several U.S. cities including Boston and Chicago, most students of the Irish Catholic experience agree that by the 1950s their ghettoization was past.[31] Understanding "ghetto" as an area of a city where members of an ethnic group live because of social, economic, political, or legal constraints, by the 1940s (perhaps even earlier) the Catholic Irish in America faced none of these constraints. The prosperity of the post–World War II economy, the G.I. Bill, subsidized suburban mortgages, the decline of invidious stereotypes, and a general decline in nativism (outside of the small town South and Midwest) resulted in the removal of these constraints. The end of the ghettos also brought about the decline of two institutions central to Catholic Irish identity: the local parish and the saloon.

We do not have good statistical data, but by the 1950s scholars widely assumed that the Catholic Irish had put aside Rose Kennedy's horror at the prospect of marrying beyond the boundaries of the group.[32] Indeed, of Rose's six children who married, only one married a person of Irish origins and two married non-Catholics.[33] By the 1980s probably no more than one-fourth of Catholic Irish marriages were to spouses of the same ancestry. Alba found that regarding the children's ethnic identity, parents of Irish ancestry, in contrast to Italian parents for example, "are no different from others of old stock background. Just one-third are concerned that their children have some form of ethnic identity. The desired identities include multiple ethnic strands and, in some cases, the Irish component is even lacking."[34]

If the theoretical understanding guiding this study is correct, the decline of Catholic Irish consciousness and identity necessarily follows cultural incorporation. That is, Hechter contends that ethnic consciousness and identity are a function of the extent of the real or perceived oppression of the group. By the 1950s the Catholic Irish faced little, and perhaps perceived less, Anglo-Saxon oppression. This is not to say that residues of anti-Catholic nativism could still be found—the 1960 election demonstrates that—but that it was considerably less than, for example, when Al Smith ran in 1928. Thus, when Kennedy was elected, the Catholic Irish were embracing what Gans refers to as "symbolic ethnicity," a vestigial attachment to a few ethnic symbols with little meaning for everyday life.[35] As Levine puts it, "Increasingly they [Irish Catholics] have memories and nostalgia in place of ethnic identity."[36] Numerous Catholic Irish intellectuals lament this outcome of the processes of incorporation. O'Connor writes:

> . . . The Irish families that had been in America for two or three generations had lost touch with their ethnic heritage. . . . It was pleasant enough for young people to celebrate St. Patrick's Day once a year, to enjoy a bit of Irish music, and to spend an evening with their friends at a local Irish pub, but few of them had any firsthand knowledge of the history or culture of Ireland. Nor did they feel any attachments to the old neighborhoods. . . .[37]

And Greeley writes: "The American Irish made it by forgetting their past and trying to be like everyone else; they successful[ly] imitated much of the achievement and style of big city Protestants. During this process, much of the poetry, the laughter, the mysticism and the style of the Irish past was lost. . . . Respectability we finally gained; now what do we have to enjoy it with."[38] Understandable lamentations perhaps; but O'Connor and Greeley understand also that loss of heritage and identity are probably the inevitably price of admission to the mainstream. A price many, if not most, African Americans would be quite willing to pay.

Greeley writes, "Irish Catholics are the most successful of the white immigrant groups."[39] Actually the Jews are the most successful of the white immigrant groups, but the Catholic Irish are second, socially and economically. Table 6.1 displays data from a composite of National Opinion Research Center surveys Greeley compiled from 1963 to 1972. The data compare the education, occupation, and income of British, Scotch-Irish, Irish Catholics, and African Americans. On each of these measures the long-oppressed Irish Catholics fare better than the Protestants, be they British, Scotch-Irish, or African American. Greeley nicely summarizes the import of the data on white immigrant economic incorporation for the purposes of this study: ". . . in the two decades between 1950 and 1970 the upward mobility system which worked extremely well for the Jews, the Irish and Italians, reasonably well for the Germans and has begun to work for the Poles, has not yet worked at all for the blacks."[40]

John Kennedy's New Frontier and Lyndon Johnson's Great Society of the 1960s provided the opening for African American political incorporation. Franklin Roosevelt's New Deal thirty years earlier provided the opening for the Catholic Irish. Prior to the New Deal, with the exception of Supreme Court Justice Pierce Butler and Joseph Tumulty,

Table 6.1. Selected Composite Data (1963–1972) on the Economic Status of Selected Ethnic Groups, British, Scotch-Irish, Irish Catholics and African Americans

Ethnic Group	Years of Education	Occupational Prestige*	Percent White Collar	Family Income
British	11.9	3.98	53	$8,309
Scotch-Irish	10.6	3.17	38	7,022
Catholic Irish	12.2	4.27	49	9,255
African American	9.7	2.47	18	5,425

*The higher the score, the greater the degree of occupational prestige.

Source: Andrew Greely, *Ethnicity in the United States* (New York: Wiley, 1974), pp. 42–56.

Woodrow Wilson's private secretary, few Irish Catholics had held influential positions in the federal government.[41] Given their population (in 1960 Catholics constituted about 25 percent of the population) and their concentration in the Northeast, Catholics in general and Irish Catholics in particular were elected in significant numbers to Congress as early as the beginning of the twentieth century. For the Catholic Irish, however, the New Deal provided the "major breakthrough from the provincial confines of city and state politics . . . [making] possible the transition from Al Smith to John Kennedy."[42] The appointment of the President's father to the then-prestigious post of ambassador to the Court of St James was symbolic of this breakthrough.

Irish Catholic political incorporation by the time of Kennedy's election was near complete. Twelve members of the Senate were Catholic Irish, as were 88 of 435 House members. Catholic Irish politicians had been elected to the Senate and to governors' chairs in states where they were a distinct minority of the electorate. Since 1928 a Catholic Irishman had chaired the Democratic National Committee (Kennedy in 1960 appointed the first Protestant in thirty-two years), and when Kennedy was sworn-in, Catholics were the majority leaders in both houses of Congress.

Another indicator of political incorporation by 1960 was the ideological and partisan diversity of the Catholic vote. Ghettoization politically has the same deleterious consequences for an ethnic group as do residential, cultural, or economic segregation. In a two-party system if an ethnic group's vote is overwhelmingly cast for one of the parties, this is usually an indicator that the group's interest and policy preferences are not bipartisan (Jews are an exception in this regard). In other words, they are ghettoized. One party will take the group's vote for granted, and the other will ignore it and its interests or concerns altogether. Since Al Smith, the Catholic vote had been overwhelmingly Democratic, and with the white Protestant South it was a cornerstone of the New Deal coalition. In the last years of the New Deal, middle- and upper-class Catholics began to turn away from Roosevelt's New Deal liberalism. The Catholic Joseph McCarthy—who enjoyed the friendship and support of the Kennedys—with his militant anti-communism encouraged Catholic affection and affiliation for the conservative Republican Party. Thus, by 1960, the Catholic vote could not be taken for granted by either party; it was a swing vote to which both parties appealed.

Eisenhower, in his two elections in the 1950s, averaged about 50 percent of the Catholic vote. Kennedy in 1960 won about 80 percent. While overwhelming, this was not a near-unanimous rallying around the flag of ethnicity. In New York City, Moynihan estimates that Kennedy got little more than half the Irish vote, and "the students at Fordham gave him as much, but it appears it was the Jewish students in the College of Pharmacy who saved this ancient Jesuit institution from going on record as opposed to the election of the first Catholic President of the United States."[43]

African American Semi-Incorporation

On board *Air Force One* on a trip to throw out the first pitch of the 2009 all-star baseball game, President Obama told Willie Mays, "Let me tell you, you helped us get there, if it hadn't been for folks like you and Jackie I am not sure I would get elected to the White House. The spirit you put in the game, how you carried yourself, all that really makes a difference. Changed peoples [*sic*] attitudes. So, you played a part in it. And, you are here on *Air Force One*; that's alright [*sic*]."[44] In paying tribute to Mays, the President recognized the significance of popular culture in shaping attitudes that brought about the cultural incorporation of African Americans and the significance of this incorporation in his election. Orlando Patterson exaggerates when he concludes that African Americans have achieved "full political and cultural incorporation";[45] he is more nearly correct with respect to popular culture when he writes, "Afro-Americans dominate the nation's popular culture: its music, its dance, its talk, its sport, its youth fashion; and they are a powerful force in its popular and elite literature."[46] In *What Obama Means for Our Culture, Our Politics, Our Future*, Jabrani Asim calls attention to how cultural changes paved the way in the American mind for Obama's election. He focuses on such things as Sidney Poitier and the movie *Guess Who's Coming to Dinner*, Motown, and "crossover" performers such as Jimmy Hendricks, Prince, Michael Jordan, and Oprah.[47] This chapter refines and extends the analyses of the President, Patterson, and Asim, first by comparing the black with the Catholic Irish experience; second, it traces the black struggle for cultural incorporation, showing the dichotomous relationship in 2008 in the African American case between popular cultural incorporation and social and cultural incorporation more generally.

The black struggle for cultural incorporation, like the Catholic Irish, started at the beginning of the twentieth century. It was a struggle against the invidious stereotypes of the group displayed on stage, vaudeville, minstrel shows, and cartoons. The depiction of the African American equivalent of the stage Irishman was more demeaning. The characters of Sambo, Buckwheat, Beulah, mammy figures, and

Amos 'n Andy depicted blacks as ignorant, shuffling, happy, comical fools. But what Robert Washington calls the "cultural subjugation" of blacks also depicted them as menaces to society, as beasts, as a savage, sexually licentious people, who if not rigidly segregated and subordinated would undermine U.S. culture, politics, and womanhood.[48] These more demeaning stereotypical portrayals of blacks are on full display in two of the most renowned movies in American cinematic history, *The Birth of a Nation* and *Gone with the Wind*.[49] In fact, the NAACP, the equivalent of the Ancient Order of the Hibernians with respect to the movies, had its first successful experience protesting the portrayal of blacks in *Birth of a Nation*, and from that time forward kept a wary eye on Hollywood because to many of its leaders the movies were "the most anti-Negro influence in the nation."[50]

The fledging NAACP mounted nationwide protests and boycotts against *Birth of a Nation* because of its depiction of blacks as stupid, lazy, violent, and sexually obsessed, and its celebration of the Klan and open justification of lynching and other forms of terror. The NAACP's protests resulted in the eventual deletions of some of the more egregious racist and white supremacist parts of the film, but the movie went on to become one of the most popular and cinematically admired in U.S. history. The NAACP did not mount protests against *Gone with the Wind*, but it continued its work against negative portrayals of blacks in the media with the simple plea that blacks be shown as complete human beings. In 1942 it held its annual meeting in Los Angeles where Walter White, its executive director, met with studio executives. Accompanied by Wendell Willkie, the 1940 Republican presidential nominee, White and Willkie attempted to invoke bonds of ethnic minority solidarity, telling the executives that they "belonged to a group which had been targeted by Hitler," and therefore "they should not be guilty of doing to another minority the things which had been done to them."[51] All this, however, was to little avail. For example in 1946 the NAACP began a concerted campaign (including boycotts of sponsors) to get CBS to stop broadcasting *Amos 'n Andy*, but the network kept the program on the air until 1966.[52] One reason that Hollywood executives could ignore the NAACP was that some black leaders and actors argued it was better to have blacks portrayed in stereotypical roles than in no roles at all.[53]

In the late 1950s and early 1960s, as a result of the growing militancy of the civil rights movement and the threat of litigation by the NAACP, Hollywood began the slow process of incorporating blacks into the industry based on their humanity. In 1956 Nat King Cole became the first African American to host a nationally televised program. Because of boycotts by southern affiliates and the failure to attract national sponsors,

NBC only broadcast the program for a year. It, however, was a milestone for black incorporation into the popular culture, setting the pattern for most future nationally acclaimed black celebrities—avoidance of activism in the cause of civil rights, indeed, avoidance of engagement with the social and political life of the black ethnic community altogether.[54] The 1950s also inaugurated the "era of Poitier," as he made a series of movies that eventually resulted in his becoming the first black to win an Academy Award. Leab describes the Poitier era as the birth of a new stereotype—the "ebony saint"—and Thomas Cripps describes Poitier's roles as "paragons of virtue." The ebony saint or black paragon of virtue was "neither Uncle Tom nor militant, he remains nonviolent despite enormous provocation, and like the ebony saint itself remains cool. He is obviously superior in skills and ability. Nevertheless, he recognizes and he implicitly accepts those that are not blatantly racist. He poses no threat to established social or sexual mores."[55]

In 1965 another ebony saint was created when Bill Cosby became the first African American to star in a weekly television series. Cosby played a multilingual Rhodes scholar CIA agent disguised as a tennis trainer for his less intellectually competent white colleague. His Emmy-award winning role in *I Spy* paved the way for the 1980s *Cosby Show*. In this long-running, award-winning, top-rated program, Cosby and his television family were an upper-middle-class family who just happened to be black.

The last of the early ebony saints was a woman—*Julia*. In this 1968 television program, Diahann Carroll played the widow of a Vietnam veteran working as a nurse and raising a son in a thoroughly integrated environment. Like *I Spy* and the *Cosby Show*, race and racism were downplayed; the characters were "human"—just like ordinary Americans.

Throughout the 1970s and 1980s the processes of cultural incorporation on-screen displayed blacks in all their diversity, from *Good Times* in the ghetto to George Jefferson, black and proud, living in a luxury midtown Manhattan apartment. In 2001 Denzel Washington and Halle Berry won Academy Awards. Washington and Berry did not portray ebony saints; instead their characters were rather despicable. But this, too, is an indicator of full incorporation because blacks could now play the full gamut of humanity; that is, once Poitier, Cosby, and Carroll established in the American mind the image of the idealized, acculturated, and good American Negro, all else was possible.

The process of cultural incorporation on television and the movies reached a high water mark with Spike Lee's movies and Oprah Winfrey's dominance of daytime television. Winfrey has been described as a "comforting, nonthreatening bridge between black and white cultures."[56] Lee is the director of the sexual libertine *She's Gotta Have It* and the radical black power films *Do the Right Thing* and *Malcolm X*. That Oprah the ebony saint and Lee the radical provocateur could both be iconic figures in popular culture is evidence that incorporation here is near complete.[57]

Lee and Winfrey endorsed Obama in 2008, and Winfrey's endorsement may have been consequential in his winning the nomination. Political scientists usually discount the effects of celebrity endorsements on how citizens vote, but Winfrey's campaigning with Obama the weekend prior to the crucial Iowa caucuses may have affected the attitudes and voting behavior of the white suburban women who constitute the bulk of her audience. Two University of Maryland economists estimated her endorsement overall may have been worth one million votes.[58] Although one million may not be accurate, rarely does one observe this kind of relationship between popular culture and political power.

Music—especially for the young and the young at heart—may in the United States be as important as cinema in shaping mass attitudes and behavior. Music is central to African American culture and in the view of some second only to religion in its cultural significance.[59] In the 1960s, black music was acculturated, became a part of the mainstream, facilitating the absorption of blackness into the popular culture. Jazz is often referred to as America's quintessential music.[60] Although the white mass public originally would not accept the music unless it was performed by white performers such as Benny Goodman, by the 1950s and 1960s jazz performers such as Duke Ellington, Miles Davis, Ella Fitzgerald, Louis Armstrong, and Thelonious Monk were considered avant-garde arbiters of America's cultural tastes (*Time* placed Monk on its cover in 1964, symbolizing the cultural incorporation of the art form). Ken Burns's 2001 multipart PBS documentary celebrating jazz's contribution to American culture and democracy was confirmation for a mass audience of the centrality of the music in the national culture.

In the 1950s the rock 'n' roll recordings of Chuck Berry, Little Richard, and Fats Domino penetrated mainstream youth culture, but their work was controversial, viewed by the establishment as "too black." Elvis Presley's blending of country and rhythm and blues contributed to cultural incorporation, but Presley, too, was viewed in some circles as "too black." The genius of Barry Gordy, then, created from black music the "sound of young America" and, ultimately, "one nation under a groove."[61] Gordy, unlike, for example, his 1960s counterparts at Stax in Memphis, deliberately produced the Motown sound for mainstream white America. Selling, in the 1960s, 70 percent of the recordings to whites, Gordy was totally committed to reaching a white audience with music that was not too black and not controversial. His carefully tailored, groomed, and monitored performers were the musical versions of ebony saints, eschewing active engagement in lyrics or otherwise with the civil rights movement. (In the late 1960s the Temptations and Marvin Gaye embraced "cause" music, but by then the cause was mainstream.) Motown, like Poitier, in the 1960s prepared the foundation for the integration of black music in all its diversity into the national culture.[62] The Beatles and the Rolling Stones played a part in this process by associating themselves with culturally authentic black musicians such as Muddy Waters, Howlin' Wolf, Buddy Guy, and John Lee Hooker.

Some African American critics lament the incorporation of black music into the mainstream culture. Nelson George, for example, contended that the development of crossover artists and music and their successful marketing to whites resulted in death of the music as an authentic ethnic cultural expression. Seeing a symbiotic relationship between ethnic black music and ethnic black politics, George concluded that in the years since the incorporation of the music, "the community that inspired both social change and artistic creativity has become a sad shell of itself: unhappily while the drive behind the movement for social change was the greatest inspiration for the music, the very success of the movement spelled the end of the R & B world."[63] The success of crossover black politicians rising in tandem with the crossover music—whose ultimate expression was the election of Obama to the presidency—raises similar concerns about the viability of an authentic black politics.[64]

But the emergence of hip-hop in the early 1980s may suggest that George's concern about the death of ethnic black music may have been premature. Rooted in the sentiments if not the conditions of the culturally, economically, and politically unincorporated ghettoized strata of the community, hip-hop or rap is in some ways authentically black—too black for many Americans, black and white.[65] President Obama, for example, a hip-hop fan, during the campaign sounded like the dicty, lace-curtain Irish embarrassed by shanty performers in the early twentieth century when he criticized hip-hop artists for misogynistic lyrics, materialism, and use of the "N-word." Hip-hop artists are not ebony saints, but the music is part of mainstream culture and as such was successfully deployed as part of the Obama campaign his lace-curtain-like criticisms notwithstanding.[66]

If the Anglo-Saxon establishment saw sports as a way to acculturate the Catholic Irish and other ethnic immigrants, the long exclusion of African Americans was seen as an effective means to maintain their cultural subjugation. From boxing to baseball, for much of the country's history, interracial sporting was prohibited. African American leaders, however, shared the "faith in sport as an arena for racial progress."[67] Thus, they struggled to integrate athletics, and celebrated the accomplishments of black athletes, and when black people "participated in nationalistic athletic spectacles, particularly in Olympic games, the intense patriotism of American athletic ideology sometimes clouded racist sentiments."[68] At the same time, this participation often reinforced the racist ideology, as black athletes were defined as the "primitive," the "savage" possessing a "primal physicality" that the more "civilized" races did not possess.[69]

Jack Johnson was the first black athlete to breakthrough nationally in American sports. Although there was no formal bar to interracial boxing, John L. Sullivan (a Catholic Irish we should note) was a nationally recognized heavyweight champion who, by refusing to fight African Americans, established in 1885 a precedent subsequent white boxers followed until 1910. In that year, Johnson broke the color barrier when he defeated Jim Jeffries to become the first undisputed black heavyweight champion. Johnson was no ebony saint; he flaunted his blackness, wealth, and violated the ultimate racist taboo by marrying and having sexual liaisons with white women. He was indicted in 1913 for violating the Mann Act, which prohibited the transportation of women across state lines for "immoral purposes." Although an international celebrity, Johnson epitomized in the white American mind the stereotype of the sexually aggressive black brute who was a menace to white women everywhere.[70]

The next African American to win the heavyweight championship was an ebony saint. Especially after defeating the German Max Schmeling in 1938 in a fight portrayed as a battle between freedom and democracy, Joe Louis was embraced as an "American" hero and patriot.[71] Thereafter, blacks dominated U.S. boxing, culminating in the phenomenal career of Muhammad Ali. Ali was no ebony saint. He was reviled by the American media when he joined the Nation of Islam and refused to be inducted into the armed services, famously declaring, "Ain't no Viet Cong ever called me nigger." But in an indication of the changing character of the national culture, by the 1980s Ali's status had been transformed from that of a radical, un-American Black Nationalist extremist to an American icon. Hailed as one of the greatest athletes of all time, he was feted by American presidents, sent on diplomatic missions, and celebrated as a hero for his principled opposition to the Vietnam War and for the courage of his religious convictions. At the 1996 Olympics in Atlanta he was granted the honor of lighting the torch that opened the games.

Jesse Owens at the 1936 Olympics became the black equivalent of the Catholic Irish John Hayes at the 1918 games, winning four gold medals in track and field. Also an ebony saint, Owens fulsomely embraced America while downplaying race and racism. Owens's acculturation may be contrasted with the behavior of Tommie Smith and John Carlos at the 1968 Olympics. Not ebony saints, Smith and Carlos raised their arms in black power salutes to protest racism in America. Owens responded indignantly, labeling Carlos and Smith as racists while downplaying the role of racism as a barrier to black achievement in the United States.[72]

Joe Louis in boxing and Jesse Owens at the Olympics symbolized the beginning of the end of the exclusion of blacks from most sports in the United States, but the seminal symbol was Jackie Robinson. Robinson was selected as the first black to play professional baseball partly because he was an ebony saint, or at least could act as if he were one. Better educated than most players (he was within a year of graduating from the University of California at Los Angeles) and clearly a gifted athlete, Robinson was selected to integrate the game because he promised to accept the expected racist indignities without protest. Robinson in his post-baseball career would speak out forcefully against racism in baseball and in America generally, but in the game he did not. His outstanding performance and his "sublime restraint" on the field made him undoubtedly the most important historical figure in the incorporation of African Americans into sports.[73]

By the time of Obama's election, African Americans dominated professional and collegiate football and basketball although their presence was declining in baseball. The preeminent symbol of this dominance was Michael Jordan. Like Barry Gordy, Jordan was completely committed to the crossover ethos. His bald head and dark skin became the essence of "cool," and he was used to market everything from cars to underwear. An ebony saint, "much of Jordan's appeal was based on the fact that he was nonthreatening . . . the condition for [his] appeal was his racial and political neutrality. . . ."[74]

However, given that African Americans have only been partially incorporated socially and economically, we find a racial undercurrent to their dominance in sports, especially basketball and football, which reinforce old racist stereotypes. As Underwood writes, "Even as the racial imbalance distorts the black youngsters [*sic*] perception of sport as the most accessible avenue up and out, it reinforces the white man's unholy stereotype of the one-dimensional black gladiator."[75] And Berkow, while noting that the old stereotype that blacks could not play quarterback because it "was the ultimate thinking and pressure position" had been broken, nevertheless, he writes, "the whispering refrain on college campuses now is, 'well, they can play all the positions but they still can't do it in the classroom.'"[76] Athletic success, thus, becomes another way to talk about black inferiority such as when the coach of a U.S. Olympic team said, "The Negro excels in the events he does because he is closer to the primitive than the white man."[77]

These racist stereotypes, however, cannot be applied so easily to tennis and golf, the aristocracies of Western sport. In the 1950s and 1970s, Althea Gibson and Arthur Ashe won tennis acclaim and the Williams sisters—Venus and Serena—dominated women's play in the 1990s and into the twenty-first century. Tiger Woods's phenomenal career in golf made him in earnings and endorsements a billionaire by age thirty. Golf in America is quintessentially the sport of the white male aristocracy and of presidents. As Mills derisively observed of America's pseudo status system, "The professional celebrity, male or female, is the crowning result of the star system of a society that makes a fetish of competition. In America this system is carried to the point where a man who can knock a small white ball into a series of holes in the ground with more efficiency than anyone else therefore gains access to the President of the United States."[78] Perhaps the most efficient ever at knocking the little white balls into holes, Woods was the ultimate symbol of popular culture incorporation; a mixed-race billionaire who did not acknowledge his blackness excelling in a sport long the preserve for rich Anglo-Saxon men.[79]

In literature during the Harlem Renaissance of the 1920s, a small group of middle-class black intellectuals and civil rights leaders began a planned effort to use art as a vehicle to integrate blacks into the American culture, which they viewed as a means to achieve broader social incorporation. James Weldon Johnson, a novelist and soon to become the first black head of the NAACP, stated the premise of the Harlem Renaissance writers: "no people that has produced great literature has ever been looked upon by the world as distinctly inferior. . . . Nothing will do more to change the mental attitude and raise [his status] than a demonstration of intellectual parity by the Negro through his production of literature and art."[80]

While the Johnson premise may have some truth, in the context of the 1920s when racist and white supremacist propaganda was high, this assumption of "civil rights by copyright" was naïve.[81] Moreover, what Robert Washington calls the "primitivist school" of the Renaissance in many ways reinforced racist stereotypes.[82] As Washington understands it, the primitivist school was based on a genetic or essentialist understanding of black culture; an equation of Africa with "primitive instinctualism"; depiction of the black lower-class culture as the principal carrier of this primitivism as manifested in its carefree, hedonistic lifestyle; depiction of the black middle class as "social misfits" alienated from their ethnic culture; and white, Western culture as emotionally repressed and sterile.[83] A literature based on these assumptions, even if Johnson's premise about the role of literature in the incorporation process is correct, was not likely to accomplish his objectives. Rather, it was more likely to reinforce the very racist stereotypes that contributed to the cultural subjugation of blacks. This was Du Bois's view of the primitivist school. Its most dogged and pugnacious critic, Du Bois was especially disturbed by the literature's tendency to portray blacks as sexual libertines, famously remarking after reading Claude McKay's *Home to Harlem* that the book "for the most part nauseates me, and after reading the dirtier parts of its filth I feel distinctly like taking a bath."[84] One critic described Langston Hughes, one of the Renaissance's leading lights, as the "poet low rate of Harlem" because of his depiction of lower-class sensuality. Hughes defiantly defended primitivist school writings, exclaiming in a famous essay in the *Nation*, "We . . . intend to express our individual dark-skinned selves without fear or shame."[85] The tension between the aristocratic, middle-aged, middle-class respectability of a Du Bois and the unvarnished ethnic authenticity of the young Hughes resembles the controversy in the Catholic Irish community about some of the works of Eugene O'Neill. But unlike O'Neill's work, the corpus of the Renaissance, whatever its literary merit, did little to further cultural incorporation of African Americans.

Nor did the publication of what is perhaps the most acclaimed novel in African American literature, Richard Wright's *Native Son*. Wright was no ebony saint, and *Native Son* was in many ways a radical novel, seeming to provide justification for black anger and violence against whites. The black middle class, while disturbed by the novel's stereotypical depiction of black lower-class life and Bigger Thomas's criminality, nevertheless celebrated the novel's mainstream acclaim and its extraordinarily honest depiction of the brutalities of American racism. James Baldwin's "moral suasionist" essays in the 1960s won acclaim in liberal circles and were literary manifestos of the civil rights movement's push for incorporation. In 1952, Gwendolyn Brooks won a Pulitzer Prize for her poetry and later was honored as the first woman elected to the National Institute of Arts and Letters. Ralph Ellison, however, was the Jackie Robinson of literature. His 1952 novel *Invisible Man*, focusing on universal themes that transcended blackness while downplaying racism, was the quintessential racial crossover novel. An ebony saint, *Invisible Man* "catapulted Ellison into America's intellectual elite, as the token representative where he operated as the leading spokesman for moderate bourgeois liberalism."[86]

In the post–civil rights era after the brief interlude of Amiri Baraka's radical Black Nationalist literary school, African American literature turned toward "exploring the black communal experience" and affirming a "distinctive black American ethnicity" within the confines of a "multicultural" America characterized by the declining significance of race and increased opportunities for the cosmopolitan black bourgeoisie.[87] These writings by the Pulitzer Prize–winning Alice Walker, the Pulitzer Prize–winning August Wilson, and the Nobel Prize–winning Toni Morrison, while rooted in the black ethnic tradition, are not about race or racism, but use the black ethnic experience to validate the cultural incorporation of the group. In other words, they treat black people like they are ordinary human beings.

In a token sense (token in the sense that their numbers are small) blacks by the time of Obama's election had also been incorporated into the nation's elite academic and media establishments. The category of black "public intellectuals" generally teach at elite, private universities and air their views in the elite, prestige media (*New York Times*, *New Yorker*, NPR).[88] Generally eschewing ethnic "identity" politics, these scholars tend to downplay the significance of racism, call attention to the pathology of the so-called black underclass and celebrate the "nothing short of astonishing" progress the United States has made in the incorporation of blacks. Astonishing, Patterson writes, because "there does not exist a single case in modern or earlier history that comes anywhere near the record of America in changing majority attitudes, in guaranteeing legal and political rights and expanding socioeconomic opportunities for its disadvantaged minorities"[89] Thoroughly incorporated, these public intellectuals "speak to the white elite about the black problem in America."[90]

Throughout this part of the chapter, Leab's idea of the ebony saint is used to describe those blacks most readily incorporated into the popular culture, but it is not used pejoratively. On the contrary, ebony sainthood—to be nonthreatening and acceptable to the majority—has always been the pathway to ethnic incorporation. Residuals of ethnicity may be maintained but ultimately the national culture trumps ethnic culture. Whether on the screen, on the playing fields, or in the White House, one cannot be too Irish, too Catholic, or too black.

The commemoration of St. Patrick's Day by Americans of all ethnic backgrounds signaled Catholic Irish incorporation. St. Patrick's Day, however, is not a legally mandated national holiday. Legally mandated holidays are perhaps the highest expression of a nation's understanding of itself, celebrating important events, rituals, and persons that define in tradition and myth the character of the nation. Thus, the enactment by Congress and the signing by the conservative Republican Ronald Reagan of the Martin Luther King Jr. Birthday holiday bill must be viewed as evidence of the incorporation of African Americans that has no parallel with the Catholic Irish or any other ethnic group. The United States celebrates officially as holidays only three persons—Jesus Christ, Christopher Columbus, and Martin Luther King Jr. That an African American would be among this select group means that the group is recognized as contributing to the nation's understanding of what it means to be American. It is the ebony saint King, however, who is celebrated; that is, King is incorporated into the national culture on the basis of the civil rights revolution he led, which represented, he said, the fulfillment of the vision and aspirations of Jefferson and Lincoln that men in the United States be treated equally. Thus, on King Day we hear "I Have Dream," celebrating the national culture's commitment to the proposition of the equality of all persons, but not King's anti-imperialist, antimilitarism, anti–Vietnam War speeches or his social democratic addresses and sermons calling for full employment or a guaranteed income. This sanitizing of King—"Americanizing"—was necessary for his cultural incorporation, a point well understood by the King family. As Vincent Harding writes, "Those who [led] the campaign for the establishment of the national holiday [chose], consciously or unconsciously, to allow King to become a 'convenient hero'; to try to tailor him to the shape and mood of mainstream, liberal/moderate America."[91] To put this another way, when King was murdered, he was the radical tribune of the unincorporated ghettoized poor; in death he became the hero of the incorporated black bourgeoisie, and a paragon to the virtues of Jefferson and Lincoln. While a part of the national culture, race divides the nation in celebrating the holiday. Ninety-six percent of blacks believe that King's birthday should be national holiday but only 67 percent of whites, and 60 percent of blacks say they do something to commemorate the day but just 15 percent of whites. Martin Luther King Jr. even in death remains to many an ethnic—not American—hero. In other words, for many whites he is still black; too black.

The best indicator of cultural incorporation—indeed incorporation generally—is the extent of interethnic marriage. From slavery to the civil rights era interracial sexual intimacy was the ultimate racial boundary; for white racists crossing it or even appearing to cross it could result in a swift, brutal death for black men. Many blacks also viewed interracial marriage with skepticism. They saw it as the ultimate act of ethnic betrayal. At the end of the civil rights, era 83 percent of whites and 52 percent of blacks were opposed to interracial marriage. At the end of the twentieth century, support for interracial marriage had increased to 68 percent among blacks and 45 percent among whites.[92] Yet blacks remain the most endogamous ethnic group in the United States. "If you want in marry in," Patterson writes of the centrality of interethnic marriages in the incorporation processes in the United States.[93] Addressing the reluctance of blacks to cross this boundary, Patterson goes on, "Even if Afro-Americans assumed they were the most successful group socially and culturally, they would be in serious error to exclude themselves from the intimate networks and cultural resources of other groups, especially the dominant one. It is no accident that Jewish and Japanese Americans are among the two most successful ethnic groups in America, as well as being the two most exogamous in spite of the fact that their source cultures strongly prohibit exogamy."[94] African Americans, for whatever the reasons, are not marrying in with the dominant group. Although the rate of interracial marriage has been increasing, in 1993 only 12 percent of all new marriages by blacks were racially mixed. This represents a substantial increase from 1963 when the figure was 0.7 percent and a near doubling from 1980 when it was 6.6 percent.[95] Exogamy is an indicator of both a lack of incorporation and the maintenance of ethnic boundaries. That is, the low rate of interracial marriages in the United States indicates both the exclusion of blacks from the dominant culture and their wish to maintain this boundary of blackness.[96]

As indicated in the analysis of Catholic Irish incorporation the most salient indicator of social, economic, and cultural incorporation is the disappearance of ethnic-specific ghettos. In all major American cities, poor African Americans are constrained to live in ethnic-specific ghettos. Ghettos are fundamentally indicators of the absence of ethnic group economic incorporation, but they are also sites for cultural isolation and sources for the negative ethnic stereotypes Greeley alludes to at the outset of this chapter. They also constitute the geography for the maintenance of ethnic identity and consciousness; sites for the strong tie of bearing one common wrong. Middle-class blacks tend to share with poor blacks this sense of a common wrong, linking their fate psychologically with the fate of the ghettoized poor. This linked fate maintains a strong black ethnic identity and consciousness that cuts across residential and class lines to sustain a black ethnic community.[97]

This consciousness of one common wrong fosters a sense of alienation toward the dominant culture, reflected, for example, in black attitudes about HIV/AIDS and the widespread availability of drugs in black communities. The dominant media reported with shock and dismay the remarks of Obama's pastor, Rev. Jeremiah Wright, alleging that the government deliberately fostered AIDS and drugs on the black community. But the views of Rev. Wright are shared widely throughout the black community. Multiple surveys conducted throughout the 1990s show that African Americans—of all social classes—are far more likely than whites to believe that the "government deliberately makes sure that drugs are easily available in poor black neighborhoods to harm black people"—64 percent of blacks compared to 18 percent of whites. And blacks are more likely to entertain the possibility that "HIV and AIDS are being used as a plot to deliberately kill African Americans," 62 percent to 21 percent among whites.[98] These striking opinion differences reflect cultural isolation not incorporation.

Finally, the existence of the ghettos gives rise to political demands on the state. Until the New Deal Americans did not look to the government to ensure employment, health, income, and Social Security. Thus, when Al Smith ran in 1928, the ghettoized Catholic Irish did not look to his campaign to develop policies to meliorate their conditions. When Kennedy ran in 1960 the economically incorporated Catholics had no such demands. However, when Obama ran in 2008 the conditions of the economically unincorporated blacks demanded ameliorative policies. Table 6.2 displays the wide differences in opinion between subordinate blacks and dominant whites on the responsibilities of government with respect to the well-being of the people. In addition, to overcome at long last and repair the common wrong done to the group, leading black thinkers support reparations for slavery and segregation.[99] Sixty-five percent of blacks support reparations, whereas 88 percent of whites oppose it.[100] In order to win the support of whites Obama had to reject or downplay these demands coming from his ethnic community. John Kennedy also ignored or downplayed the demands on the state coming from Catholics in 1960, but those demands were minor when compared to the demands of blacks in 2008.

Table 6.2. Racial Differences in Opinion on the Social Welfare Responsibilities of Government (Percent saying Government Responsibility)

Goverment Responsibility	Black	White
To provide jobs	74%	33%
Health care	69	33
Assure decent standard of living	70	33
Decent living for the unemployed	77	43
Financial aid to college students	62	30
Decent housing for all	50	14

Source: General Social Survey, 1996, University of Chicago, National Opinion Research Center.

The persistently high rate of poverty among African Americans is the single most important indicator of the lack of African American incorporation into the economy. In general, the black community can be divided into three strata of roughly equal size; a stable black middle class, a struggling working class, and an impoverished class of poor people living in the cities and the rural South.[101] The relative size of the three classes varies with the state of the economy; that is, there is some movement between the working and the middle classes, depending on the level of growth and employment in the economy. For example, during the Clinton administration, the economy grew at unprecedented peacetime rates. As a result the percentage of blacks in poverty declined from 31 percent to 22 percent, and the size of the working and middle classes, measured by family income, increased. Yet the reality confronting the first black president was stubborn, racialized, concentrated poverty. Stephan and Abigail Thernstrom state this reality starkly: "The persistent poverty rate is the single most depressing fact about the state of black America today. . . . After three decades of falling very substantially, the figure has been struck within three or four points of the 30 percent mark for about twenty-five years."[102] Dealing with this reality is the central demand of the black ethnic group. But only one American president—Lyndon Johnson—has been willingly to forthrightly tackle this difficult problem because to do so is politically unpopular among the dominant ethnic groups. The incentive structures of winning the presidency and governing make it even less likely that the first black president would be willing or able to do so.

The breakthrough to the beginnings of the political incorporation of African Americans occurred in the 1960s during the Kennedy and Johnson administrations. Prior to the 1960s, only a handful of blacks had served in Congress, on the courts, or in senior positions in the executive branch. President Kennedy was the first to appoint blacks to senior-level positions in the executive branch, including an unsuccessful effort to name Robert Weaver as the first black in the cabinet. President Johnson did appoint Weaver to the cabinet, as secretary of the newly created Department of Housing and Urban Development. Yet in the Kennedy–Johnson years, blacks were appointed to only 2 percent of Senate confirmed positions. The real breakthrough came in the Carter administration when blacks were appointed to 12 percent of Senate confirmed positions. President Reagan and the first President Bush appointed 5 percent and 6 percent, respectively, and President Clinton appointed 13 percent, including four black members of the cabinet. Ten percent of President George W. Bush's appointments were African American, including Colin Powell and Condoleezza Rice as secretary of state. The appointment of such a high proportion of blacks to senior, highly visible positions by a conservative, Republican president suggests that incorporation at this level of government was near complete. The appointments of Powell and Rice to arguably the second most visible and important position in the government may have helped to adjust the mind of white America to seeing blacks exercise power "responsibly" in behalf of the nation.[103] In Powell's case, early polling data in 1995 indicates he was the first African American with a real chance of winning the presidency. Gallup poll data show that he might have defeated Bob Dole for the Republican nomination, defeated Clinton in the general election, or both Clinton and Dole if he had ran as an Independent. The Gallup data are from 1995—a year before the election—thus they are only suggestive of what results might have been had Powell decided to run. But what is clear is that after the Persian Gulf War, Powell became the first genuine national leader who was black—an ethnic African American leader who transcended race.[104]

In Congress only three blacks have been elected to the Senate, and never has there been more than one in that body at the same time. Only two blacks have been elected governors of one of the states and two have been elected as national party chairs, Ron Brown chair of the Democratic National Committee in 1989, and Michael Steele, chair of the Republican Committee in 2009. In the House when Obama was elected, forty-two African Americans served, near full incorporation at 9 percent of the membership. This near full incorporation, however, came about only because interpretations of the Voting Rights Act in 1990 allowed for the deliberate drawing of congressional district lines to create a large number of majority black districts. (In 2008 only three of the black members of the House were initially elected from majority white districts.) When Obama was elected, James Clyburn of South Carolina was House majority whip, the third ranking position in the House leadership. Earlier William Gray, an African American from Philadelphia, had held this position. African Americans also chaired four of nineteen House committees, including three of the most important—Ways and Means, Judiciary, and Homeland Security.

The Thernstroms indicate—correctly—that statistical data on the political incorporation of blacks as measured by the percent of elected offices held is misleading because blacks are disproportionately Democratic and liberal and therefore generally do not compete in large parts of the country that are conservative and Republican.[105] Looking in 1994 at the percentage of Democratic seats blacks held in the House, the proportion increases from 9 percent to 18 percent.[106]

The Thernstroms' observation, however, also indicates the absence of full political incorporation. As discussed earlier with respect to Catholic Irish political incorporation, when one party monopolizes the vote of an ethnic group, this suggests a lack of complete incorporation. The group's interests are near inevitably marginalized because one party takes its vote for granted and the other ignores it altogether. For African Americans, unlike the Catholic Irish, this "one-party system" has been the case for all of American history except for the brief period from 1936 to 1964. In 1964 the Republican Party abandoned its long identification as the party of Lincoln with black interests, and members embraced a rigid ideological conservatism that, in its effects, was tantamount to an embrace of racism.[107] Related to this absence of bipartisan incorporation, blacks are politically unincorporated because of their monolithic liberalism in a nation that is at a minimum right of center, and on race-related issues profoundly conservative.[108] Unlike the Catholic Irish in 1960, in 2008 blacks displayed ideological and policy preferences that located them far to the left of dominant ethnic groups.[109] These distinctive ideological and policy preferences are marginalized in a two-party system in a right-of-center nation, even when—perhaps even more so when—the more liberal of the two parties nominates and elects an African American as president.

This study is centrally concerned with this marginalization and the Obama campaign and presidency when compared with Kennedy and the Catholic Irish experience. This comparison is the subject of the next four chapters, but it is useful to conclude here where we begin with an observation from Greeley, the most prolific student of the Catholic Irish. Greeley wrote, "Despite the strong similarities between the Irish experience and that of blacks, few American Irish are willing even to consider the possibility that the black quest for dignity and freedom in the United States demands their support."[110] Stephanie Rains, an Irish scholar of the Catholic Irish experience in the United States, writes Irish ethnicity in this country was "an innocent version of whiteness" allowing the group to "maintain the inherent privileges of whiteness while simultaneously making claims on ethnic victimhood and exclusion, based upon the historical experience of Ireland's colonization [*sic*] and the discrimination experienced by earlier generations of Irish Catholics in America."[111]

In the 1960s Bernadette Devlin, a leader of the Irish resistance, came to the United States and attempted to get her countrymen to make common cause with African Americans in their struggle for civil rights. In her lectures at Catholic Irish venues, black civil rights leaders sometimes accompanied her. At these lectures she was almost always heckled, and the hostile audiences frequently prevented her black companions from entering the room.[112] Devlin soon realized that the Catholic Irish public and its organized leadership had absolutely no sense of the solidarity of the oppressed with blacks. They were interested only in the liberation of Northern Ireland. As a result of Devlin's solidarity-building efforts, her fundraising tour fell far short of its goals in solicitations from the Irish American community, and her speeches in Boston were sometimes interrupted by the chant, "Niggers out of Boston, Brits out of Belfast."[113]

When Devlin visited in the mid-1960s, Catholic Irish ethnicity was increasingly symbolic, and identification with Ireland was a more important attribute of their ethnicity than consciousness of oppression in the United States. Fully incorporated, the old Catholic Irish identity had withered away to be replaced by a broader European American immigrant identity, an identity they shared with immigrants from southern and eastern Europe, who came to America poor and dispossessed but who, through family, church, and hard work made it. This European, white, ethnic immigrant experience creates bonds of solidarity that unites European ethnic groups, while at the same time excluding blacks. Uniting them and excluding blacks because they say blacks have failed to pull themselves up like their ancestors from Poland, Italy, and Ireland.[114] In other words, blacks had failed to become incorporated, to become white because of their own shortcomings.

The ephemeral, symbolic incorporation of blacks in the popular culture reinforces this Euro-American immigrant identity and its disparagement of blacks. In the popular culture—on television, in the movies, in sports—blacks have made it, have become white. But the nightly news and the morning papers often show impoverished, ghettoized blacks as welfare recipients and criminals. If Oprah, Tiger, Condi, and Cosby can make it, why can't they? Indeed, Cosby himself reassures them, and he tells them their perceptions are correct: that if blacks in the ghettos would only abandon the ways of the ghetto, work hard, go to church, and take care of their families, they too could make it, become white, and perhaps even become president.[115]

7

Kennedy and Obama

Charisma, Character, and Ethnic Identity

"Coolness, detachment, rationalism." "Ultimate pragmatist, deliberate thinker." "Nimble mind, wide ranging intellect, astonishingly self-contained." "The combination of a first class intellect and first class temperament." "Bright and attractive, an air of calm and a wonderful speaking voice." "Calm and cool, not just intellectualism but judgment." "Cerebral, intellectual, detached." "Natural gravitas." "Erudite nature." "A man of raw ambition." "Ambition now as visible as a radio tower . . . been thinking about the presidency for more than a decade." "A cult of personality." "Charismatic."[1]

"Aristocratic, intellectual, coolly self-contained." "Cool, analytical mind; detachment, objectivity, candor." "Classic American pragmatist." "Aloof, witty, ironic." "Handsome, charismatic, glamorous political celebrity." "Extraordinary political intelligence." "Detached, cool, reluctant to commit himself ideologically." "Pragmatic liberal." "Elusive detachment." The most important thing . . . was his own political ambition. He refused to wait his turn." "Agent of generational change." "A cult of personality." "Charisma."[2]

Although they come from extraordinarily different backgrounds and their paths to the presidency could not be more different, as the quotes above indicate (the first paragraph refers to Obama; the second to Kennedy), the character and personality of Kennedy and Obama are frequently characterized in identical or near-identical words; "JFK in Sepia," a "Kenyan Kennedy." Of Kennedy and Obama, Paul Street writes, both were "handsome, young, ethnically novel, charismatic and highly telegenic."[3] Like Gary Hart and other ambitious young politicians before him, Obama saw Kennedy as a role model, and, as the Introduction discusses, the President's brother and daughter in endorsing Obama said he reminded them of their brother and father. Obama even has a touch of the green; his maternal great-great-great-grandfather was an Irish immigrant.[4] These comparisons can be overdrawn, but important similarities exist between Kennedy and Obama in their style, rhetoric, intellectualism, and in their interactions with subordinates; both also exhibited extraordinary ambition, egoism, confidence, caution, and daring.[5] Kennedy's 1960 campaign was to a great extent based on marketing a narrative of a handsome, charismatic, youthful, gallant, cool celebrity with a thrilling rhetoric of change, a new generation of leadership committed to "getting the country moving again."[6] Charisma and change were also the "master narratives" of Obama's campaign. The most comprehensive study of media coverage of the 2008 Democratic primaries found that the media fairly conveyed each candidate's "master narrative" (Clinton's and Obama's). The most prevalent narrative about Obama was that he represented "hope and change" (28 percent of media coverage projected this idea). The second most prominent narrative (17 percent) about Obama was that he had a "special and rare charisma, someone whose rhetorical skills could move crowds in ways not often seen."[7] Obama even goes so far as to claim that his final decision to run was based on the response of crowds to his rhetoric: "After seeing the responses I was getting around the country, I had to step back and ask: Is there something about my message that is sufficiently unique and could be useful enough to moving the country forward? And ultimately the answer was yes."[8]

Yet we know that in both Kennedy's and Obama's cases that much of the success of their narratives rested on manufactured images, rhetoric, political posturing, and an all-too-frequent fawning press corps. *In a Question of Character: The Life of John F. Kennedy*, Thomas Reeves concludes by warning, ". . . the American people must resist the temptation to be won over by a handsome face, expensive campaign efforts, and thrilling rhetoric."[9] In 2008 as in 1960 this resistance proved difficult.

This chapter's primary concern, however, is not with presidential character or personality in general, but rather with Kennedy's and Obama's "ethnic character" to discern the extent to which their character or personality is shaped by their Catholic Irish and African American heritages, and the extent to which those heritages influenced their campaigns and conduct of the presidency. Here the differences are striking. Kennedy was reared in a wealthy quasi-aristocratic, patriarchal Catholic Irish household attended by governesses, butlers, maids, and nurses. Obama was raised largely by his white, working-class grandparents because his white mother was often away and his Kenyan father was but an inchoate dream, having abandoned him when he was a baby. In

Kennedy's household his devout, puritanical mother urged the children to always "Be Irish, Be Catholic." His father, however, looked down on the Catholic Irish, and in many ways urged his children (especially the sons) to abandon or at least thoroughly downplay their ethnic heritage and become more like aristocratic Anglo-Saxons. Meanwhile, the biracial, dark-skinned Obama, aided by his mother and grandfather, embraced blackness. Finally, by the time Kennedy ran for president in 1960, what it meant to be Irish Catholic in America was becoming increasingly unclear as the group's distinctive ethnic identity and culture was rapidly withering. But when Obama ran in 2008, the boundaries of blackness—psychological, cultural, and political—were distinctive and politically relevant. And, predictably, in the campaign and the presidency, Obama like Kennedy downplayed his ethnic identity. In other words, although Obama was blacker than Kennedy was Irish or Catholic and his ethnicity was more salient and politically relevant than Kennedy's, the constraints of a presidential campaign and the presidency itself required similar behavior: ethnic avoidance.

Kennedy's Ethnic Character

President Kennedy's father left Boston to escape the oppression of the Anglo-Saxons and raise his children in a less hostile ethnic environment. He also wanted to escape the ties that bound the family to Boston's omnivorous Irish Catholic culture and community; that is, the wealthy, aristocratically pretentious father came to view his ethnic origins as a barrier to his aspirations for inclusion in Anglo-Saxon society. Moreover, like many nouveau riche members of oppressed ethnic minorities, Joe Kennedy not only wanted to escape his ethnic heritage but also wanted as well to embrace the heritage of the oppressor. Kennedy wanted his children to grow up Celtic Anglo-Saxons. Joe Kennedy, Garry Wills writes, "ceased deliberately to be Irish in the accepted sense" and the children were brought up "not to respect their own."[10] Unlike Tip O'Neill, among the Kennedys there was no long memories and hatred of the English oppressor. On the contrary, there was an "affinity for things British."[11] Thus, at best John Kennedy was "Semi-Irish; Semi-English."[12] As Jacqueline Kennedy said on the eve of the 1960 campaign, "It was unfair for the Kennedys to be treated as Irish, they were such poor Irishman; they tried so hard to be anything but."[13] Growing up in the plush environs of Bronxville, London, Miami, and Hyannis Port, Jack admitted he personally faced little Anglo-Saxon prejudice or discrimination: ". . . I had gone to private school, I came from New

York instead of Boston, my father had some money and was well known. I may have had a little feeling of barrier but not acute."[14]

Kennedy perhaps confronted the first little feelings of an ethnic barrier at Harvard. There he was part of an Irish contingent of students that set him apart from the Anglo-Saxon cliques and ethos that dominated the university in the 1930s. Although his father was rich and famous and he had attended exclusive Anglo Saxon prep schools, he was still to his Anglo-Saxon classmates "such an obvious Boston-Irish type . . . he had a Boston accent. . . . And older more puritanical Bostonians regarded the Kennedys as coarse, loud noveaux [*sic*] riche upstarts . . . just irretrievably Boston Irish."[15] At Harvard, Kennedy gained entry into the Spee Club, "the inner sanctum of Boston's WASP world." Thereafter "as long as he lived, could anyone look down on Jack Kennedy."[16] He had made it, and from thereon he was as his father wished: an "intense Anglophile."[17]

But to those who knew and cared about such things, he was discernible Catholic Irish. The working-class people of South Boston did know and did care, which was of enormous benefit when he came to Boston to run for Congress. His Catholic Irish constituents viewed him as one of them. Wealthy, Harvard educated, a bit pretentious but still "Honey Fitz's grandboy." Cool, immaculately dressed, he fit none of the stereotypes of the traditional Irish politician—he was not given to the blarney, did not sing Sweet Adeline or Danny Boy, could not dance a jig, and did not wear a derby.[18] He was a "changeling" who "disdained his Irish background," Murray Kempton wrote.[19] Perhaps. But he and his father had national ambitions, and they knew that a Boston Irish politician like Honey Fitz or Tip O'Neill would never make it to the White House. Thus, for Kennedy, like any ambitious third-stage ethnic politician, ethnic identities are often embarrassing. He may use his ties to the group to awaken sentiments of pride and solidarity at the ballot box, but usually third-stage ethnic politicians have to be or appear to be something of a changeling, postethnic. Kennedy was perhaps both "part-Irish" and "semi-English because both were requisites for a successful transethnic Catholic Irish politician in 1960.

Kennedy genuinely admired his grandfather Honey Fitz and enjoyed the presence of his company and the storytelling, but in the course of his first campaign Honey Fitz was usually shunted aside. His close buddies and political aides Dave Powers and Kenneth O'Donnell in their memoir write of his love for Irish stories, jokes, and songs, but these sentimental, symbolic ethnic ties were for private pleasure not public display.[20] In Congress most of his aides were Catholic Irish, but in the White House the O'Donnells, O'Briens, O'Gormans, and Maguires were absent or relegated to non–policy-making roles.

For many years after his election to the Senate, Kennedy was one of the few prominent Catholic Irish politicians in Massachusetts who did not participate in Boston's St. Patrick's Day parade, and the rhetoric around his standard St. Patrick's Day speech usually avoided the issue of Irish unification. The speech (written by Sorensen, who recalls that his first assignment was to write a St. Patrick's Day speech) usually avoided the Northern Ireland question, focusing instead on tributes to various Irish American patriots and extolling the contributions of Irish immigrants to U.S. society.[21] Often he would compare the colonial oppression of Ireland with Soviet and Chinese communist oppression.[22] Similarly, in his 1963 address to the Irish parliament (Kennedy was the first sitting U.S. president to visit the country), he ignored the question of unification while once again praising the virtues of Irish patriots and immigrants and celebrating and encouraging the contributions of Ireland to the anticommunist struggle and international peacekeeping.[23] As a young congressman, Kennedy had supported resolutions calling for the unification of Ireland; his avoidance of the issue later was partly a response to the fact that Great Britain was America's principal ally in the international struggle against communism and his prioritizing of that struggle over the liberation of Northern Ireland or any other place.[24] Kennedy's posture here, too, reflects an axiom of ethnic politics for "one of your own to get elected, he must go out of his way to prove he is not *just* one of your own."[25] As Mitchell writes, "I suspect the word of this strategy was sent out in Irish American circles. . . . If you want one of your own to make it to the top, don't expect him to be yammering about Irish unification."[26] But Mitchell also wondered if Kennedy could have gotten away with avoiding the Irish government's request for intervention if he had served eight years or if Irish American opinion had "weighed in on the matter, could the Kennedys have withstood the charge that they were false to their Irish heritage."[27]

Similarly, as chapter 10 discusses, Kennedy as a young congressman supported federal aid to parochial schools, leading the Catholic press to laud him as the "Galahad in the House."[28] But, like Irish unification, he flip-flopped on this issue once he began to seriously contemplate the presidency. The issue of aid to church schools was more important than Irish unification because his Catholic identity was more troubling to the American electorate than was his Irishness, although Kennedy was probably more Irish than he was Catholic.

If the President's father disdained his Irishness and aped the English, his mother was the opposite, especially with respect to Catholicism. Hamilton describes Rose Kennedy as a "fanatical Catholic" with a "neurotic determination to make the Kennedy family stick at least publicly to the tenets of the Catholic faith."[29] Wills writes, "Rose

Kennedy belonged to the last generation of Catholic women who could combine, in some measure, the two vocations held up to them by the nuns—marriage and the convent."[30] Joe Kennedy, however, was clearly the patriarch, the dominant and domineering force in the household. And he, for sure, was no puritanical Catholic. On the contrary, Hamilton writes, he was a "political and public Catholic who was not Catholic in any of his practices."[31] A frequently encountered story in Kennedy family histories is of Joe openly rebuking Rose for her belief that sex was only for procreation.[32] Wills suggests that Joe's attitudes about sex were another case of his affinity for things English and the wish to escape from his ethnic heritage. "Irish Catholics in America," he writes, "have been if anything puritanical about sex and Kennedy wanted people to know that he had escaped that particular form of ethnic narrowness."[33] Rejecting the sexual morality of his mother, John Kennedy was his father's son. Hamilton concludes that perhaps the most damaging example the father set for his sons was his sexual ethos "inciting in [Jack] a deliberately degrading, exploitative attitude toward women."[34]

Like his father, then, John Kennedy was a public, symbolic Catholic. He attended mass regularly, ate fish on Fridays, and observed Catholic rituals.[35] But unlike, for example, Senator Eugene McCarthy,[36] he had no intellectual, spiritual, or philosophical commitments to the faith. Nor did he see any connections between Catholicism and the way he conducted his private life or his ideological or political commitments.[37] Thus, he was undoubtedly sincere when he said repeatedly during the 1960 campaign—most famously in his speech to the Houston clerics—that his religion would have no affect—none—on his conduct of the presidency.

Obama's Ethnic Character

The story of John Kennedy has been told and retold in countless family histories, biographies, memoirs, and studies of his presidency. By contrast, Barack Obama is, even according to his semiauthorized campaign chronicler, "a mystery."[38] Not until the 1970s do we begin to get beyond Kennedy's manufactured image and the Camelot myth toward a more fully accurate account of Kennedy, his family, and presidency, and we are still learning.[39] As of this writing, there is still not a fully-researched, comprehensive biography of Obama, and he is just completing the third year of his presidency.[40] Thus, at this point this analysis or any other of Obama is tentative; little more than a good first draft in long-form journalism. In addition, at this point, much of what we think we know about Obama is based on his memoir, *Dreams from My Father: A Story of Race and Inheritance.* Like any memoirist Obama tells us that he "tried to write an honest book," but he also tells us the account is not completely honest because many of the persons portrayed in the book are "composites" (in order to protect their privacy) and many of the events are most likely reconstructed to enhance the flow of the narrative. He emphasizes certain persons, places, and events, while downplaying others. *Dreams* is also about creating, manufacturing a marketable political narrative because although it is about his coming-of-age, it is written at a time when he is thinking about starting a political career. Thus, his "raw ambition" undoubtedly, too, gave shape to the narrative. Not having Joe Kennedy's wealth and vast public relations machinery, a well-crafted telling of his own story would have to suffice; that is, the young, rational, ambitious Obama surely was aware of what Joe told Jack on arranging the publication of his undergraduate thesis: "You will be surprised how a book that really makes the grade with high-class people stands you in good stead for years to come." *Dreams* certainly did that for Obama.

Dreams is a remarkably compelling story of a young man searching for blackness, for an ethnic mooring and heritage, and this chapter draws extensively on it. But journalists who interviewed Obama's teachers and classmates suggest that he perhaps exaggerates the roles of race, racism, and racial ambiguities in his quest to become black.[41] Moreover, in a book about his struggles to become black, he does not address at all his transformation from "Barry" to "Barack." In school in Hawaii, Obama (following his father's example) referred to himself as "Barry" because "he didn't want to have to explain his name. Barry was just a way of simplifying things—a small compromise to smooth the way in society."[42] However, when he transferred from Occidental College in Los Angeles to Columbia in New York, he asked people to call him "Barack". One would surmise that this change of name was a reflection of a growing black consciousness, a wish to more assertively reclaim his African heritage. One would especially surmise this since he tells us in *Dreams* that he transferred to Columbia because there were more black students there and because of the university's proximity to a black community.[43] Yet Obama insists—rather adamantly—that the name change had nothing to do with blackness. "It was not," he told Richard Wolfe, "some assertion of my African roots . . . not a racial assertion. It was much more of an assertion that I was coming of age. An assertion of being comfortable with the fact that I was different and that I didn't need to try to fit in a certain way."[44] In other words, in New York he could be assertively black and proud—and comfortable with his African name?

The ambiguities surrounding how "Barry" became "Barack" are but one example of the mystery of Obama. Although the evidence in this chapter suggests that Obama is black—blacker than Kennedy was Irish or Catholic—his blackness and how he became black seems to reflect a little of Du Bois's famous double consciousness formulation; that is, he may feel more so than Jesse Jackson, for example, "twoness—an American, a Negro, two souls, two thoughts, two unreconciled strivings, two warring ideals in a dark body."[45]

If Kennedy and his father sought to escape their ethnic heritages, the mixed-race Obama, his mother, and maternal grandfather deliberately sought to develop a black ethnic identity. Obama claims that he had no choice about his ethnic identity. When asked on *60 Minutes* when he had "decided" to become black, he replied that it required no decision on his part since he looked black, and "if you look African American in this society, you're treated as an African American."[46] But, he did have choices; not a choice of colors as Curtis Mayfield sang about, but a choice of ethnicity.[47] As Randall Kennedy points out, he could have, like Tiger Woods, manufactured an identity for himself by blending his mixed heritage becoming a "Kencaucasian."[48] In addition, he was born and, except for a few years in Indonesia, raised in Hawaii. In the 1970s Hawaii had a black population, according to one survey, of only 409—one-tenth of 1 percent—excluding military families, which if included would still have made the population less than 10,000.[49] Thus, unlike Chicago or Boston, Honolulu has no "geography for blackness." Furthermore, in the 1970s more than half of Hawaiians were "hapa" or mixed race, and the state was the only place in the country that embraced biracialism in its language and ethos. Glauberman and Burris rightly observe that Obama then rejecting "hapa or white identity while living with his white grandparents" is all the more remarkable.[50]

Finally, in *Dreams*, which Obama says is about his "fitful internal struggle . . . to raise himself as a black man in America," he writes of how he might have chosen another ethnic identity. At Occidental he recalls the biracial "Joyce" (Italian father) who proclaimed, "I'm not black, I'm multiracial."[51] He could have followed Joyce's choice or "Tim's." Also at Occidental, "Tim was not a conscious brother, planned to major in business, wore argyle sweaters and looked like Beaver Cleaver . . . white girlfriends, listening to country music."[52] Finally, he could have married the wealthy, upper-class white woman that he loved and disappeared into her world. But he rejected this option, writing that while standing in her grandfather's library surrounded by photographs of famous people, "I realized that our two worlds . . . were as distant from each other as Kenya from Germany. And I knew that if we had stayed together I'd eventually live in hers. After all, I'd been doing it most of my life."[53]

Obama, therefore, had "ethnic options." Although a self-conscious, organized biracialism movement did not emerge in the United States until the 1970s,[54] in Hawaii biracialism was more than a movement; it was a way of life. Living this DuBosian twoness, Obama "learned to slip back and forth between my black and white worlds, understanding that each possessed its own languages and structures of meaning, convinced that with a bit of translation on my part the two worlds would eventually cohere."[55] Du Bois's "two souls, two thoughts, two un-reconciled strivings, two warring ideas" in his "dark body" achieved their ultimate DuBosian reconciliation and coherence in his presidential campaign; eloquently and elegantly articulated in his Philadelphia race speech, which chapter 8 discusses.

In Hawaii Obama's blackness was shaped by his mother, grandfather, and his grandfather's drinking buddy Frank with his "old black power dashiki . . . living in a sixties time warp."[56] Obama describes his mother—Stanley Ann Dunham—as a "lonely witness for secular humanism."[57] Others have described her as a "free spirited woman" and a "1960s Beatnik era cultural rebel."[58] In 1960 while studying at the University of Hawaii at age eighteen, she met and married Obama's father, who was twenty-three. This in a sense was an act of rebellion, since even in Hawaii black–white sexual intimacies were unusual. Obama relates that his maternal grandfather had found "swallow[ing] the idea of his daughter marrying a black man,"[59] difficult and that his paternal grandfather was opposed to the marriage writing, "He didn't want the Obama blood sullied by white women."[60] A year after Obama's birth, his father abandoned the family to study at Harvard. Several years later, his mother married another "person of color," an Indonesian graduate student, and from age four until ten, Obama lived in a small village in Indonesia. In the late 1970s he returned to Hawaii, and when his mother again left, he stayed and lived with his grandparents while his mother engaged in anthropological field work around the world. Although his mother (who died of ovarian cancer in 1995) was away during his formative years, Obama describes her as the "one constant in his life" and an early source of his blackness.[61] First, he writes, she provided an idealized, positive image of his father as a handsome, charismatic, intellectually gifted Anglophile who returned to Kenya to contribute his knowledge to his country's postcolonial development. Learning later that this was not the case, that his father was an alcoholic, a womanizer, and an unsuccessful bureaucrat, becomes the basis for *Dreams* "mediations" on the absent father. His father, Obama suggests, might be a source of his ambition: "Someone once said that every man is trying to live up to his father's expectations or make up for his father's mistakes, and I suppose that may explain my particular malady as well as anything else."[62] In addition to giving her young son a positive image of a black role model in his father, his mother, he claims, also attempted to instill in him a black consciousness and identity.[63]

Obama's grandfather—Stanley Armour Dunham—nurtured Obama's blackness principally by introducing him to Frank Marshall Davis. In *Dreams,* Obama is vague about "Frank's" impact on his development. Davis was an accomplished poet, a black nationalist, and perhaps a former communist.[64] Glauberman and Burris describe Davis as a " 'cultural mentor, . . .' [Obama] visited him right up until he left Hawaii. Davis was the *Kupuna* who had cultural knowledge. . . ."[65]

Davis would certainly have been able to anchor the young Obama in blackness. Born in rural Kansas in 1905, after studying journalism at Kansas State University, Davis moved to Chicago where he worked for several Chicago weeklies and later as editor for the *Gary American,* the *Atlanta World*, and the Associated Negro Press. Working as a journalist in the 1930s and 1940s brought him into contact with some of the most noted figures of the time, including Duke Ellington, Richard Wright, Louis Armstrong, W. C. Handy, Melville Herskovits, Sterling Brown, Gwendolyn Brooks, and Langston Hughes.[66] Davis was also a poet, photographer, and political activist, as well as a student of black history, culture, and music, especially jazz and the blues. In recognition of his promise as a poet, in 1937 he was awarded a Julius Rosenwald prize in poetry. However, in 1948, Davis left the United States and his promising literary career and moved to Hawaii to escape "the chains of white oppression."[67]

Married to a white woman, Davis found Hawaii's climate and more racially tolerant atmosphere congenial and essentially went into exile.[68] In the 1970s as the black power and black arts movements flourished, Davis was "rediscovered" and "hailed as a *black* poet who had written before being *black* was politically correct" and as a repository of "living history."[69]

Thus, to the extent the young Obama listened and learned, Davis had a lot to teach about blackness, as well as how being black was not inevitably compromised by having whites as part of one's family. In other words, blackness could exist along with, as he put it in his memoir, "people of all colors working together."[70] But the old dashiki-wearing poet and activist had an abiding commitment to a multidimensional blackness. Following is an example of what he might have taught the young Obama:

> We as a group are learning our identity. Our young people know who they are. We are through producing carbon copy

> Caucasians and we are learning to do our own thing, man, without shame. At last we have learned to take pride in our hair, clothing, color, food, music and history as well as other traits setting us apart as a people. We are saying at last "America, this is how we really are. This is what we have given the nation and the world, and we glory in our history and achievements. Whitey, we have had enough of your bullshit. From now on, treat us like equals, or the whole damn mess called America will go up in flames."
>
> And for the first time the white power structure is finding difficulty in locating "different Negroes" to save itself from Niggers, for today many of the formerly different Negroes have blossomed into blacks. The old ploy was to locate a talented Afro-American basically white under his skin, accept him into the club as a courtesy Caucasian with limited membership privileges because he was "different from the rest of the people" and prop him up as a puppet leader in the ghetto. He would receive a comfortable salary and promises of a few crumbs to be flung to the masses in return for keeping them from grumbling too loudly. But that no longer works. Today black is not only beautiful but far wiser.[71]

In *Dreams* Obama recalls that Davis told him in one of his last visits that a college education .could offer an "advanced degree in compromise." The price of admission: "leaving your people behind."[72]

Aside from acquainting Obama with Davis, his grandfather and grandmother, who was the principal breadwinner in the family, did something else to shape Obama's character—they secured his admission and financially supported his study at Punahou, the most exclusive prep school on the islands. At this wealthy, largely white academy, Obama entered the rarefied atmosphere of the nation's elite that Davis had cautioned him about, where he would remain for the rest of his life.

"Blackness," as the Davis quote suggests, is a problematic concept; that is, it is difficult to define, and when defined it has multiple meanings.[73] Blackness is a cultural phenomenon, meaning that it cuts across lines of class, gender, ethnicity, region, religion, and residence although these variables shape how blackness is experienced.[74] It is also shaped by the omnipresence of racism, for African peoples, whatever their status and wherever they are in the Diaspora, they sometimes encounter racism. Even Obama, who has spent most of his life in the rarified heights of Punahou, Columbia, Harvard, and Hyde Park, reports the "usual litany of petty slights: security guards following me as I shop, white couples who toss me their keys as I stand outside of a restaurant waiting for the valet, police cars pulling me over for no apparent reason."[75] Thus unlike Irishness when Kennedy was elected, blackness was more than symbolic; it had in 2008 a substantive, material basis, providing identity, consciousness, and solidarity. And Randall Kennedy is correct: "most blacks want to retain for the foreseeable future, if not permanently, a sense of group solidarity and its attendant manifestations in social, cultural and political life."[76]

Blackness is an ethnic boundary-maintenance concept that separates or distinguishes individuals on the basis of their presumed identification with the ethos and interests of the black community. It has multiple dimensions or meanings, four of which may be identified. First, the psychological dimension requires a consciousness of one's identity as black, a rejection of negative stereotypes, and expressions of pride in identification with one's African and African American heritage.[77] The second dimension is cultural, requiring awareness or involvement in the cultural life of the black community. However, given that experts disagree as to what constitutes or distinguishes black culture in the United States, giving this dimension any definitive meaning is difficult; that is, what it means to be culturally black in the United States is amorphous and ambiguous, but nevertheless certain values and rituals are found in religion, music, sports, and dance that over the years have been identified as at least partially distinctive cultural attributes. These, however, may vary to a considerable extent by age, class, region, and residence. The third dimension of blackness—the political—involves the belief that the fate of all blacks is linked. To be identified as politically black requires individuals to evaluate political issues in terms of their impact on the interests of the group, and to make political choices on the basis of whether they benefit or harm the group. This dimension is akin to Tommie Shelby's notion of black solidarity where "the only interests that blacks share on account of their being black and that can serve as a stable and legitimate basis for political unity are race-related ones—fighting racism, promoting racial equality, eliminating racialized poverty, and reducing racial antagonism."[78] The fourth dimension of blackness—the ideological—is the most contentious. The African American political culture is relatively homogeneous in terms of adherence to the liberal ideology; therefore to be black is to embrace liberalism. And, since the 1960s the Democratic Party has been the more liberal of the two parties, to be black is to be Democratic, or at least not Republican. To put this another way, since the 1960s, conservatism as it has been advanced by the Republican Party is viewed in the black political culture as hostile to black interests, as "antiblack," and as the functional equivalent of racism.[79] Thus, to be a black Republican or a black conservative is to be beyond the boundaries of blackness.

On each of the four dimensions Obama appears to be black. Psychologically, his mother apparently instilled in him at early age identification with blackness. He then built on that by reading blackness. In his memoir, Obama recalls his friend Ray telling him, "I don't need no books to tell me how to be black."[80] But Obama did and he "read black": Baldwin, Hughes, Wright, Du Bois, and above all Malcolm. Malcolm's heroic transformation from "Negro to black" especially appealed to him, writing "only Malcolm's autobiography seemed to offer something different."[81] As countless post–civil-rights-era black men will attest, reading Malcolm will deepen the blackness of even the most racially conscious African American.

At Occidental, Obama self-consciously continued to read blackness and radicalism: "To avoid being mistaken for a sellout, I chose my friends carefully. The more politically active black students, the Chicanos. The Marxist professors and structural feminists and punk rock performance poets. We smoked cigarettes and wore leather jackets. At night in the dorms we discussed neocolonialism, Frantz Fanon, Eurocentric and Patriarchy."[82] Realizing that reading was not enough to anchor his blackness he claims he "needed a community . . . a community [greater] than the common despair that my black friends and I shared when reading the latest crime statistics or the high fives I might exchange on the basketball court."[83] So, he transferred from the near all-white environs of Occidental to Columbia so he could be around more black people. After graduating from Columbia rather than accept a congressional internship or position with a group like the Urban League, with the heroic image of Student Nonviolent Coordinating Committee (SNCC) workers in his psyche, he became a community organizer in the ghettos of Southside Chicago.

As an adolescent Obama embraced black culture—he listened to music from jazz to soul, learned to "dance all the soul train [*sic*] steps," and above all playing basketball.[84] Basketball, Mendel writes, became a "source of solace,"[85] while Glauberman and Burris write, it was his "heart and soul and helped to shape his character . . . [making him] one of the brothers."[86] Michael Eric Dyson writes that Obama's "rhetoric is firmly rooted in black soil."[87] Obama's gift with words in addressing white America was widely commented on during the campaign (Hillary Clinton charged he was all rhetoric with little substance, while the McCain campaign ran ads mocking his rhetorical appeal). His rhetorical appeals to whites (or mixed audiences to be precise) were elegant and intellectual, however, before largely black audiences he could speak in cadences of Martin Luther King and in the tradition of Malcolm X. For example, in a speech before a largely black audience in South Carolina in January 2008 he sounded like Malcolm, "They are trying to bamboozle you. It's the same old okie-doke. Y'all know about the okie-doke right. . . . They try to bamboozle you. Hoodwink ya. All right, I'm having too much fun up here."[88] Dyson refers to this speech as "signifying—in which the speaker hints at ideas or meanings that are veiled to outsiders."[89] Nia-Malika Henderson refers to it as "dog whistle politics" appealing to the cultural sensibilities of black people while not alarming whites.[90] Dyson concludes, "Obama was making a risky move that played to the insider-group understanding even as he campaigned to the white mainstream: while denying he was a Muslim, he fastened onto the rhetoric of the most revered Black Muslim, mimicking his tone and rhythm beat for beat."[91] Another example of Obama's "signaling cultural authenticity" that escaped whites occurred in his visit to Ben's Chili Bowl shortly before the inauguration. An iconic place in black Washington, when the waiter asked him if he wanted his change after Obama purchased a chili dog he responded "nah, we straight." Henderson writes, "The video of the exchange became an instant Internet hit among blacks who got a kick out of their Harvard-educated president sounding 'mad cool.'"[92] And the "swagger, the rhythmic lope that says cool and confident and undeniably black—seen on the first postelection visit to the White House."[93]

Politically Obama is also undeniably black; a traditional liberal Democrat he is located well within the mainstream of the political culture, and might be described as a "soft black nationalist."[94] On the important nationalism-integration cleavage in black politics Obama clearly comes down on the integrationist side.[95] However, his "strategic rejection of nationalism" as presented in *Dreams* is nuanced and sophisticated, rooted in an understanding of the well springs of the nationalist tradition's hold on the black imagination. "Desperate times," he writes, "called for desperate measures, and for many blacks times were desperate. If nationalism could create a strong and effective insularity, deliver on its promise of self-respect, then the hurt it might cause well-meaning whites or the inner turmoil it caused people like me would be of little consequence."[96] For Obama "if nationalism could deliver" becomes the central question; a question of effectiveness not sentiment. He concludes—correctly—that historically, Black Nationalism has not been able to deliver. Rather, it frequently "dissipated into an attitude rather than any concrete program, a collection of grievances and not an organized force, images and sounds that crowded the airwaves and conversations but without corporal existence."[97] Only the Nation of Islam, Obama argued, had a significant following, and the failure of its program "finally explained how nationalism could thrive as an emotion and flounder as a program."[98]

Obama attended Farrakhan's 1996 Million Man March, which reinforced the strategic rejection he sketched out in *Dreams*: "What I saw," he told the *Chicago Reader* "was a powerful demonstration and impulse and need for African American men to come together, to recognize each other and affirm our rightful place in the society. There was a profound commitment to bring about change in our communities and in our lives. But what was lacking among March organizers was a positive agenda, a coherent agenda of change."[99] Thus of this historic nationalism–integrationism conflict in black politics, he concluded, black leadership must move "out of the twin cul-de-sac [of] the unrealistic politics of integrationist assimilation—which helps a few upwardly mobile blacks to 'move up, get rich and move out'—and the equally impractical politics of black rage and black nationalism—which exhorts but does not organize ordinary folks or create realistic agendas for change."[100] One way out of the cul-de-sac for Obama was the black church. Religiosity and the church are pillars of blackness. Thus, the agnostic Obama found faith and joined a black church. What is noteworthy is that he did not join a traditional black Baptist congregation but Rev. Jeremiah Wright's Trinity United Methodist Church, a militant, activist, Afro-Centric, Black Nationalist congregation. Ironically, another way out of the cul-de-sac was to run for office, eventually the presidency, although knowing that "change won't come from the top," but from "a mobilized grassroots."[101] The presidency may be the ultimate cul-de-sac for one interested in changing the chronically desperate condition of blacks. This, however, is a subject for the next three chapters.

Obama, one must conclude, is black—psychologically, culturally, and politically. Because of his rootedness in all the relevant dimensions of blackness, when questions about how black he was were raised during the campaign, they had little resonance with ordinary blacks. Obama is, however, and to some extent always has been an incorporated, integrated, assimilated black, raised by whites, and gaining entry into the nation's elite institutions at an early age. Although not an Irish Brahmin like John Kennedy, he is close; cut-glass for sure. Meanwhile, a good part of the black community is shanty. How a lace-curtain or Irish Brahmin Catholic president would have dealt with the chronic desperation of the shanty Irish we can never know. There were none when Kennedy was elected. How Obama deals with this problem is a prinicipal concern of this book, which the next chapter begins to address.

8

Religion and the Election of 1960

It is paradoxical. In 2008 Barack Obama faced no organized opposition to his candidacy based on race, whereas John Kennedy faced well-organized opposition—overt and clandestine—because of religion. This is paradoxical first because the ideology of white supremacy and racism are historically more deeply rooted in American culture than anti-Irish sentiments or anti-Catholic nativism. Second, as has been pointed out throughout this volume and analyzed in detail in chapter 6, by the time Kennedy was nominated the Catholic Irish were fully incorporated, whereas when Obama was nominated blacks were semi-incorporated. Related to this, invidious negative stereotypes about the Catholic Irish were largely things of the past in 1960, but such stereotypes about blacks were widespread in 2008. Third, the biracial, light-skinned, elitist, bourgeois Obama was to many whites an ebony saint, but he was also undeniably black—perhaps not as black as Jesse Jackson, but black nevertheless. Kennedy, on the other hand, was not discernibly Irish or Catholic; certainly he was no Al Smith or Tip O'Neill. So in 1960 there was a fully incorporated Catholic community that constituted approximately 25 percent of the population and a thoroughly assimilated Catholic candidate. In addition, there existed well-established principles of the separation of church and state and an explicit constitutional prohibition on any religious test for public office. But in 1959, polls indicated that 25 percent of Protestants said they would not vote for a qualified Catholic for president, compared to about 5 percent of whites in 2007 who said they would not vote for a qualified African American.

Opposition to a Catholic president in 1960 included not only Protestant fundamentalists and bigots but liberals and civil libertarians; not just the Rev. Norman Vincent Peale but the Rev. Martin Luther King Sr. and perhaps his son as well. In 1960 there was, among thoughtful, enlightened segments of the public, a perception that there might be legitimate reasons to apply an unconstitutional religious test for the presidency. No such legitimacy—none—was suggested in 2008 concerning race. This is not to suggest that race and racism were not factors in the 2008 election. They demonstrably were. Rather, it is to suggest that they were near universally considered as irrelevant considerations.

In addition to this paradox, both Kennedy and Obama had to deal with skepticism about their candidacies within their own ethnic communities. Whether it was time for a Catholic or black to run, whether a Catholic or black could win, whether a Catholic or black candidacy might set back the interests of the group, whether these particular candidates had the requisite experience for the office, and, finally whether they were Catholic or black enough, Both Kennedy and Obama had to run "de-ethnicized" campaigns while at the same time not alienating their ethnic bases. Both—reluctantly—found giving major speeches on religion and race strategically necessary in an effort to balance or blend ethnic and mainstream sentiments and concerns.

In both 1960 and 2008 political elites and especially media elites played important roles in holding candidates to the norm of religious and racial tolerance, and in calling out campaign tactics that appeared to go beyond the boundaries of legitimate discourse. Finally, although both Kennedy and Obama were victorious the available evidence indicates that both suffered an "ethnic deficit." When Joe Kennedy was asked shortly after the 1960 election how many states his son would have won if he been Episcopalian, without hesitation he responded, "Fifty."[1] Kennedy would not have won fifty states if he had been Protestant, and Obama would not have won fifty if he had been white, but given the strategic electoral environments in 1960 and 2008 both would have won by larger margins if they had been white Anglo-Saxon Protestants.

The Kennedy family's long quest for the presidency began in earnest at the 1956 Democratic Convention. In that year with the presidential nomination firmly secured, Adlai Stevenson leaked to the press the idea that he might select a Catholic—either New York City Mayor Robert Wagner or John Kennedy—for the vice presidential nomination. The Kennedy family organization under the leadership of Joe Kennedy immediately swung into action to secure the nomination.[2] Theodore Sorensen was directed to prepare a memorandum showing the size and strategic significance of the "Catholic vote." Sorensen argued that the Catholic vote, which comprised 25 percent of the electorate, was concentrated in California and 13 other states with 261 electoral votes (two more than the 259 needed to win). The memorandum noted that in 1952 Eisenhower had carried nearly half the Catholic vote and as a result many of these electoral vote-rich states. The memorandum also argued that Al Smith's defeat in 1928 was inevitable, and prohibition was more of a factor in his defeat than religion. Thus, Sorensen concluded, a Catholic vice president could swing the Catholic vote to Stevenson with relatively little risk of a Protestant backlash.

The Kennedys, however, did not wish to be openly associated with discussion of a Catholic bloc vote (in 1960 John Kennedy would argue there was no such thing as a Catholic vote), and thus they arranged for Sorensen's memorandum "The Catholic Vote in 1952 and 1956" to be released in the name of John Bailey, the Catholic chair of the Connecticut Democratic party.[3] The "Bailey Memorandum" was circulated widely in the media (*US News and World Report* published virtually the entire document) as a means to pressure Stevenson to choose Kennedy. The vacillating Stevenson, however, decided to leave the choice to the convention and in a spirited contest Tennessee Senator Estes Kefauver narrowly defeated Kennedy.[4]

In retrospect, losing the vice presidential nomination in an open contest with Kefauver was probably advantageous. It provided a good test of the Kennedy organization, and Kennedy received valuable national media exposure, delivering the principal Stevenson nominating speech. In addition, Stevenson's inevitable defeat could not be blamed—as Joe Kennedy feared—on the presence of a Catholic on the ticket. Finally, Kennedy's race for the vice presidential nomination led him to conclude that he did not have to settle for the vice presidency. Rather he said the contest with Kefauver taught him "it should be as easy to get the nomination for president as it was vice president. Until then I thought I would have to work first toward the vice presidency."[5] Kennedy's performance at the 1956 convention transformed him into a rising star. In 1957 the Kennedy publicity machine went into high gear. Earlier in 1955 Kennedy's second book, *Profiles in Courage*, had won the Pulitzer Prize. Although he and his father had to threaten lawsuits over allegations that Sorensen had actually written the book, the Pulitzer Prize gave him credentials as an intellectual and the book became a bestseller.[6] A year after the 1956 convention "saw the beginning of a publicity buildup unprecedented in U.S. political history. For the first time, a very junior and relatively unimportant member of the Senate became the subject of glowing articles that paid little attention to politics and instead presented to their readers an arresting political personality, a celebrity."[7] By 1960 Kennedy was the acknowledged frontrunner for the nomination, receiving hundreds of invitations a week to make speeches and drawing large crowds and autograph seekers as he traveled throughout the country.[8] Reeves estimates that between 1958 and 1960, Joe Kennedy spent more than $1.5 million promoting his son.[9]

In May 1959, Gallup released a poll on the likely impact of Kennedy's religion on the 1960 election. Based on a large sample, the results were published in a five-part series in newspapers throughout the country. While 62 percent of Protestant respondents said they would vote for a well-qualified Catholic, 28 percent said they would not. On the other hand, 95 percent of Catholics said they would vote for their party's nominee if he was a Catholic, and 52 percent indicated they might switch parties in order to vote for a Catholic nominee.[10] Overall, Gallup concluded that Catholicism had declined as a negative issue for the electorate, but on balance Kennedy would be hurt more than helped by his religion. In a projection that nearly matched the election outcome, Gallup concluded that when religion was not a part of the voters' decision calculus, Kennedy would defeat Nixon 57 percent to 43 percent, but when voters took religion into consideration the results were a virtual stalemate.[11]

As he began the campaign, Kennedy knew three things could defeat him: his religion, his health, and his womanizing. Of the three, he made plans to deal only with the first. He was more worried about his health derailing his campaign then he was about his serial adultery.[12] Gossip about Kennedy's "sexual permissiveness" was circulating,[13] and he knew that he could be "just one news story away from a cataclysmic scandal."[14] Yet the adultery continued with Kennedy apparently concluding that the "gentleman" (the press in 1960 was virtually all male) of the media would consider it ungentlemanly to delve into the muck. As it turned out he was correct; the media did not begin reporting on the sex lives of presidential candidates until 1984. Although he blatantly lied about it, Kennedy suffered from Addison's disease among other maladies. When rumors surfaced about the illness (Lyndon Johnson at one point referred to Kennedy as a "sickly boy" unfit for the presidency),[15] Kennedy stated flatly that he did not have Addison's disease. Like his womanizing, the public did not learn of the poor state of the President's health until after his death although he took daily doses of cortisone and other medications to control the disease.[16] Richard Reeves writes, "In a lifetime of medical torment, Kennedy was more promiscuous with physicians and drugs than he was with women."[17] Luck and the forbearance of the press and his opponents kept sex and his health from undermining Kennedy's candidacy. With religion, however, he knew he could count on neither the press nor his opponents, so how to deal with the Catholic question became the central strategic problem of the campaign.

Kennedy inaugurated the first modern presidential campaign. First, the 1960 campaign was the first to use sophisticated, computerized polling and marketing to sell a personality to the voters. Second, this selling of the candidate involved direct appeals to voters over the heads of party leaders through the primaries, requiring for the first time the extensive use of television. Third, Kennedy traveled about the country on the "Caroline," his father's personal jet while Hubert Humphrey, for example, campaigned in mountainous West Virginia and snow-bound Wisconsin on a bus. Finally, big money—his daddy's—was employed on a then-unprecedented scale.

Kennedy employed these formidable resources first in his quest for the nomination. Although he was the frontrunner, he knew that he faced formidable opposition within the Democratic Party establishment. This opposition included leading Catholic politicians and the church hierarchy. Catholic opposition—or at least skepticism—about his candidacy discussed below, but Kennedy first had to deal with the opposition of leading liberals, blacks, and white southerners. Some of this opposition was based on religion as discussed later in the chapter, but liberals and blacks were skeptical about Kennedy for other reasons as well. Eleanor Roosevelt, the iconic leader of party liberals, and President Truman opposed Kennedy's nomination. Truman was opposed partly because of his disdain for Joe Kennedy, telling reporters "I like Jack. He is a nice person. But, I don't like his daddy and never did."[18] Truman also said Kennedy was too young and inexperienced, and he was hoping as well that in a deadlocked convention the nod might go to Stuart Symington, his home state senator.[19] Eleanor Roosevelt disliked Joe Kennedy even more so than did President Truman, owing to his isolationist views and strident opposition to the New Deal. As the 1960 campaign approached, Joe Kennedy kept himself out of the public eye,[20] and John Kennedy declared that he was in "total" disagreement with his father's views. Yet to many liberals "it seemed unlikely that his opinionated, domineering parent, a nineteenth-century pater familias would tolerate real dissent under his roof."[21] Eleanor Roosevelt also charged that Joe Kennedy was trying to buy the election; a charged Humphrey echoed. Describing Kennedy as a "spoiled candidate," Humphrey exclaimed, "I don't think elections should be bought."[22]

Eleanor Roosevelt and other liberals were also upset with the Kennedys because of their close associations with Senator Joseph McCarthy. The Catholic McCarthy, a close family friend, had dated one of the Kennedy daughters and hired Bobby Kennedy to work on his Senate investigative staff. John Kennedy was the only Democratic senator not to vote to censure McCarthy (he was hospitalized at the time), leading Eleanor Roosevelt to sneer that he was "someone who understands what courage is and admires it, but has not quite the independence to have it."[23] Finally many liberals were skeptical about Kennedy because he always disdained calling himself one of them. Preferring Humphrey's "ideologically pure" liberalism to Kennedy's "pragmatic" version, many liberals in 1960 agreed with Humphrey's description of Kennedy as an "election year convert to liberalism"[24] and as a "Democratic Nixon, who only joined the liberal ranks to win the nomination."[25]

African Americans, even in 1960 the most liberal bloc in the party, were skeptical because of Kennedy's "zigzag" behavior on civil rights.[26] As Burns described it if not "a profile in cowardice . . . a profile in caution and moderation."[27] Kennedy was certainly not a racist or white supremacist, but he had no black acquaintance or staffers (unless one includes his longtime valet, George Thomas) and had little interest or concern about civil rights or the problems of blacks. His knowledge of blacks was, according to Arthur Schlesinger Jr., based on his acceptance while at Harvard of the "Dunning School" interpretation of Reconstruction, which taught that blacks were mentally incapable of exercising civil rights and that the South was unjustly treated. One gets a sense of his racial views from the portrait of Senator Edmund Ross in *Profiles*. Ross was the senator whose "not guilty" vote prevented the removal of President Andrew Johnson from office after his impeachment. Kennedy described Ross's vote as "the most heroic in American history." However, it is most likely that Ross was bribed to cast his vote in favor of Johnson's acquittal.[28] Kennedy's jaundiced view of Reconstruction is clear when he writes:

> The event in which the obscure Ross was to play such a dramatic role, was the sensational climax to the bitter struggle between the President, determined to carry out Abraham Lincoln's policies of reconciliation with the defeated South, and the more radical Republican leaders in Congress, who sought to administer the downtrodden Southern states as conquered provinces which had forfeited their rights under the Constitution. . . . Andrew Johnson, the courageous, if untactful Tennessean who had been the only Southern member of Congress to refuse to secede with his state, had committed himself to the policies of the Great Emancipator. . . .[29]

Meanwhile, Kennedy described Thaddeus Stevens, the leader of the civil rights forces in the House, as "the crippled fanatical personification of the extremes of the Radical Republican movement."[30]

In the Senate Kennedy generally voted with the liberal civil rights bloc, although in 1957 he joined Majority Leader Lyndon Johnson and the southern segregationists in approving jury trials for persons accused of voting rights violations (making it virtually impossible to win convictions). But as he turned his attention toward 1960, he was haunted by the ghost of the 1948 election. When President Truman embraced the cause of civil rights in 1948, he split the Democratic coalition and nearly lost the election. Although Truman won a narrow, surprise victory, the defection of four southern states to the Dixiecrat party caused northern Democrats with presidential ambitions to downplay civil rights. Adlai Stevenson had pursued this course in 1952 (naming a southern segregationist as his running mate) and 1956, and Kennedy was determined to do the same in 1960.[31] Thus, his principal concern about civil rights was strategic rather than principled. That is, he wanted to simultaneously maintain the support of blacks and southern racists.[32] African American political and civil rights leaders clearly preferred Hubert Humphrey, the liberal Minnesota senator who had established his reputation in national politics by insisting that the Democratic Party adopt, for the first time, a civil rights plank in its 1948 platform. But Harlem Congressman Adam Clayton Powell (who had endorsed Eisenhower in 1956) went even further, declaring in effect that any candidate would be better than Kennedy.[33] Meanwhile, Kennedy won the endorsement of the governors of Alabama and Mississippi, with the latter describing Kennedy as "Dixie's favorite Yankee."[34] With Kennedy's agreement, the Democratic Party adopted the strongest plank on civil rights ever, but to placate the South he selected the South's favorite son—Lyndon Johnson—as his running mate.

While working to balance the shaky coalition between the liberal and black civil rights forces and the conservative southern segregationists, Kennedy also had to pay attention to his own Catholic and Catholic Irish base. Many of the Catholic Irish leaders of the urban machines in the Northeast and Midwest were opposed to Kennedy's nomination because they did not think a Catholic could win. Haunted by the ghost of the Al Smith campaign, these leaders thought that another Catholic loss would be a setback to the cause of full political incorporation. The Catholic governors of California and Pennsylvania were skeptical about Kennedy's candidacy because it would ruin their chances for the vice presidential nomination. Finally, some were concerned that if elected, Kennedy would bend over backward to prove he was not pro-Catholic. By contrast, a Protestant—even the Republican Richard Nixon—in order to appeal to Catholic voters would most likely be more sympathetic to Catholic interests and concerns. In a 1960 speech Sorensen said as much. Denying that Kennedy would be vulnerable to pressure from Catholics, Sorensen said, "In fact, he would be less vulnerable to any possible pressure from the so-called Catholic vote than some non-Catholic politicians who might feel the need to cater to Catholics."[35] These concerns were reinforced in the minds of many Catholic leaders and clergy by Kennedy's flip-flopping on issues of Catholic concern. As a young Congressman Kennedy had strongly supported federal aid to Catholic schools, but by 1958 he had completely abandoned this position and was militantly opposed to any such aid arguing that it was patently unconstitutional. (As discussed below, Nixon was more sympathetic on this issue than was Kennedy.) Similarly, in 1945 Kennedy said he supported the initiatives of Franklin Roosevelt and Truman to appoint an ambassador to the Vatican. By 1959 he said he was opposed. These flip-flops resulted in regular criticism of Kennedy in the Catholic press. The Jesuit journal *America*, for example, lamented the "earnest Senator's efforts to appease the bigots."[36] Other critics noted his reluctance to be photographed with Catholic prelates but how quickly he was to "summon the photographers whenever Billy Graham or some other protestant churchman comes a calling."[37] The Catholic Church hierarchy—with the exception of Boston's Cardinal Cushing, a family friend—was thought to favor Nixon.[38] Although no Catholic prelate endorsed Nixon, New York's Cardinal Spellman's high-profile appearances with Nixon to some implied support.[39] The church hierarchy was upset about Kennedy's flip-flopping on recognition of the Vatican and aid to church schools. And on what Sorensen calls "the most sensitive issue of all," Kennedy opposed the church's attempt to reduce foreign aid to nations using public funds for birth control. On birth control generally Kennedy declared, "without minimizing the moral implications . . . [this] is essentially a political issue to be decided on the basis of the general welfare."[40] In the view of many Catholics these views suggested that Kennedy was not Catholic enough. "Why don't you support Catholic schools," the *Catholic Review* queried, "why don't you receive communion more often?"[41]

In a 1959 *Look* magazine interview, Kennedy outraged many in the Catholic theological community when he averred that in his view a radical separation existed between private religious beliefs and public life. He was quoted as saying, "whatever one's religion in private life may be, for the officeholder, *nothing* takes precedence over his oath to uphold the Constitution in all its parts—including the First Amendment and the strict separation of church and state."[42] Kennedy was to pursue this line of thinking in his famous speech to Protestant clergy in Houston, but to many religious people—not just Catholics—this was nonsense. The Catholic press was overwhelmingly hostile.[43] Kennedy's "privatization" of religion, *America* editorialized, was inexplicable: "We were somewhat taken aback by the unvarnished statement that nothing takes precedence over one's oath. Mr. Kennedy doesn't really believe that. No religious man, be he Catholic, Protestant or Jew, holds such an opinion."[44]

Whether Kennedy believed it or not, strategically he felt it was imperative to make this unequivocal declaration. Calculating that in the end Catholics would support one of their own notwithstanding his semi-Catholicism; Kennedy concluded that reaching out to Protestants was necessary, even at the risk of alienating part of his base. This was not without risks. Catholics were now near fully incorporated and the ethnic bonds of solidarity were weaker than in 1928. Thus his Protestant outreach "threatened to undermine Catholic support as [he] appeared to pander to anti-Catholic conservative Protestants."[45]

In 1989 Donald Robinson wrote of the primaries that "once a useful means for informing and checking the judgments of party leaders about the popularity of candidates, [they] have assumed a dominant role in the nominating process, though they are clearly unfit for it."[46] In 1960 Kennedy used the primaries for this "informing and checking" role, whereas in 2008 Obama used them to actually defeat the preferred candidate of party leaders.

From the 1830s to the 1970s the choice of the Democratic nominee was in the hands of party leaders—governors, senators, big-city mayors, and the leaders of major interest groups such as labor unions. In contrast to 2008, when all the states and territories used binding primaries or caucuses, in 1960 only sixteen non-binding "beauty contests" were held. Although he would get few delegates from winning the primaries, Kennedy knew he had to enter and win some of them in order to exorcise the ghost of Al Smith by proving that a Catholic could win, especially in Protestant areas. At the beginning of 1960. a majority of party leaders and delegates expected Kennedy to be the nominee, but they were worried that he would lose the general election because of religion.[47] Even the Catholic "bosses" of the urban machines, who viewed him fondly as a fellow Hibernian, thought that he was "hopelessly doomed to defeat."[48] And because to them winning was everything, even ethnic bonds of solidarity could not lead them to back a loser. So Kennedy had to show them.

If he could show them by winning in Protestant parts of the country, the Catholic Irish party leaders would fall in line and the nomination would be his because, he judged, his rivals were less viable nominees than he. His major rival was Humphrey. Kennedy dismissed him as a "far out liberal," whom southerners and conservatives would reject. This meant that if Humphrey was to have any chance he would have to contest Kennedy in the primaries. His other rivals expected to win the nomination by default. Lyndon Johnson, the Senate Majority Leader with his base in the South and Southwest, assumed that at a deadlocked convention, party leaders might turn to him. But skeptical about his support outside his base, he was unwilling to enter the primaries. Similarly, Missouri Senator Stuart Symington, a former Air Force secretary, assumed that with President Truman's support he might be the compromise choice. But the possible candidacy of Adlai Stevenson worried Kennedy the most. Assuming that Humphrey was too liberal, that no southerner could be nominated, and that Symington was too bland and little known, Kennedy thought a deadlocked convention would most likely turn to Stevenson. Eleanor Roosevelt supported the urbane, erudite Stevenson, who was a hero to liberals yet acceptable to the South. Although he had lost twice to Eisenhower, experts believed that no Democrat could have defeated the popular general but virtually any Democrat could defeat Nixon. Thus, Kennedy's strategy was to decisively win in the primaries, thereby avoiding a deadlocked convention.

He entered seven of the sixteen primaries, avoiding mainly those in heavily Catholic states. The first contest was in Wisconsin (31 percent Catholic), the neighboring state to Humphrey's Minnesota. Louis Harris, Kennedy's pollster, did detailed surveys in Wisconsin and concluded that Kennedy faced a delicate religious balancing act. First, he had to mobilize his Catholic base by not overly stressing his opposition to issues of concern to them such as federal aid to their schools. He also had to prevent his Catholic supporters from making religion an issue with allegations of anti-Catholic bigotry. On the other hand, while mobilizing his base he also had to win significant Protestant support otherwise a victory would be meaningless. Above all, Harris wrote, he had to avoid allegations of "reverse bigotry"—that Catholics were voting for him simply because he was Catholic. This was imperative because perception of a "Catholic bloc vote" could arouse a "sleeping Lutheran and Protestant majority" backlash.[49] In the end, Harris concluded, the best strategy was to in effect take his ethnic base for granted and "bend over backward not to demonstrate any pro-Catholic bias in his campaigning. No social appearances with Catholic clergy or at Catholic venues."[50]

Kennedy defeated Humphrey decisively 56 percent to 44 percent, but it was largely an ethnic-base vote. He lost all of the predominantly Protestant counties, while winning in Catholic areas probably with a heavy crossover vote from Catholic Republicans.[51] Experts estimate that the Catholic vote was three or four to one for Kennedy, whereas the Protestant vote for Humphrey was three to two.[52] While Kennedy had won decisively, the results did not put the religious issue to rest, and thus he went on to West Virginia. Humphrey's defeat in Wisconsin effectively meant that his chances for winning the nomination were over. Having lost in his region of the country and with little money, many liberals urged Humphrey to pull out of the race because a bloody fight might leave both candidates damaged, deadlock the convention, and give the nomination to a more conservative candidate. But if Humphrey withdrew, Kennedy knew that the religious issue would continue to haunt his campaign. Thus, he needed a showdown with Humphrey. For reasons that are not clear, Humphrey decided to contest the West Virginia primary although polls indicated Kennedy was leading 70 percent to 30 percent.

West Virginia in 1960 was virtually an all Protestant state. The Kennedy organization had been anticipating a possible West Virginia showdown and started to conduct polling in the state in 1958.[53] Estimates as to how much money Kennedy spent in the state vary. Rorabaugh gives a "realistic estimate" of from $1.5 million to $2.5 million, and Hersh suggests it might have been twice that much.[54] Meanwhile, Humphrey's estimated expenditures were $30,000; Kennedy spent $30,000 on television alone.[55] The Kennedys' limitless money allowed the campaign to conduct saturation ads, including a statewide broadcast dealing with the religious issue.[56] The campaign also arranged for the distribution of an open letter from prominent national Protestant clergy addressed to "Fellow Pastors in Christ" in West Virginia, decrying anti-Catholic bigotry in the election. Kennedy won West Virginia 61 percent to 39 percent. Humphrey withdrew, and although Kennedy went on to win several other largely uncontested primaries, with his victory in West Virginia he had effectively won the nomination. Lyndon Johnson formally entered the race shortly before the convention opened, and there was a long, emotional, and apparently spontaneous demonstration for Stevenson on the floor, but Kennedy easily won the nomination on the first ballot: Kennedy, 806; Johnson, 409; Symington, 86; Stevenson, 79½; and others, 140½.

Winning the nomination, however, did not put to rest the ghost of Al Smith. His fellow Democrats he knew did not—could not—fully exploit the religious issue given that Catholics were a core constituency necessary for victory in the fall. Republicans would be less constrained, and West Virginia and Wisconsin were not barometers of the nation. Kennedy candidly acknowledged that the party was taking a risk. Anticipating ideas that he would develop in detail later in his speech to the Houston clergy, Kennedy told the delegates:

> I am fully aware that the Democratic Party, by nominating someone of my faith, has taken on what many regard as a new and hazardous risk—new at least since 1928. The Democratic Party has once again placed its confidence in the American people, and in their ability to render a free and fair judgment. To uphold the Constitution and my oath of office, to reject any kind of religious pressure or obligation

> that might directly or indirectly interfere with my conduct of the presidency in the national interest. My record of fourteen years in supporting public education, supporting complete separation of church and state and resisting pressure from sources of any kind should be clear by now to everyone. I hope that no American—I hope that no American, considering the really critical issues facing this country, will waste his franchise and throw away his vote by voting either for me or against me because of my religious affiliation. It is not relevant. I am telling you what you are entitled to know: As I come before you seeking your support for the most powerful office in the free world—I am saying to you that my decisions on every public issue will be my own, as an American, as a Democrat, and as a free man.[57]

In 1960 the Democratic Party was unambiguously the majority party. The New Deal philosophy and coalition Franklin Roosevelt established in the 1930s still commanded the loyalties of a majority of the electorate, and Democrats still maintained majorities in both houses of Congress, the state legislatures, and governorships. Although the Republican Eisenhower had won two impressive victories in 1952 and 1956, political scientists referred to those elections as "deviating elections," which are elections based on short-term influences on the "normal vote" of the majority party that brings about its temporary defeat.[58] The principal short-term force in the elections of 1952 and 1956 was General Eisenhower. Both parties had attempted to recruit the popular, nonpartisan World War II hero. Eisenhower's decision to run as a Republican almost ensured a Democratic defeat, given the stalemate in the Korean War and President Truman's low approval rating (at one point falling to as low as 23 percent). "We Like Ike," however, did not translate into "We like Republicans," as was demonstrated by the high rate of ticket splitting and the Democrats regaining control of both houses of Congress in 1954. Therefore, once he got the nomination, Kennedy knew that if his religion did not constitute another short-term influence, he should easily defeat Nixon because the normal Democratic vote was 54 percent.[59] Thus, Kennedy's New Frontier was firmly anchored in the tradition of majority party New Deal liberalism, including Medicare, federal aid to education, and assistance to economically distressed areas. These were the bread-and-butter issues of the campaign, but like Obama nearly fifty years later, Kennedy also promised "change" to "get the country moving again" with a "new a generation of leadership—new men who are not bound by the traditions of the past—men who are not blinded by old fears, hates and rivalries—young men who cast off the old slogans and delusions."[60]

In order to get this New Frontier beyond the old hates and fears, Kennedy knew he would have to develop a strategy to deal with the old hates and fears based on religious bigotry and the anti-Catholic wariness among "the thoughtful people," liberals and civil libertarians who objected to the "imposition on Catholics and non-Catholics alike of Catholic standards through legislation and economic and political pressure on education, marriage, divorce, contraceptives, legal abortion and other matters."[61]

In 1947, in *Emerson v. Board of Education,* the Supreme Court ruled in a 5–4 decision that local school board payments to parochial schools to cover transportation costs did not violate the Establishment Clause of the First Amendment.[62] Although the majority for the first time declared that the clause was intended to establish "a wall of separation between church and state," and that no amount of money however small could be used to "support any religious activities or institutions," it concluded that subsides for pupil transportation did not constitute support for religious schools. The dissenting justices disagreed with Justice Wiley Rutledge, writing that helping children get to school in a substantial way helped them to secure "religious training and teaching."[63] Shortly after *Emerson,* Protestants and Other Americans United for Separation of Church and State (POAU) was organized to protest the Court's decision. By the 1960s, POAU was a coalition of liberals and conservatives committed to overturning *Emerson,* and opposing the influence of the Catholic Church hierarchy on public life. POAU was to be a major source of organized opposition to Kennedy's election.[64]

Beginning in 1947, Paul Blanchard, who was subsequently to become POAU general counsel, wrote a series of articles in the *Nation* inveighing against Catholic influence in the United States. In 1958 he published a best-selling book attacking the "intolerant and separatist policies of the Catholic church."[65] Blanchard wrote, "In the name of religion, the church hierarchy fights birth control and divorce laws in all states. It tells Catholic doctors, nurses, judges, teachers and legislators what they can and cannot do in many of the controversial phases of their professional conduct. It segregates Catholic children and censors the cultural diet of the children."[66] Blanchard also attacked the doctrine of papal infallibility.

The traditional southern Protestant fundamentalists and evangelicals, including African Americans, joined these liberal opponents of the church. The National Association of Evangelicals announced their opposition to Kennedy on the grounds that a "Protestant president would better preserve that religion's position as defining U.S. culture."[67]

In his 1953 sermon, "Paul's Letter to the American Church," Martin Luther King Jr. joined the critics preaching:

> I am disturbed about Roman Catholicism. This church stands before the world with its pomp and power, insisting that it possesses the only truth. It incorporates an arrogance that becomes a dangerous spiritual arrogance. It stands with its Noble Pope, who somehow rises to the miraculous heights of infallibility when he speaks *Ex cathedra*. But I am disturbed about a person or an institution that claims infallibility in this world. I am disturbed by any church that refuses to cooperate with other churches under the pretense that it is the only true church. I must emphasize the fact that God is not Roman Catholic, and that the boundless sweep of his revelation cannot be limited to the Vatican. Roman Catholicism must do a great deal to mend its ways.[68]

In September 1960, the Atlanta Baptist Ministers Union, with the powerful support of Rev. Martin Luther King Sr., specifically endorsed Nixon because of its opposition to Kennedy's religion.[69] Then Kennedy called Mrs. King after Dr. King was jailed in Georgia, and his brother Robert, the campaign's manager, intervened with a judge and secured King's release. At this point the senior King reversed his position and endorsed Kennedy. "I had expected to vote against Senator Kennedy because of his religion. But now he can be my president, Catholic or whatever he is. It took courage to call my daughter-in-law at a time like this. He has the moral courage to stand up for what he knows is right."[70] An amused Kennedy on hearing of King's statement remarked "That was a hell of a statement, wasn't it. Imagine Martin Luther King having a bigot for a father. Well we all have our fathers, don't we?"[71] The night of his release from the Georgia jail Dr. King delivered a sermon declaring "anti-Catholic bias and religious bigotry is as immoral, undemocratic and unchristian [*sic*] as racial bigotry."[72] Jackie Robinson, among others, had urged Nixon to intervene after King's arrest but he refused. Many observers believe that Kennedy's intervention helped to increase his margin of the black vote in enough states to swing the election.[73]

Recognizing the diversity of the opposition based on religion, Kennedy did not wait for incidents like the King arrest to deal with the problem. Although he distrusted Catholic clergy, he met with John Wright, the highest ranking American at the Vatican and a family friend, to solicit his advice.[74] Wright advised him to reach out to prominent Protestant clergymen, which he did. In addition, he and his brother met privately with Blanchard, POAU, and other liberal critics. Sorensen developed a comprehensive strategy to address the problem, including hiring two staffers (one Catholic, one Protestant) to work full-time on the issue, running ads in Protestant religious media; soliciting prominent Protestant clergy to denounce religious bigotry while maintaining "public distance from Catholic leaders."[75]

Kennedy was particularly worried that Billy Graham, the nation's best-known Protestant clergyman, might endorse Nixon. Graham was definitely opposed to Kennedy on religious grounds, but he wished to maintain his reputation as a religious statesman above the political fray. Graham, however, engaged in a secret campaign to manipulate anti-Catholic sentiments and mobilize support for Nixon.[76] A part of Graham's clandestine activities was helping to plan the most famous, highly publicized attack on Kennedy's candidacy by Protestant clergy on September 1960, the so-called Peale Manifesto.

On September 7, 1960, Norman Vincent Peale convened more than 150 Protestant clergymen in Washington at what was called the National Conference of Citizens for Religious Freedom. Peale, the pastor of a prestigious New York City church, the nationally renowned author of the best-selling *The Power of Positive Thinking*, and a close friend of Nixon's, was sometimes referred to as the "chaplain to conservative political forces."[77] At the end of the conference a five-point "Peale Manifesto" was issued that openly declared Kennedy unfit to be President because "it is inconceivable that a Roman Catholic president would not be under extreme pressure by the hierarchy of his church with respect to foreign policy."[78] The manifesto went on to say that Kennedy would be unable to resist pressures from the church to gain federal funds for its schools and institutions and "otherwise breach the wall of separation of church and state."[79]

The Peale Manifesto generated enormous controversy, and other leading Protestant clergy and the national media widely criticized Peale. Converse writes that the media served as an "integrative mechanism" during the 1960 election by "emphasizing religious tolerance and question[ing] some of the more garrish [*sic*] anti-Catholic stereotypes. . . ."[80] In addition, by portraying Kennedy as a Harvard-educated, poised, urbane intellectual, the media—television in particular—undermined old Catholic stereotypes. The media's relentless attacks on the Peale Manifesto resulted in several newspapers canceling his syndicated column and some called for his resignation as pastor of his New York City congregation. Reinhold Niebuhr, Paul Tillich, and other leading Protestant clergy in a *New York Times* ad labeled the Peale Manifesto religious bigotry of the worse kind and itself a violation of the principle of the separation of church and state. The manifesto, the ad declared, "certainly [did] not represent American Protestantism as a whole" and "most of the people in the forefront of the attacks on Roman Catholicism as an influence on the presidency are social conservatives who generally oppose liberal policies."[81]

The Peale Manifesto was a turning point for the religious issue in the campaign. Condemned across the political spectrum, from the Catholic conservative William F. Buckley to liberal Jewish rabbis, Peale was forced to recant the statement. Meanwhile, Nixon, while distancing himself from the manifesto, refused to denounce his friend as President Truman and the chair of the Democratic National Committee called on him to do. Four days after the manifesto, Kennedy delivered his address on religion before the Greater Houston Ministerial Association. The address, before this conclave of conservative fundamentalists, Casey describes as the "single most dramatic moment in the entire campaign."[82] Like Obama's race speech in 2008 in response to his pastor's controversial remarks, Kennedy's speech in response to the Peale Manifesto helped him to survive "a near death campaign experience."[83] As usual the crafting of the speech was given to Sorensen. After consulting with Catholic theologians Sorensen's draft was a balancing act, "walking a tightrope" between "the Protestant audience to which it was addressed and the large Catholic population that might be sensitive to any perception that he somehow might sell out his religion or church in the name of political expediency."[84]

By most contemporaneous and historical accounts, Kennedy successfully walked this tightrope. Writing contemporaneously Theodore White concluded, "when he had finished, he had not only closed round one of the election campaign—he had for the first time more fully and explicitly than any other thinker of his faith defined the personal doctrine of a modern Catholic in a democratic society."[85] Looking at the speech historically, Massa concludes that it was a "landmark in American politics" that represented the "mainstreaming of American Catholicism."[86] The speech did not break new ground. Rather, it simply presented in a more polished way Kennedy's "privatization" of religion that he had advanced in an earlier address to the American Association of Newspaper Editors, in his *Look* magazine interview, and in his acceptance speech at the Democratic Convention. While declaring that he did not "intend to disavow either my views or my church in order to win this election,"

Kennedy went on to say that neither his church nor his religious views would have any impact on his conduct of the presidency.[87] To some Catholics, then and now, this was paradoxical. Massa writes, "Part of the irony in the debate over religion is the fact that the Houston speech, which marked an America well on its way to a secular White House no less than to a Catholic presidency, was the product of Protestants like Norman Vincent Peale, who had themselves made Kennedy's religion an issue. The issue they created helped to ensure the privatization of religion that they would later bemoan and attack as a betrayal of the close religious—political relations that had always shaped the presidential office."[88]

On the religious issue Nixon operated in an environment of strategic uncertainty. On the one hand, he certainly wished to benefit from anti-Catholic sentiments in the electorate. On the other, he was sensitive to charges of pandering to bigotry and wished as well to try to hold at least some part of the Catholic vote Eisenhower won in 1952 and 1956. Thus, the strategic dilemma. As Lasky writes, "Nixon got it from both ends: Republican Catholics were being urged to vote for Kennedy because he was of their religion; and Republican Protestants were being urged to vote for him to prove they were not biased against Catholics."[89] Nixon flirted with the idea of addressing this dilemma by naming a Catholic—Labor Secretary James Mitchell—as his running mate.[90] But Billy Graham told him it would not resolve the problem because "[Kennedy] will capture the Catholic vote—almost 100 percent of it—no matter what concessions you make."[91] Nixon, while not naming Mitchell, did make concessions to Catholics. He waffled on the issue of recognition of the Vatican and in a compromise suggested that the question of federal aid to church schools be left up to the states rather than a complete prohibition as Kennedy proposed. And, by repeating that he would not use the religious issue, Nixon could remind Protestants that a religious issue did indeed exist.

As best we can tell religion was a major issue in determining the outcome of the election. Kennedy won one of the narrowest victories in the history of presidential elections if indeed he won at all.[92] The final official vote tally shows Kennedy winning by margin of .1, or 49.7–49.6. Kennedy won twenty-five states, including the heavily Catholic states of New England, the Northeast, and Midwest, and five states of the old confederacy including Texas (Louisiana and Mississippi were won by the racist Harry Byrd of Virginia). Although the popular vote was essentially a tie, because of the distortions of the winner-take-all provisions of the Electoral College, Kennedy's electoral vote was less close, 303–219. Ironically, Kennedy won in the most Catholic and anti-Catholic parts of the country; the heavily Catholic New England and northeastern states and the heavily Protestant, fundamentalist, white evangelical southern states. Nevertheless, he was the first person to win the presidency without winning a majority of the white Protestant vote.[93] He won 80 percent of the Catholic vote, 38 percent of Protestants, 48 percent of southern whites, 68 percent of African Americans, and 81 percent of the Jewish vote.[94]

Because the Catholic Irish population was thoroughly incorporated by 1960 with its population residing in heterogeneous, suburban neighborhoods, reliably determining the distribution of the Catholic Irish vote is difficult. Experts estimate, however, that Kennedy did better by an increment of five points among Irish as compared to non-Irish Catholics.[95] Shannon guesses that he may not have won a majority among well-to-do suburban Catholic Irish voters.[96] It is striking that Kennedy did as well among Jews as he did among Catholics generally or his fellow Hibernians specifically. And as pointed out in an earlier chapter, the Scotch-Irish vote, North and South, was indistinguishable from the vote of other Protestant ethnic groups.

Shannon writes, "Kennedy's religion elected him and it also nearly defeated him."[97] In 1956 Eisenhower won 50 percent of the Catholic vote, but this was a deviating vote due to short-term forces. Converse calculates that in 1960 the normal Catholic Democratic vote was 63 percent thus Kennedy the Catholic added a surge or increment of 17 points.[98] Overall, Converse estimates that Kennedy's Catholicism resulted in a gain of 4.3 percent of the national two-party votes and a simultaneous loss of 6.5 percent. Calculating gains and losses, the religion deficit in 1960 was 2.2 points.[99] In other words, if Kennedy had been a Protestant, he would have won with at least 52 percent of the vote. Converse summarizes the import of these calculations for the role of religion in the election: "Not only did Kennedy possess a type of personal appeal which the television debates permitted him to exploit in unusual measure, but he was also the candidate of a party enjoying a fundamental majority in the land. Even the combination of these circumstances was barely sufficient to give him a popular vote victory. Lacking such a strong underlying majority, which Al Smith certainly lacked in 1928, it is doubtful that the most attractive of Catholic presidential candidates would have had much chance of success."[100]

Kennedy ran fifteen points behind Democratic congressional candidates, doing better in only 134 of 435 districts, "undermining his capacity for governance."[101] Shortly after the election, Kennedy was asked whether his narrow margin of victory deprived his administration of a mandate. Without missing a beat he responded, "One vote is a mandate." A mandate perhaps, but Kennedy's narrow margin and his failure to win a majority of the Protestant vote was clearly to him a mandate to continue to practice the politics of ethnic avoidance once he assumed the presidency.

9

Race and the Election of 2008

In no other democratic polity in the world could Barack Obama—a young backbencher with about three years' experience in national office and unknown to party leaders just four years before—have been selected by a major party as its nominee to run for the highest office in the land. This is because "no other nation, none ever, anywhere has chosen its candidates for leader of the government by a direct popular election."[1] In most nations, as it was in the United States until 1972, the choice of a party's candidate for national executive is made by party leaders in convention. At the 1968 Democratic Convention, Vice President Humphrey was the choice of party leaders, winning the nomination although he had not competed in any primaries and was clearly not the choice of most Democrats. The violent disorders at the convention resulted in establishing a commission to democratize the nomination process, essentially placing the choice of the nominee in the hands of the people rather than the politicians. Headed by Senator George McGovern—one of the defeated 1968 candidates—the reform commission mandated henceforth all states (and territories) use open primaries or caucuses to select delegates. In 1968 only seventeen states used primaries to select delegates and the rest used selection processes state party leaders controlled. Subsequently, Democratic Party reformers required that each state use some form of proportional allocation of delegates, instead of the winner-take-all approach many states used. As pointed out in chapter 5, a more exacting proportional allocation of delegates was one result of the Jesse Jackson campaigns.

Many political scientists were skeptical about the democratization of the nominating process contending—as had many of the Framers of the Constitution—that the people were not competent to choose among the candidates.[2] Academic students of presidential elections also contended that the primaries and caucuses would weaken the parties and empower the media, particularly television. "Television," Donald Robinson wrote in the late 1980s, "has become virtually a substitute for party organization. The candidate who can afford to advertise on television hardly needs to come to terms with his party's national organization at all. He must raise a great deal of money, meaning that virtually all his gatherings must be fundraisers, and to do that, he must have a substantial personal organization. But he can dispense with the party organization."[3] Reacting to these academic concerns as well as to the nomination, election, and defeat of Jimmy Carter, the relatively unknown one-term governor of Georgia, Democratic Party leaders attempted to place some limits on the unvarnished power of the people to select the nominee. In 1984 this resulted in the creation of "superdelegates" (members of Congress, governors, and national and state party leaders) who could be seated at the convention without having run in the primaries or caucuses and could vote for any candidate they wished. Until 2008 the superdelegates were not in a position to play a role in determining the nominee, but in general they were expected to and generally did give more support to establishment candidates then to insurgents or outsiders. In 1988, for example, Jesse Jackson got 20 percent of the primary vote but only 9.3 percent of the superdelegates, while Dick Gephardt, a congressional leader, received 15 percent of the primary vote but 19 percent of the superdelegates.[4] Although Hillary Clinton assumed that her nomination was inevitable based on a sweep of the twenty-four state Super Tuesday contests, the superdelegates, she also assumed, would be a firewall against the unlikely prospect of a successful insurgent candidate. The assumption of the inevitability of a Super Tuesday triumph and the superdelegates as a firewall were two crucial miscalculations of the Clinton campaign.

Television, as Robinson postulates, certainly played a major role in the rise of Barack Obama. As indicated in chapter 4, one of the fortunate events in his rise was the adulatory press coverage that he received after his 2004 keynote speech at the Democratic convention. Like John Kennedy in 1959, Obama in 2006 received intense coverage in the media probably unlike anything except the coverage of Kennedy preceding the 1960 election. Unlike Kennedy, however, Obama's coverage was largely spontaneous not partly manufactured by a father's multimillion-dollar public relations machine. In 2006 Obama published his second book, *The Audacity of Hope*. Largely a campaign manifesto—unquestionably written by Obama—the book became a bestseller. The book tour, his campaign manager David Plouffe writes, "unexpectedly turned into a presidential draft. . . . The crowds and chatter around the book tour bred a great deal of speculation in the political community and the media about a possible Obama candidacy."[5] Also, like Kennedy in 1958, Obama was the most sought-after Democratic politician—more so than Bill or

Hillary Clinton—for fundraising and campaign appearances on behalf of Democratic candidates. Hundreds and frequently thousands turned out to see him; cheering, they would sometime shout, "Run, Obama, run!" Local and national media widely covered these appearances, leading some commentators to remark that the crowds recalled the enthusiasm of "the jumpers" during Kennedy's 1960 campaign.[6]

When Obama begin to plan his campaign in late 2006, the inevitability of Hillary Clinton was the major strategic concern. However, several other candidates also had some prospect of winning the nomination, including John Edwards, the fifty-one-year-old 2004 vice presidential nominee. Edwards, anticipating that Clinton would be his major opponent, positioned himself to her left with an emphasis on the problem of poverty in America. The first candidate to focus on this issue since McGovern in 1972, Edwards hoped to chip away at Clinton's strong support among African American leaders and voters. The other major candidates included Bill Richardson, the sixty-year-old Latino governor of New Mexico, former energy secretary, and U.N. ambassador; Christopher Dodd, the sixty-three-year-old, twenty-eight-year Senate veteran and chair of the Banking Committee; and Joseph Biden, the sixty-five-year-old, thirty-six-year Senate veteran and chair of the Foreign Relations Committee. Richardson, Dodd, and Biden were running on their resumes, although Richardson may, on the basis of ethnic solidarity, have hoped to attract the support of the growing Latino electorate. But Clinton was clearly the frontrunner. The sixty-year-old former activist first lady and two-term senator was the establishment candidate, endorsed by many party leaders, ahead in the polls, and widely viewed as most likely to become the first female president. When Obama entered the race, Clinton was running substantially ahead of him among African Americans, and leading members of the Congressional Black Caucus had already endorsed her. Indeed, Clinton considered the black vote her base vote, based on the widespread adoration of her husband in the black community.

Although President Clinton on race had governed "in the shadows of Ronald Reagan" embracing conservative positions on crime, welfare, and to some extent affirmative action,[7] he was nevertheless widely admired among blacks, elite, and mass. When he left office in January 2001, 87 percent of blacks approved of his performance as president, compared to 45 percent of whites. Nearly a decade later, a poll indicated that, among blacks, Clinton was more popular than Jesse Jackson, 93 percent to 87 percent.[8] Nobel laureate Toni Morrison described Clinton as the first black president, writing that he displayed "almost every trope of blackness—single parent household, born poor, working-class, saxophone-playing, McDonald's junk food-loving boy from Arkansas."[9] More seriously, *USA Today* columnist Dewayne Wickham concluded after interviewing more than two dozen black intellectuals and political leaders. "Bill Clinton was not the first black president, but in the long line of white men who ascended to this nation's presidency he was the next best thing."[10] Better, Wickham averred, than Lyndon Johnson, who risked his presidency and his party's future to enact the most comprehensive civil rights and antipoverty policies of any U.S. president. Aware of and relying on sentiments of this sort, the Clintons assumed the black vote was a Clinton base vote. They did not—could not—anticipate the meteoric rise of a talented, handsome, charismatic, young black candidate relying on the bonds of ethnic solidarity to make the black vote his base vote in becoming the first black president.

Obama's strategy for winning the nomination was clearly based on ethnic solidarity among blacks, but like Kennedy he assumed he could take that vote for granted while appealing to the mainstream of the Democratic Party electorate. Thus, like Kennedy, he would flip-flop on issues of concern to blacks hoping they would understand this was necessary if one of their own was to be nominated and elected. That is, the Obama campaign was aware of polls showing that as much as half of whites thought he would favor blacks if he became president. Of that number, only 32 percent said they would vote for him.[11] Clearly, then, like Kennedy, he would have to bend over backward to show his ethnic evenhandedness.

Again, in a paradox, Obama's task was somewhat easier than Kennedy's. Although blacks were not fully incorporated, ghettoized, and stigmatized,[12] in 2008 only 5 percent of whites said they would not vote for a qualified black candidate for president compared to 25 percent of Protestants who said in 1960 they would not vote for a qualified Catholic. Indeed, more Americans in 2008 said they would not vote for a qualified woman (11 percent) or a Mormon (24 percent).[13] Thus, Obama faced a much smaller—almost nonexistent—overtly ethnically hostile electorate than Kennedy (in 2008 only 4 percent of Protestants said they would not vote for a Catholic for president). The 5 percent is for expressions of overt, publicly stated racial animus toward a black president. The actual degree of racial animus, though difficult to measure, was undoubtedly higher.[14] But for Obama strategists this data meant that the campaign, unlike Kennedy's, was not required to go out of its way to address the race issue. Certainly, he would not be required to make a speech on race or tell the Democratic Convention in his acceptance speech that nominating him was a "hazardous risk."

On race, for Obama the less said the better. Obama would eventually give a race speech, but it was dictated by circumstances, not strategy.

Hoping to ignore race, Obama's campaign was based on charisma and change, much like Kennedy offering himself as a new generation leader that could get beyond the old debates of the past. When the forty-three-year-old Kennedy sought the presidency in 1960, he had been in Congress fourteen years, had traveled throughout Europe and Asia, and because of his father's contacts knew the leading statesmen and journalists of the era. The forty-six-year-old Obama in 2007 was just two years in the Senate and virtually unknown to national political and media elites. Obama argued that the issue was judgment not experience, and he claimed that on the signature issue of the campaign—the Iraq War—he had shown better judgment than his more experienced opponents. In a speech on the eve of the Iraq War, Obama argued that the war was a mistake, whereas Edwards, Clinton, Biden, and Dodd had supported the congressional resolution authorizing the conflict. Thus, Obama framed the issue as judgment versus Washington experience, a frame likely to play well in Iowa and New Hampshire where the war was extremely unpopular among Democrats.[15]

Aside from Obama's early opposition to the war, little else appeared to distinguish among the candidates. All were conventional liberals, favoring modest increases in taxes on the wealthy; more expenditures on education, national health insurance, energy-climate change legislation; and comprehensive immigration reform with a "pathway" to citizenship for undocumented residents. With little to distinguish the candidates ideologically, Obama's campaign was premised on the idea of change—"Change you can believe in," and the idea that after twenty years of Bush–Clinton–Bush the American people wanted change and a new kind of postpartisan politics. In a more fundamental sense, however, Obama's campaign was premised on personality—his story, his biography. In his March 2008 race speech, Obama summarized the biographical basis for his campaign:

> I chose to run for president at this moment in history because I believe we cannot solve the challenges of our time unless we solve them together, unless we perfect our union by understanding that we may have different stories, but we hold common hopes; that we may not look the same and may not have come from the same place, but we all want to move in the same direction toward a better future for our children and grandchildren. And this belief comes from my unyielding

> faith in the decency and generosity of the American people. But it also comes from my own story. I am the son of a black man from Kenya and a white woman from Kansas. I was raised with the help of a white grandfather who survived a Depression to serve in Patton's army during World War II and a white grandmother who worked on a bomber assembly line at Fort Leavenworth while he was overseas. I've gone to some of the best schools in America and I've lived in one of the world's poorest nations. I am married to a black American who carries within her the blood of slaves and slave owners, an inheritance we pass on to our precious daughters. I have brothers, sisters, nieces, nephews, uncles and cousins of every race and every hue scattered across three continents. And for as long as I live, I will never forget that in no other country on earth is my story even possible.[16]

In order to become competitive in the primaries, Obama's strategists (the principal strategists David Plouffe, David Axelrod, and Robert Gibbs were all white) knew they would have to first become competitive in the money race. The Obama campaign, the *Washington Post* wrote, "shattered fundraising records and challenged ideas about the way presidential bids are financed."[17] Relying heavily on the Internet and small donors (less than $100) and ads on Yahoo, Google, and Microsoft search engines, the campaign received small donations from more than 1.5 million donors, the largest in campaign history. Although Obama relied disproportionately on small donors, like all presidential campaigns his was largely financed by wealthy, corporate-connected individuals and Hollywood celebrities. In the crucial first quarter of 2007 the campaign established its credibility as a serious alternative to Clinton by nearly matching the Clinton campaign, $24.7 million to $29.1 million. Overall, Obama raised $429 million compared to Clinton's $210 million. By the end of the primaries Clinton's campaign was in debt more than $20 million having to use $10 million of her own money in order to remain competitive. Obama finished the primaries with $43 million in cash on hand and a debt of only $300,000.[18]

Having won the money race, Obama strategists knew that the key to winning the nomination was Iowa. Campaign manager David Plouffe writes, "Hillary Clinton had to be disrupted early in the primary season for us to have any chance of derailing her. . . . It was Iowa or bust. . . . [thus,] we focus[ed] like a laser on Iowa."[19] This focus resulted in a stunning victory; Obama won 38 percent of the vote, Edwards 33 percent, and Clinton 29 percent. Immediately after Iowa, Biden and

Dodd dropped out. Although Richardson and Edwards continued on to New Hampshire (Edwards on to South Carolina), at this point it was essentially a two-person race between the first woman and the first black man with realistic chances of becoming president. Within hours of Iowa, internal Obama campaign polling begin to show Clinton's support collapsing among blacks, with Obama's support rising to 75 percent and then to 80 percent.[20] With a compelling nationally televised speech in Iowa, Obama went into New Hampshire with a double-digit lead over Clinton in the polls. But in what Plouffe described as "one of the biggest surprises in modern campaign history" and as a "devastating blow," Clinton won New Hampshire 39 percent to 36 percent.[21] Some commentators attributed Obama's defeat to the so-called Bradley Effect—the difference between actual election results and the polls, in which black candidates win fewer votes than are predicted by the polls. (The phenomenon was first identified in Los Angeles Mayor Tom Bradley's 1982 loss of the California governor's race.) Although there may have been some Bradley Effect, the major explanation for Clinton's upset was a dramatic shift among white women after Clinton's "emotional moment" where she appeared to cry in the course of discussing her candidacy (there may also have been problems with the statistical models used in the polls to estimate likely voters). Plouffe described the New Hampshire upset as a devastating blow, but in retrospect it was probably a disguised blessing because it allowed the candidate and the organization to hone their skills and develop a campaign presence in all fifty states. The Obama campaign was "thrilled" that the next major contest was in South Carolina because "African Americans made up about 50 percent of the primary electorate, and though Hillary had a huge lead in the African American community at the moment, we believed that if we could show some competitiveness through 2007, and if voters became familiar with Obama . . . our support level would increase. If we could topple Clinton in Iowa or New Hampshire, our support in the community would skyrocket."[22] Obama easily won South Carolina (with 90 percent of the black vote and 20 percent of the white vote) with 54 percent of the vote. Bill Clinton tried to downplay the significance of the victory by noting that Jesse Jackson had won the state in 1984 and 1988, suggesting that Obama's win was based mainly on ethnic solidarity. Clinton was largely correct but that was the strategic significance of South Carolina after Iowa: It demonstrated that the black vote was now the Obama base vote.

Losing the black vote to Obama was a blow to the Clinton strategy but not necessarily a fatal one since the major premise of her campaign was winning the big states in the twenty-four-state Super

Tuesday elections. From the outset of the campaign, Clinton predicted that she would wrap-up the nomination on February 5, Super Tuesday. Obama, conversely, focused on winning delegates in the small, largely white caucus states while holding down Clinton's margin in the big states so that on Super Tuesday he would get a reasonable share of their delegates. His strategy worked. On Super Tuesday, Clinton won eight states (including all of the big ones except Illinois) but Obama won the smaller states winning fourteen, and 847 delegates to her 834. Thereafter he went on to win eleven consecutive states, which gave him a small but mathematically insurmountable delegate lead.

The ties of ethnic solidarity were indispensable to Obama's triumph. His delegate lead was in large part based on the overwhelming support he received in African American congressional districts. The Democratic Party awards bonus delegates to districts with a history of strong party support, giving them in some cases twice as many delegates as less loyal Democratic or Republican districts. Since African Americans are the party's strongest supporters, winning in their districts gave him an advantage over Clinton in the big states she won, like Ohio, Texas, Pennsylvania, California, and New York. Paradoxically, then, Obama won the nomination by winning in the blackest and most Democratic places and in the whitest and most Republican places—states like Alaska, Idaho, Utah, Wyoming, and Nebraska.

Examining the outcome in more detail, Obama won majority support in only three demographic categories: blacks where he had a sixty-seven-point advantage, young whites (ages eighteen to twenty-nine) where he had a nine-point advantage and the cities where the advantage was eight points. Clinton had a twenty-four-point advantage among white women, three points among white men; Latinos, twenty-six; whites without a college education, thirty-one; seniors (those age sixty-five and older), thirty-four; and she won suburban voters by four points. Clinton and Obama received roughly the same proportion of the white, college-educated, upper-income vote.[23] Obama won most of the southern primaries because of his black base, but he did not do well among southern whites. The demographic pattern of his support in the South was consistent with the national: the young, the well-educated, and the upper income. But his support among young whites in the South resembled more his support among elderly whites elsewhere in the country, as did his support among the college-educated and upper-income population. For example, nationally Obama received 53 percent of the white youth vote, but in Kentucky, Alabama, and Louisiana, he received about one-third, which is about the same as the 29 percent of his white elderly vote nationally.[24] Obama narrowly won the Jewish vote in California and Massachusetts, with an overall average of 42 percent in the five states (New York, Pennsylvania, New Jersey, Massachusetts, and California), where there was a significant Jewish vote (excluding Florida because the party set aside its primary results because of violations of party rules on scheduling). Some Israeli and Jewish commentators raised questions about Obama's commitment to Israel, and rumors and lies about his being a Muslim were circulated to Jewish voters. In response, the leaders of nine major Jewish organizations issued a joint statement: "Attempts of this sort to mislead and inflame voters should not be a part of our political discourse and should be rebuffed by all who believe in our democracy. Jewish voters, like all voters, should support whichever candidate they believe would make the best president."[25] The long contest between Clinton and Obama ended in a virtual tie. Including Florida, Clinton actually won a slightly larger proportion of the popular vote (48 percent to 46 percent), and Obama's final delegate lead was about 150. The superdelegates, therefore, could have made the difference as Clinton anticipated they would. But once it became clear that Obama had a small but insurmountable lead in elected delegates, most of the unpledged superdelegates begin to announce support for Obama. They had little choice because, as Plouffe reports, telling a group of Obama supporters "if the Clintons and party leaders try to steal this nomination, to assert their will and judgment in the place of the voters, we will burn the house down. It will make Kennedy-Carter and Hart-Mondale look like fairy tales. We will win this ugly if we have to. They are not taking this from us."[26]

At the Democratic National Convention in Denver's Invesco Field—the first held in an outdoor sports arena since John Kennedy's—Obama, unlike Kennedy, barely alluded to race in his acceptance speech.[27] At the beginning of the address he noted that he was the product of a "brief union between a young man from Kenya and a young woman from Kansas." Then, a bit more directly he said, "I get it. I realize that I am not the likeliest candidate for this office. I don't fit the pedigree. . . ." Finally the day of the speech was the forty-fifth anniversary of the March on Washington. So, near the end of the speech, Obama referred to a "young preacher from Georgia . . . before Lincoln's [*sic*] Memorial" talking about the promise of America.[28] The acceptance speech reflected how the campaign intended to deal with race during the fall campaign and how it had dealt with it during the primaries—with winks, nods, and disguises.

In *The Audacity of Hope* Obama embraced William Julius Wilson's policy analysis of how to deal with the problem of racialized poverty. In his widely read and influential book (both Bill Clinton and Al Gore said their thinking on the problem of the so-called black underclass was influenced by the book) *The Truly Disadvantaged*, Wilson rejected race-specific or targeted public policies. Instead, he called for universal, class-based programs that would target the poor of all races with the intent to "equalize the life chances" of all disadvantaged Americans.[29] Wilson favored this deracialized, universal approach not because he believed it was the most effective way to deal with the problem of concentrated, ghettoized poverty, but because he believed the more efficacious race or ghetto-specific approach would not command the support of the majority white electorate. Thus, programs to help the "truly disadvantaged" must be disguised as programs to help all Americans. "In the final analysis," Wilson writes, "the question of reform is a political one. Accordingly, if the essential political message underscores the need for economic and social programs that benefits all groups in society, not just minorities, a basis for generating a broad coalition would be created."[30] Wilson called this approach the "hidden agenda."[31] Without directly referring to Wilson, Obama writes, "Rightly or wrongly, white guilt has largely exhausted itself in America. . . . An emphasis on universal as opposed to race-specific programs isn't just good policy, it's also good politics."[32] Obama also embraced Wilson's view that racialized poverty is both systemic and cultural. This is typical of the balancing acts Obama performed on race throughout the campaign and in the first years of his presidency, not unlike Kennedy's tightrope walking on religion. This balancing act was best shown in his race speech delivered in the wake of the Wright imbroglio, which is discussed later. But of the cultural causes of poverty, Obama wrote, "I think much of what ails the inner cities is a breakdown in culture that will not be cured by money alone. . . . [And] . . . the single biggest thing we could do to reduce such poverty is to encourage teenage girls to finish high school and avoid having children out of wedlock."[33] But this conservative and neoconservative, white mainstream view of the problem is immediately balanced with the black mainstream, left-liberal systemic view:

> . . . African Americans understand that culture matters but that culture is shaped by circumstances. We know that many in the inner city are trapped by their own self-destructive behaviors but these behaviors are not innate. And because of that knowledge, the black community remains convinced that if America finds its will to do so, then circumstances for those trapped in the inner city can be changed, individual attitudes among the poor will change in kind, and the damage of [historical racism] can gradually be undone, if not for this generation then at least for the next.[34]

In the course of the campaign on specific public policies related to race Obama flip-flopped and waffled. On President Clinton's welfare reform legislation—opposed by virtually the entire black leadership establishment—as an Illinois state senator, Obama expressed opposition. However, as the campaign for the presidency unfolded he ran ads touting the legislation as having "slashed the rolls by 80 percent." As *ABC News* noted, "The shift in Obama's rhetoric has proceeded in stages. When former President Clinton was poised to sign welfare reform while running for re-election in 1996, Obama called it 'disturbing.' A decade later, as an underdog running for president against Clinton's wife, he spent 2007 avoiding the subject. By the time Obama emerged as the Democratic frontrunner in the Spring of 2008, he began to leave the impression he was for it all along."[35]

On the death penalty—which the black leadership also overwhelmingly opposed because of its racially discriminatory use—when he was running for the state Senate in 1996, he opposed it, but in his 2004 U.S. Senate race, he said he accepted it as punishment for the most "heinous crimes."[36] On affirmative action, he waffled by remarking on several occasions that he did not think his daughters should be eligible for affirmative action university admission, implying that it should be a class- rather than race-based policy.[37] But, as Justice William Brennan pointed out in his opinion in the seminal *Bakke* case, a class-based approach could not achieve the necessary degree of racial diversity because the population of poor and lower-class whites is so much larger than the comparable black populations.[38] In the early 1990s, when Bill Clinton mused about turning affirmative action into a class-based policy, Jesse Jackson considered it such a serious breach of faith with the black community that he made it clear that if Clinton adopted such an approach he would challenge his renomination, reelection, or both.[39]

Obama's strategists thought he could flip-flop or waffle on these and other race-related issues because the bonds of racial solidarity would link black voters to him, notwithstanding any specific policy stances. Princeton University Professor Cornel West argued against Obama's "hidden agenda," stating he should speak out directly on the history of racism and not cast its legacy of racialized poverty as problems shared by all Americans. Yet West understood that "he's got a large number of white brothers and sisters who have fears and anxieties. He's got to speak to them in such a way that he holds us at arm's length; enough to say he loves us but not too close to scare them away."[40]

Throughout the early phases of the campaign questions were raised about Obama's blackness. Indeed, shortly before he was to address the National Association of Black Journalists, the group held a panel discussion on the subject. Debra Dickerson, an African American essayist, penned a widely publicized article in which she claimed that Obama was not black because he was not "descended from West African slaves."[41] She went on "and more subtly, when the handsome Obama doesn't look eastern (versus western) African, he looks like his white mother; not so subliminally, that's partially why whites can embrace him but blacks fear that one day he'll go Tiger on us and get all race transcendent (he might well not be in the running without a traditionally black spouse and kids)."[42] Jesse Jackson accused Obama early in the campaign of ignoring (along with all the other candidates except Edwards) the problems of the poor and "acting white" although he subsequently denied the "acting white" comment.[43] Later in the campaign, Jackson ignited a controversy when he was recorded using crude language suggesting he wanted to castrate Obama because he was "talking down to black people."[44] Congressman Jesse Jackson Jr., an Obama national campaign cochair, denounced his father for his "outrageous, reckless, divisive and demeaning comments."[45] Jesse Jackson's comments were an outlier, although they probably reflected some underlying unease throughout the black leadership establishment, partly because Obama was a newcomer and partly because he had not come up through the traditional black leadership recruitment processes.[46] However, the widely publicized Jackson comments most likely helped Obama among segments of the white electorate by highlighting his distance from Jackson and independence from the civil rights establishment.

Although there was a great deal of chatter in the media about Obama's blackness, at the mass level, once he became well known (after Iowa), he was fully embraced. Even earlier in a 2006 Zogby poll, when respondents were told about the ethnic origins of Obama's parents and asked to identify his ethnicity, two-thirds of blacks labeled him black, while more than three-fourth of whites, Latinos, and Asian identified him as multiracial.[47] In a poll conducted in the fall of 2008, 70 percent of blacks said there was such a thing as the "black experience in America," and 89 percent said Obama was "in touch with it."[48] And contrary to the view of many black academics, journalists, and politicians, 71 percent of the respondents said Obama was addressing issues of special concern to blacks.[49] Finally, and probably most alarming to the old-guard black establishment, a July 2008 Gallup poll asked blacks to name the one individual or leader who spoke for them on racial issues. A full 29 percent named Obama, while Al Sharpton and Jesse Jackson followed at a distance with 6 percent and 4 percent, respectively.[50]

Aware of the data about black attitudes, Obama strategists (in addition to the top strategists who were white, Cornell Belcher was a top pollster and Valerie Jarrett, a long-time associate from Chicago, African Americans, were in the inner circle) assumed the black vote could be taken for granted. Thus, the central strategic concern was to maintain the base black vote in the primaries and general election while reaching out to mainstream white America. This balancing act was possible because while "black" to blacks, the image of Obama the campaign crafted for whites was an ebony saint, a "no-demand black," like Tiger, Oprah, and Michael Jordan.[51] In Iowa Obama walked this racial tightrope in Iowa as skillfully as Kennedy had walked the religious tightrope in Wisconsin. Although the relatively small black population in Iowa was surgically targeted for turnout, Obama avoided appearances at black churches or campaigning with black leaders except for the ebony saint, Oprah. Al Sharpton is nobody's ebony saint. Thus, when it was rumored that he was planning to visit Iowa during the closing days of the caucuses the campaign went into crisis mode. Apparently someone close to Sharpton informed Obama of Sharpton's planned visit and told him that he might be able to persuade Sharpton not to come depending on Obama's wishes. Plouffe writes:

> . . . it was clear that his presence would not be helpful. We had polled him . . . his ratings in Iowa were less than 20 percent and over 60 percent negative. Our research showed that voters were always interested in whom Obama would surround himself with in the White House. . . . This was an instance where race, which had been largely a nonfactor to date, could have got into the equation. If undecided voters get the impression that Sharpton was an influential advisor for us, it could undermine their willingness to take a chance on Obama.[52]

Obama conveyed Plouffe's views back to his contact and Plouffe writes the campaign "never heard back one way or another. But he did not come to Iowa. And throughout the rest of the campaign, I found Sharpton to be a reasonable and constructive force."[53]

If Plouffe is to be believed, keeping race a "nonfactor" sometimes bothered Obama. On one occasion during Iowa, he writes, Obama "sheepishly brought up the idea of buying ads on BET to spike our numbers" among blacks. Plouffe rejected the idea, arguing that his numbers would not significantly improve among blacks until he "proved" his "viability" by winning Iowa or New Hampshire. Obama demurred and "that was that. But it became clear to us how much pressure he was getting from all sides. . . ."[54]

On another occasion, Plouffe tells us Obama became more insistent:

> Yes, Iowa is the pathway [but] I'm going to ask one concession that should not harm our Iowa efforts. We are doing good African American politics in the early states. And that's as it should be. But I am going to insist that we start spending more time on African American leaders in states down the road. . . . It is psychologically draining for me to get emails and calls from people about how upset they are that we lost another prominent African American to Clinton and that it appears we don't care. Win or lose, I just can't have that. We have to do more.[55]

The concession was to have Valerie Jarrett begin daily calls to influential blacks urging them to wait for Iowa before making any endorsements. Obama also established a small "advisory board" of influential blacks so that he could personally stay in touch with sentiments in the black community.[56] In addition, he appeared more than a dozen times on the Tom Joyner radio program. Broadcast in more than 100 cities, Joyner's program has a large, mainly African American audience and is a major media venue for communication with black voters. Tavis Smiley, an African American radio and television talk show host, was a major contributor to the Joyner program. Just prior to Obama's formal announcement, Smiley invited him and Clinton to participate in his annual "State of the Black Union" conclave broadcast on C-SPAN. Clinton accepted; Obama declined, offering to send his wife instead. Smiley then began to routinely criticize Obama, implying that in declining to attend the gathering he was "dissing" black people. Smiley's criticisms of Obama resulted in waves of criticisms of Smiley on the Joyner program and elsewhere, ultimately resulting in his departure from the program. Inside the campaign what was described as the "Smiley backlash" was exhilarating, proving as one adviser said, "Barack [was] untouchable in the black community."[57]

As the campaign progressed, Obama did become untouchable. The black community rallied around him after Iowa and stayed firmly with him for the duration of the election. As the black community became "increasingly protective" of Obama,[58] others raised questions about the blackness of those blacks supporting Clinton. Members of the Congressional Black Caucus came under increasing pressure, leading several to switch their support to Obama. Several Caucus members were challenged in their primary elections, with their opponents asserting that their opposition to Obama proved they were "out of touch with the black community."[59] In Brooklyn one voter went even further, telling the *New York Times* that it was "racial self-hatred. It was [as] if they [black leaders, supporting Clinton] were saying: we people of color are not ready yet, we're not ready to be in the White House. Self-hatred does that to you."[60] In this atmosphere of heightened race consciousness, the bonds of blackness transcended partisan and ideological divisions in the black community, leading even well-known conservative Republicans to consider supporting Obama.[61]

Obama's balancing deracialization act was proving quite successful until his pastor, Rev. Jeremiah Wright exploded on the scene in mid-March. The theory of deracialization was developed after the 1989 elections, in which several blacks were elected to office in majority white places, including most prominently Douglass Wilder as governor of Virginia and David Dinkins as mayor of New York City. McCormick and Jones understand deracialization as "conducting a campaign in a stylistic fashion that defuses the polarizing effects of race by avoiding explicit reference to race-specific issues, while emphasizing those issues that are perceived as racially transcendent, thus mobilizing a broad segment of the electorate for the purpose of capturing or maintaining public office."[62] The fundamentals of this theory require the candidates to avoid references to issue of concerns to blacks such as affirmative action or antipoverty policies. The theory also requires that the candidate project a "nonthreatening" image and avoid association or identification with race leaders such as Jesse Jackson or Al Sharpton. In other words, the black candidate should avoid any overt association with blackness. Wright disrupted this strategy when on March 10 *ABC News* first broadcast excerpts from his sermons. Plouffe describes the Wright situation as the "the greatest threat to Obama's candidacy" that put the campaign in a "desperate fight for survival."[63] Robert Gibbs describes it as "the most perilous point in the campaign . . . that easily could have been the end."[64]

Obama joined Wright's Afro-Centric Church as part of his quest to become black. He was aware that Wright—whom *Ebony* magazine named in 1998 as one of the fifteen leading black preachers in America—adhered to black liberation theology, which holds that God is committed to the liberation of his most oppressed peoples—Africans—and it requires preachers to be unapologetically committed to militant opposition to racism and white supremacy.[65] He was aware that Wright preached jeremiads, often prophetic, sometimes apocalyptic, and always passionate outcries against injustices. Obama was also to drawn to Wright's Trinity United Methodist Church because its congregation cut across class lines, and it was an activist church, ministering to the psychological and material as well as spiritual needs of the dispossessed. In other words, in the context of the theory guiding this book Wright was a minister to the unincorporated black America—the oppressed, the ghettoized, the stigmatized, and the marginalized. For sure, then, Obama joined Wright's church because of its theological and ideological distinctiveness. Wright's influence on Obama and his admiration for him is clear in *Dreams*, and is evidenced further by his drawing the title of *The Audacity of Hope* from one of Wright's sermons. Thus although Obama may have been unaware—as he claimed—of the specifics of Wright's sermons as *ABC News* broadcast, he certainly could not have been surprised. Indeed, we know he was not because on the weekend before Obama announced his candidacy, *Rolling Stone* published an article in which Wright was quoted as preaching:

> Fact number one: We've got more black men in prison than there are in college. Fact number two: racism is how this country was founded and how this country is still run! . . . We are deeply involved in importing drugs, the exporting of guns and the training of professional killers. . . . We believe in white supremacy and black inferiority and believe in it more than we believe in God. We conducted radiation experiments on our own people. . . . We care nothing about human life if the end justifies the means! And, And, And! Gaud GOT TO BE SICK OF THIS SHIT![66]

Wright was scheduled to give the invocation at Obama's announcement of his candidacy but after the *Rolling Stone* story appeared, Axelrod and Plouffe called Obama and told him the campaign was facing its first crisis and Wright had to be uninvited. Plouffe writes, "This would be an obviously painful call to make but he immediately agreed. . . . 'I'll call him and tell him it will overshadow everything. I still want him to come, maybe he can do a private prayer with my family before I go to speak.'"[67] Wright did the private prayer. The statement explaining Wright's removal from the program did not indicate it was because of his views, but rather because he did not "want the church to face negative attention."[68] According to Wright, Obama told him, "You can get kind of rough in the sermons, so what we've decided is that it's best for you not to be there in the public."[69] Wright also said, "when his enemies find out that in 1984 I went to Tripoli [to visit Libyan leader Muammar Gaddafi, then labeled a 'rogue' terrorist leader] with Farrakhan, a lot of his Jewish support will dry up quicker than a snowball in hell."[70] Although *Fox News* and other conservative media criticized the Obama–Wright relationship, the story quickly disappeared in the glow of the media's coverage of Obama's triumphant announcement. Similarly, Al Sharpton and other black clergy murmured about Obama "not standing by his pastor," but the issue quickly faded among blacks as well.[71] The handling of this initial Wright incident was yet another example of Obama balancing, walking the racial tightrope, and trying to keep race a nonfactor. Inexplicably assuming that the issue was dead, Obama's strategists forgot about Wright. After the campaign survived the near disaster of the second Wright incident, Plouffe writes, "he still kick[s] myself for how terribly we mishandled our internal Wright work."[72]

Excerpts from Wright's sermons first aired on ABC were broadcast repeatedly on television and talk radio, as well as appearing all over the Internet. In the excerpts, Wright suggested that 9/11 was God's punishment for the injustices of U.S. foreign policy and that the government purposely created AIDS to harm blacks. Regarding 9/11, Wright preached, "we bombed Hiroshima, we bombed Nagasaki, and we nuked far more than the thousands in New York and the Pentagon, and we never batted an eye. . . . America's chickens are coming home to roost. . . . The government gives them [African Americans] drugs, builds bigger prisons, passes a three-strike law and then wants us to sing 'God Bless America.' No, no, no. God Damn America."[73]

Almost immediately Obama told his staff he had to give the "race speech." From the start of the campaign Obama had mused about giving a speech on race, but Axelrod and Plouffe "strenuously disagreed, believing we should not inject into the campaign an issue that for the most part was not on the voters' mind."[74] This time, however, Axelrod and Plouffe quickly agreed. Obama wanted to deliver the speech in the next several days and, for the most part, he wanted to write it himself telling his aides, "I already know what I want to say in the speech. I've been thinking about it for thirty years."[75] Thinking about it since he was sixteen because as he told his campaign biographer:

> Actually, this week, with the whole Wright thing, [it] was very personal for me because I understood it on both sides in a very visceral way. I know the sadness and the sense of pain and hurt that my mother would feel from a sense that blacks were painting whites with a broad brush. Because I actually remember her saying to me once "I don't feel white" that's not my identity. And I remember wanting to make sure that she understood that me embracing an African American identity in no way meant that I wasn't affirming or embracing her.[76]

The speech, "A More Perfect Union," delivered at Philadelphia's Constitution Hall at midmorning on March 18, was broadcast live on all the cable news outlets. Immediately compared to Kennedy's Houston speech, it was widely hailed in the national media and well received by the public.[77] Typical of the accolades, the *New York Times* titled its editorial, "Mr. Obama's Profile in Courage," writing, "inaugural addresses by Abraham Lincoln and Franklin D. Roosevelt come to mind, as does John F. Kennedy's speech on religion, with its enduring vision of the separation of church and state. Senator Barack Obama, who has not faced such tests of character this year, faced on Tuesday. It is hard to imagine how he could have handled it better."[78] Andrew Sullivan was even more effusive, almost lyrical: ". . . this searing, nuanced, gut-wrenchingly loyal and deeply, deeply Christian speech is the most honest speech on race in America in my adult lifetime. It is a speech we have been waiting for a generation. Its ability to embrace both the legitimate fears and resentments of whites and the understandable anger and dashed hopes of many blacks was, in my view, unique in recent American history."[79] And one distinguished white scholar of race in America went so far as to describe it "as surely the most learned disquisition on race from a major political figure ever."[80] The black commentary was generally also positive, but Vanderbilt University Professor Houston Baker Jr., the distinguished scholar of African American literature, dissented describing the speech as "a bizarre moment of mimicry, aping Martin Luther King, Jr., while even further distancing himself from the real economic, religious and political issues so courageously articulated by King from a Birmingham jail. In brief, Obama's speech was a pandering disaster that threw once again, his pastor under the bus."[81]

Obama's balancing act on race was more difficult than Kennedy's on religion. More difficult because Kennedy's strategists knew religion would not be a nonfactor. Therefore, they developed plans to deal with it early on in interviews and speeches. Thus, the Houston speech was the culmination of ideas developed over many years. Obama's speech—his thirty years of thinking about race notwithstanding—was drafted on the run (Obama did not wish to disrupt his daily campaign schedule to prepare the address for fear it would suggest panic) in the midst of a crisis. Yet, it was as good a balancing act as Kennedy's. Like Kennedy, he knew he had to address mainly the broad mainstream of the majority white electorate, but without making his ethnic base feel that he was selling out the race, his church, or his pastor. Obama performed this balancing act brilliantly.

The balancing started with the Constitution. Speaking in the city where the document was written, Obama said, "a Constitution that had at its very core the ideal of equal citizenship under the law; a Constitution that promised its people liberty and justice. . . . And yet words on parchment would not be enough to deliver slaves from bondage. . . ."[82] Next Obama established his twoness, balancing himself: "I am the son of a black man from Kenya and a white woman from Kansas. . . . I am married to a black American who carries within her the blood of slaves and slave owners. . . ." Next he spoke of his racially balanced campaign: "Despite the tendency to view my candidacy through a purely racial lens, we won commanding victories in states with some of the whitest populations in the country." Then, he sought to provide a balanced understanding of Wright, whose "comments were not only wrong but divisive, deeply divisive when we need unity," but he is also the "man who introduced me to my Christian faith, a man who spoke to me about our obligations to love one another; to care for the sick and the poor." To further the balance of his pastor, Obama sought to equate the "black" anger he expressed with a "similar anger in the white community: For the men and women of Rev. Wright's generation, the memories of humiliation and doubt and fear have not gone away. . . . That anger is not always productive. . . . But the anger is real; it is powerful. . . . In fact a similar anger exists within elements of the white community. . . . When they hear that an African American is getting an advantage in landing a good job or a good spot in college because of an injustice they never committed. . . ." Next Obama presents his policy balancing act by "continuing to insist on a full measure of justice in every aspect of American life. But it also means binding our particular grievances . . . to the larger aspirations of all Americans. . . . And it means taking full responsibility for our own lives—by demanding more from our fathers and spending more time with our children." Then, the penultimate balance: Ashley's story. Earlier, Obama had balanced his pastor and his grandmother. "I can no more disown him [Wright] then I can disown the black community. . . . No more disown him than I can my white grandmother who helped raise me, . . . but a woman who more than once . . . has uttered racial or ethnic stereotypes that made me cringe." Ashley was a young white woman who worked in Obama's South Carolina campaign. When asked at a meeting of volunteers why she was there she replied that she wanted to do something to help people like her mother who had to file bankruptcy when she got cancer. Obama then says someone asked an elderly black man why was he there and he replied, "I am here because of Ashley." Obama concluded his address by saying that this "single moment of recognition between that young white girl and that old black man" was the starting point of his campaign's efforts to complete the work of the Founders in perfecting a more perfect union.

Shortly after the Philadelphia address Obama met with Wright at the pastor's Chicago residence and came away saying, "The person I saw yesterday was not the person I met twenty years ago."[83] The next week Obama unequivocally condemned—disowned—Wright after Wright's histrionic appearance at the National Press Club, where he repeated his damnations of America and suggested that Obama's criticisms of him and his views were based on political expediency rather than conviction. At this point Obama and his wife resigned from the church.

Tracking polls in Indiana and North Carolina—the next primary states—during the Wright incident indicated that Obama's support was eroding. The speech, his resignation from the church, and his aggressive campaigning in both states apparently made a difference. He won North Carolina by fifteen points and lost to the heavily favored Clinton in Indiana by only one point. On election night after the polls closed in Indiana and North Carolina, Tim Russert, the respected NBC political analyst, declared that the election was over and that Obama would be the Democratic nominee.

Neither race nor racism were nonfactors in the 2008 election, but compared to prior post–civil rights era presidential campaigns, appeals based on race or racism were rare and inconsequential.[84] In the primaries Clinton was constrained from aggressively "playing the race card" because she could not risk alienating African American voters she would need if she won the nomination. In the general election the race card in the sense that Tali Mendelberg uses it was difficult to play because the "norm of racial equality" made explicit appeals to race or racism unacceptable.[85] Beginning with the Nixon campaign in 1968 Republican strategists employed implicit, subtle racialist appeals focusing on busing, welfare, crime, and racial quotas. In 1992 Bill Clinton co-opted Republican positions on these issues and effectively removed them from partisan debate.[86] Thus from 1996 to 2008, Republican strategists found using images of the "Welfare Queen" or Willie Horton to appeal to racialist sentiments in the electorate difficult.

The McCain campaign might have used Wright in a racialist way against Obama, but to the dismay of vice presidential nominee Sarah Palin and neoconservative pundits like William Kristol, McCain told his strategists Wright was off-limits.[87] Why McCain made this decision is not clear, but he may have been concerned that the media would accuse him of playing the race card, which some almost certainly would have.

Although the race card was not played, ironically the religion card was almost its surrogate, used in the words of one columnist to "otherize" Obama by suggesting he was a Muslim.[88] Mark Penn, the Clinton campaign's chief strategist, recommended using Obama's

Hawaiian and Indonesian backgrounds to otherize, by suggesting they "exposed a very strong weakness" because those places were not "centered in basic American values and culture."[89] Although the Clintons ultimately decided not to play the "Hawaii card," Obama rarely spoke of his Hawaiian roots instead emphasizing that his values "spring from his forebears in the Kansas heartland."[90] This may have been the appropriate strategy since in the American mind Hawaii may not quite be American. Television commentator and NPR correspondent Cokie Roberts expressed this otherized view of the state on *ABC News*'s Sunday morning talk program. Commenting on Obama's decision to vacation in Hawaii, she said, "I know his grandmother lives in Hawaii and I know Hawaii is a state, but it has the look of him going off to some sort of exotic place. He should be in Myrtle Beach, you know, if he is going to take a vacation at this time."[91]

But the main push to otherize related to religion. Obama's middle name—Hussein—and four years living in Indonesia (the world's most populous Islamic country) led to rumors that he was or had been a Muslim (one frequent posting on the Internet suggested he had attended an Islamic religious school while in Indonesia). Clinton dismissed one of her campaign workers after it was reported that she was forwarding e-mails alleging Obama was a Muslim.[92] But the Clinton campaign distributed a photo of Obama dressed in traditional Kenyan clothing (a turban and wrap around white robe) while visiting relatives in Kenya.[93] On *Meet the Press* Colin Powell said he had heard "senior members of my own party drop the suggestion 'He's a Muslim and he might be associated with terrorists.'"[94] In July the *New Yorker* ran what the Obama campaign called a "tasteless and offensive" display on its cover, a cartoon depicting Obama in the White House wearing traditional Muslim clothing and his wife—Michelle—carrying an assault rifle dressed in camouflage and wearing her hair in a huge Afro. As a log burns in a fireplace they exchange fist bumps. The magazine's editor defended the cover as a satire with something to say: "I can't speak for anyone else's interpretation, all I can say is that it combines a number of images that have been propagated, not by everyone on the right but by some about Obama's supposed 'lack of patriotism' or his 'soft on terrorism' or the idiotic notion that somehow Michelle Obama is the second coming of the Weathermen or the most violent Black Panthers. That somehow all of this is coming to the Oval office."[95] John McCain condemned the cover as "totally inappropriate . . . and offensive."[96]

Although McCain condemned the *New Yorker* cover and refused to make Wright's association with Obama an issue, his campaign attempted also to otherize Obama by portraying him as a radical because of his association with University of Illinois professor and former Weatherman Bill Ayres. Although Obama's association with Wright was longer and more substantive than with Ayres, the campaign nevertheless focused on Ayres, and Palin frequently accusing Obama of "palling around with terrorists" (the Weathermen were responsible for bombing the Capitol and the Pentagon during the 1960s). The media pointed out that Obama was eight years old when the bombings occurred and that he and Ayres were not friends, but merely lived in the same Chicago neighborhood, served on charitable boards together (in 1997 Chicago named Ayres its citizen of the year), and Ayres had hosted a coffee for Obama when he first ran for office. The Associated Press went further. A widely distributed news analysis suggested the McCain campaign was playing the race card. Palin's comments, the wire service wrote, were "tinged with racism," were "incendiary," and "whether intended or not . . . portraying Obama as 'not like us' is another potential appeal to racism. . . . Palin's words avoid repulsing voters with overt racism. But there is a subtext for creating the false image of a black presidential nominee 'palling [*sic*] around' with terrorists while assuring a predominantly white audience that he doesn't see their America."[97] The Associated Press's response to Palin's comments about Ayres suggests that the media might have been equally hostile to the campaign's use of Obama's association with Wright. In any event, the first campaign with an African American as a major party nominee was remarkably free of racist or racialist appeals.

Unlike when Kennedy was elected in 1960, in 2008 the Democrats were not the majority party, having lost that status in 1968. When President Johnson signed the Civil Rights Act of 1964 he told Bill Moyers, "I think we have just delivered the South to the Republican Party for a long time."[98] Johnson was only partly correct. He should have told Moyers that he had just delivered the white majority to the Republicans for a long time. By 2008 the robust 1960 56 percent "normal" Democratic vote had declined to well below 50 percent. The role of race and racism in this decline is well established.[99] Since Johnson in 1964, no Democratic nominee has won a majority of the white vote (Johnson won 59 percent of the white vote and 95 percent of the black vote), while averaging 88 percent of the black vote. In the forty years between 1968 and 2008 the Democrats lost seven of ten presidential elections. In this period the Republicans averaged 49 percent of the national vote, compared to the Democrats 45 percent. In their seven winning elections the Republican average of the national vote was 50.1 percent; the Democrats average in their three victories was 47 percent. The two parties in 2008 were racially polarized and neither enjoyed majority status, although in presidential elections the Republicans enjoyed a modest advantage. But fundamentally the parties were evenly balanced. Party identification is volatile, but the Democrats and Republicans have the support of little more than one-third of the electorate with the one-third or so who identify as Independents exercising the balance of power in national elections. Since the Reagan presidency, the Republican Party has become a fairly cohesive conservative party ideologically, whereas the Democrats are predominantly liberal but include also a significant moderate-centrist faction. In the party's three wins since 1968, the Democrat's nominee represented this moderate-centrist faction. Obama thus was the first nonsouthern, ideologically liberal Democrat to win the presidency since Kennedy in 1960. He was also the first member of the Congress to win the presidency since Kennedy.

In 2008 exit polls indicated that 39 percent of the electorate self-identified as Democratic, 32 percent Republican, and 29 percent as Independent. Although Obama, unlike Kennedy, did not have anywhere near a partisan majority, the strategic environment of the 2008 election pointed to a Democratic victory. (Obama ultimately won 52 percent of the Independents and 89 percent of the Democrats.) Most presidential elections are "retrospective"; that is, they are referendums on the past four years.[100] This made for an ideal strategic environment for Obama or any Democratic nominee in 2008. Throughout the year the "generic" ballot (which asks voters which party they would like to see win the presidency) showed a double-digit Democratic lead. As the general election approached, 90 percent of the electorate thought the country was headed in the wrong direction; the nation had faced rising gasoline prices, a collapse of the housing market, a massive budget deficit, rising unemployment, an unpopular war, and an incumbent president whose popularity was in the mid-30s. A month before the election the stock market dramatically declined and the credit markets collapsed, requiring a $700 billion bailout from the federal Treasury. Newspaper headlines and television newscasts raised the spectra of another Great Depression. Under these circumstances it hardly mattered who the Republicans or Democrats nominated; the Republican was going to lose.

For several generations political scientists have worked on mathematical models that do reasonably well in forecasting the outcome of national elections.[101] Using the state of the economy as the main variables, the models also typically include the relative standing of the two parties and the popularity of the incumbent president. Using variations of the model forecasters predicted a Democratic landslide in 2008, 55 percent or more of the vote.[102] However, once variables were introduced into the model to take account of Obama's race—to measure what Lewis-Beck, Tien, and Nadeau labeled "ballot box racism"—Obama wins by only 50.7 or perhaps even loses. In other words, like the religion deficit in 1960, the race deficit in 2008 might have caused a Democrat who should have won easily to lose. Lewis-Beck and his colleagues suggest that if the "economic meltdown" had not occurred in late September, ballot box racism may have cost Obama the election. They acknowledge that this conclusion is not easy to demonstrate conclusively, but:

> the time trends in the polls indicate that, across mid-June to mid-September Obama support was decreasing, while McCain support was increasing, with the two never that far apart. At some points in August and September, McCain actually took the lead. . . . Only after the bailout, and the unfolding economic crisis, did these trends reverse themselves. . . . An obvious implication is that, without the full force of an economic meltdown, Obama might not only have been denied a landslide, he might have been denied victory. We think the roots of Obama's underperformance can be laid at the feet of race prejudice.[103]

Obama won 53 percent to 46 percent, winning 65 million votes to McCain's 57 million. Obama won 28 states and the District of Columbia with 364 electoral votes to McCain's 163. Turnout was estimated at 62 percent, the highest since 1968. Although Obama won a clear majority of the national vote, among whites he lost by twelve points winning only 43 percent losing among both white men (47 percent) as well as white women (41 percent). However, he won 54 percent of the young white vote (ages eighteen to twenty-nine). Among whites he did not do as well as Carter or Clinton in 1996, but he did a couple of points better than Gore and Kerry. In the South he won the "suburban" states of Virginia, North Carolina, and Florida, but he lost by substantial margins in the other eight states of the Old Confederacy.

Ethnically, Obama's winning coalition resembled the typical post–civil rights era Democratic vote. He lost white Protestants (34 percent), evangelicals (24 percent), and Catholics (47 percent), while winning among Jews (86 percent), Latinos (67 percent), and Asian Americans (66 percent). The black vote was his base without which he could not have won. But this is no different than Carter and Clinton. His 94 percent of the black vote was several points above the Democratic average since 1964 and a point below Lyndon Johnson's 95 percent. It was not, however, his margin of victory among blacks that was crucial it was the turnout. While the number of non-Hispanic white voters remained the same as in 2004, in 2008 2 million more blacks turned out. In 2004 about 60 percent of blacks turned out, but in 2008 65 percent, nearly equaling for the first time ever the white turnout (66 percent).[104] In several states—Maryland, Mississippi, Missouri, Nevada, Ohio, and South Carolina—turnout among blacks surpassed 70 percent, and among young people and women, blacks voted at higher rates than whites.[105] Obama's campaign mobilized his ethnic base in other ways as well, with black participation greater than whites with respect to volunteering (14 percent to 7 percent) and campaign contributions (31 percent to 21 percent).[106] This relatively high turnout and participation of blacks suggest that Obama was successful because he was black; that is, among whites Obama suffered a race deficit because of ballot-box racism, but among blacks because of race consciousness and solidarity, he benefited from ballot-box blackness. In conclusion, with respect to race and the 2008 election, one can almost paraphrase William Shannon regarding religion and the 1960 election: Obama's race elected him and it almost nearly defeated him.

Obama had other advantages. First, McCain had a self-styled reputation as a maverick and so was not especially popular among white conservative, evangelical Republican base voters, and he was particularly distrusted for his 2000 attacks on the Reverends Pat Robertson and Jerry Farwell and his vote against Bush's 2001 tax cuts. The seventy-two-year-old Senate veteran and Vietnam War hero was the default nominee; that is, he was more acceptable to Republican base voters than his principal opponents, former New York City mayor Rudy Giuliani and former Massachusetts governor Mitt Romney. Giuliani was a supporter of abortion and gay rights, as was Romney when he was governor of Massachusetts. But McCain was not viewed as a reliable conservative. Thus, his choice of Alaska governor Sarah Palin, an ideological conservative and opponent of abortion and gay rights, was an effort to shore up his base. Palin probably did help McCain among base voters, but her lack of experience and poor performance in a series of television interviews led even some conservative commentators to question McCain's judgment in a selecting a person with such minimal qualifications to assume the presidency. (By early October, only 43 percent of voters thought Palin was qualified to be president.) McCain's ambivalent relationship to the conservative base explains why the percentage of Republican voters declined by 1.3 percent between 2004 and 2008. By contrast, Obama's nomination enchanted the Democratic base with Democratic voting increasing by 2.6 percent.[107]

Second, Obama had an enormous financial advantage. Although Obama had promised to participate in the public finance system established in 1976 to fund presidential campaigns, shortly after he won the nomination he changed his mind becoming the first major party nominee not to participate in the system since it was established. In his statement explaining his decision, Obama charged that Republicans had become "masters at gaming the system" by using unaffiliated groups that could raise unlimited funds (so-called 527s) to launch "smear attacks" on Democratic nominees. While Obama's allegations have an element of truth (the so-called swift boat ads against John Kerry in 2004 were an often-cited example), Obama's extraordinary fundraising capabilities were most likely the decisive factor in his change of mind. Under the public system, each nominee in 2008 was limited to $84 million. Meanwhile, Obama raised more than $318 million during the general election campaign. This financial advantage allowed Obama to outspend McCain in television and radio ads by an estimated 4–1 margin. It also allowed Obama to fund a fifty-state strategy and run an extensive nationwide, grassroots voter registration, mobilization, and get-out-the-vote campaign. The Obama organization, for example, directly contacted (in person, by phone, e-mail, or text message) a much larger percentage of likely voters than McCain's, especially blacks and young whites.[108]

Third, experts generally agree that Obama won each of the three televised debates. Certainly, the voters thought so. For example, in the crucial first debate a CNN poll found that 51 percent of voters thought Obama won, 24 percent McCain, and the remainder undecided.[109]

With all of these advantages and a highly favorable strategic environment, Obama should have won a landslide. That he did not is probably because he was black.

10

The Politics of Ethnic Avoidance in the Kennedy and Obama Administrations

The first ethnic presidents were, by coincidence, also liberal reform presidents. Elected on campaigns promising change, Kennedy and Obama in their first year proposed extensive programs of progressive change. Both also came to power in perilous times, with crises or incipient crises at home and abroad. Both had large majorities in both houses of Congress, but Democratic Party factionalism and antiquated congressional procedures threatened to delay, water down, or defeat their major legislative initiatives. Finally, both men came to office pledging to be transethnic presidents who would avoid issues and interests of particular concern to their ethnic communities. Although neither was wholly successful in the politics of ethnic avoidance, Obama was more successful than Kennedy. Yet, in the end, his presidency was confronted by much more ethnic animus than Kennedy's.

The Kennedy Presidency and Religion

The first indication of the politics of ethnic avoidance (or embrace) is selection of the cabinet and senior White House staff. Like all liberal reform presidencies, liberals in the Kennedy administration "had to be satisfied with secondary posts."[1] And like any first of its ethnic group, Kennedy could not appoint too many Catholics in highly visible positions. Speaking to Kenneth O'Donnell, Kennedy said, "If I string along exclusively with Galbraith and Schlesinger and Seymour Hersh and those other Harvard liberals, they'll fill Washington with wild-eyed Americans for Democratic Action (ADA) liberals. And if I listen to you and Powers and [John] Bailey . . . we'll have to organize a White House Knights of Columbus."[2] Kennedy's "ministry of talent," to use Sorensen's phrase, included one Republican among the four senior positions in the cabinet; C. Douglass Dillon, undersecretary of state in the Eisenhower administration and a Nixon supporter, as Treasury secretary; and a corporate executive, Robert McNamara, the president of Ford Motor Company, as Defense secretary. Responding to liberal criticism of his choice of Dillon for the senior financial post, Kennedy said, ". . . we need a Secretary of Treasury who can call a few of those people on Wall Street by their first names."[3] The cabinet was ethnically diverse for the times, including two southerners (secretaries of State and Commerce), two Jews (secretaries of Labor and Health, Education and Welfare), and two Catholics (attorney general and postmaster general). If it had not been for the intervention of his father there may have been only one Catholic in the cabinet. The President was reluctant to appoint his young, inexperienced brother as attorney general but, Joe Kennedy insisted, "Bobby is going to be the attorney general."[4] No women or blacks were appointed to the cabinet. The administration did arrange to have Chicago Congressman William Dawson leak to the press that he had declined the postmaster general post and Robert Weaver, an African American was appointed administrator of the Housing and Home Finance Administration with the promise that it would be elevated to cabinet status, making Weaver the first black member of the cabinet. Andrew Hatcher, a deputy White House press secretary, was the most visible African American in the administration.

The President brought many of his longtime Catholic Irish aides onto the White House staff, but mostly as non–policy-making functionaries (O'Donnell as appointments secretary and Larry O'Brien as liaison to Congress). Arthur Schlesinger, the liberal historian, was appointed assistant to the president, but he too had little involvement in decision making. John Kenneth Galbraith, the celebrated liberal economist, instead of being named chair of the Council of Economic Advisors, was sent away as ambassador to India. Although Kennedy enjoyed Galbraith's witty, sardonic conversation and memoranda, he thought him too liberal to advise him formally on the economy.[5] Instead, he named Walter Heller, a mainstream, centrist University of Minnesota economics professor. The senior foreign policy staff position—national security advisor, went to Republican MacGeorge Bundy, the Brahmin dean of the Harvard faculty. The only liberal of stature on the White House staff was Sorensen, and he was Kennedy's alter ego. Kennedy had two appointments to the Supreme Court. The liberal, Jewish Arthur Goldberg left the cabinet as Labor secretary to replace Felix Frankfurter, and Byron White, a friend of the president, Protestant and centrist, replaced Charles Evans Whittaker.

Kennedy's main preoccupation in the presidency was foreign policy, especially the cold war conflict with the Soviet Union and combating the spread of international communism. But he had an extensive domestic reform agenda, including medical insurance for the elderly, federal aid to education, aid for depressed areas, an increased minimum wage, antirecessionary measures, and civil rights. In the 1960 election the Democrats lost twenty-one seats in the House and two in the Senate. There was hardly, therefore, a mandate for Kennedy's agenda of liberal reform. Nominally the Democrats enjoyed comfortable majorities in both houses, 263–174 in the House and 64–36 in Senate, but in reality the conservative coalition of Republicans and southern Democrats largely controlled Congress. In addition, conservative southern Democrats chaired twelve of twenty House committees and ten of sixteen Senate committees. The conservative coalition had blocked most New Deal initiatives after Franklin Roosevelt's first term and had been completely hostile to Truman's Fair Deal. The leaders of Congress—the speaker and the majority leader—were liberals and supportive of Kennedy's agenda, but clearly this would be no easy task. Unlike Obama in 2008, Kennedy's major problem in terms of congressional rules and procedures was the House Rules Committee rather than Senate filibusters because the latter was rarely invoked except on civil rights. Five Republicans and two conservative Democrats controlled the twelve-person Rules Committee, which the racist, reactionary Howard Smith of Virginia led.[6] The Committee, operating under Smith's autocratic leadership, could deny a bill a "rule," thereby preventing it from coming to the full House for a vote. Worse than the filibuster, the power of the Rules Committee allowed a mere seven members of the House to determine what bills the other 428 members would debate and vote on. Kennedy knew if his program was to have any hope of enactment something would have to be done about the Rules Committee. One thing that might have been done was to make the Democratic members of the Committee directly accountable to party leadership, which was done in the 1970s. But House Speaker Sam Rayburn supported the autonomy of the committee. Therefore, rather than reform it, Rayburn elected to end its control by the conservatives by increasing its size. Although Kennedy did not become openly involved in this internal House conflict, he let it be known that he supported Rayburn's efforts. The resolution to increase the size of the Committee passed by a five-vote margin, 217–212. One-third of southern Democrats opposed it, and it would have been defeated without the votes of twenty-two Republican liberals from the urban Northeast.[7] The closeness of the vote suggested that

Kennedy would probably have to rely on liberal Republicans to enact his agenda. Rayburn appointed two reliable liberals to the committee (Carl Elliott of Alabama was a liberal on domestic issues except for civil rights), giving it a one-vote liberal majority (the Republicans were also given an additional seat). Three of the eight Democratic liberals were Catholic, including Tip O'Neill.

Kennedy sent his legislative agenda to Congress in the first weeks of his presidency. It included five priority "must-pass" bills: federal aid to education, Medicare, aid to depressed areas, an increased minimum wage, and an omnibus housing bill. Republicans said the President was moving too fast and overwhelming Congress with too many bills. Charles Halleck, the House Republican leader, labeled each of the bills a "child of the Kremlin,"[8] and prospective 1964 Republican nominee Barry Goldwater in speeches on the Senate floor and around the country repeatedly attacked Kennedy's "socialist, left-wing" program.[9]

Kennedy, James Giglio writes, "was not a strong president in dealing with the Congress."[10] Unlike Lyndon Johnson (with whom he rarely consulted on legislative strategy), Kennedy had few friends or even intimate acquaintances in Congress and was reluctant to engage in "cajoling and bargaining[; instead] he relied on reason; if that failed, he surmised that the time was not ripe, quoting Jefferson "Great innovations should not be forged on slender majorities."[11] Nevertheless, relying on a fairly sophisticated congressional liaison operation he was able to pass three of the five must-pass bills—a modest increase in the minimum wage, aid to depressed areas, and a housing bill. Neither house acted on Medicare during his time in office, but the Senate did pass a bill authorizing federal aid to education. It however was defeated in the House Rules Committee. The defeat of this bill is the penultimate case of the politics of ethnic avoidance during the Kennedy presidency.

The politics of ethnic avoidance was impossible with federal aid to education. It was a major issue during the campaign and was perhaps Kennedy's major legislative priority in his first year in office. It was also the Catholic issue of his presidency. Some in the Irish Catholic community might have expected the first Catholic Irish president to have considered change in foreign policy with respect to Northern Ireland, but Kennedy felt no pressure about this issue during his presidency.[12] Not so with federal aid to education. One month after taking office, Kennedy sent his first message to Congress dealing with education. In it he declared unequivocally, "In accordance with the clear prohibition of the Constitution, no elementary or secondary school funds are allocated for constructing church schools or paying church schools' teacher salaries."[13] A week later Archbishop Karl Alter of Cincinnati, speaking for the U.S. Conference of Catholic Bishops, was just as unequivocal: "In the event that a federal aid program is enacted which excludes children in private schools, . . . there will be no alternative but to oppose such legislation."[14] New York's Cardinal Spellman said, "It is unthinkable that any American child be denied federal funds allotted to other children . . . because his parents choose for him a God-centered education."[15] Later, the National Catholic Welfare Conference called for the bill's defeat unless loans for church schools were included. Thus the religious conflict that Kennedy dreaded was joined.

The effort to provide federal financial help to the nation's schools goes back to the Reconstruction era. Confronting the enormous illiteracy rate in the South (especially among blacks), in 1882 Senator Henry Blair of New Hampshire introduced legislation to provide grants to the states of more than $100 million over ten years. No provision was made for assistance to private schools, but the legislation did require the states to distribute the funds on a racially nondiscriminatory basis. With the strong support of President Benjamin Harrison, Blair's bill passed the Republican-controlled Senate three times between 1884 and 1890, but the Democratic House always refused to take up the bill. Between 1948 and 1959, the Senate four times passed aid to education bills.[16] Each explicitly prohibited aid to church schools. In 1949 John Kennedy helped to kill the Senate passed bill in the House because of this prohibition. Representing his heavily Catholic district, Kennedy was angered by what he said was the clearly anti-Catholic bias of the legislation and cast the deciding vote to kill it in committee.

By 1960 nonpublic schools—mainly Catholic—educated 15 percent of the nation's schoolchildren in 10,000 elementary schools and 2,400 high schools with faculty and staff of more than 100,000.[17] Many members of Congress—Protestants and Catholics—thought that given these numbers, excluding Catholic schools from aid would undermine the objective of improving the overall education of the nation's young people. In the House, John McCormack of Massachusetts, the Catholic majority leader and soon to be speaker, was the informal leader of the Catholic bloc in the House, and he favored providing some kind of aid to Catholic schools. In the Senate, Wayne Morse, Protestant and chair of the Senate Subcommittee on Education, also favored including something for Catholic schools in any bill.

Shortly after the election the President appointed study groups or task forces to prepare recommendations for legislative proposals on the priority items on his agenda. Frederick Hovde, the president of Purdue University, chaired the task force on education. The Hovde Report recommended a program of general aid to public elementary and secondary schools exclusively. Abraham Ribicoff, the Jewish secretary of Health, Education and Welfare, insisted that the Hovde recommendation could not pass unless "there was something in it for the Catholics," such as loans for school construction and maintenance.[18] For Kennedy, however, it was a "closed issue," believing that as the first Catholic president he could not go back on his campaign promise to deny assistance to Catholic schools. Evidently irritated that as a Catholic he was being pressed on the issue when Eisenhower had not been when he proposed similar legislation without aid to Catholic schools, Kennedy declared at a March 1 press conference, "There isn't any room for debate on the subject. It is prohibited by the Constitution and the Supreme Court. Therefore, there would be no possibility of recommending it."[19] Kennedy met with Paul Blanchard and POAU members to discuss the Hovde Report, but he refused to meet with members of the Catholic Church hierarchy because he had made his decision. The case was closed; there was nothing to discuss.

Despite his unequivocal public opposition, however, Kennedy did agree to a surreptitious effort to provide a "sweetener" for the Catholics. He authorized Ribicoff and Sorensen to secretly negotiate a compromise with the Catholic bishops on an amendment to the National Defense Education Act (NDEA) to expand loans beyond defense-related facilities (which were provided to Catholic schools) to include government-guaranteed loans to construct "virtually any structure short of a chapel."[20] Fearing once again that as a Catholic he could not publicly be identified with the amendment, Kennedy insisted the sponsors of the bill in the Senate introduce the amendment while denying that the administration played any role in its development. In the words of Sorensen's "administratively confidential" memorandum, "there was to be no mention of or indication that the administration played any role or [had] taken any position on this amendment or course of strategy."[21] The bill with the NDEA amendment passed the Senate 49–34, with the support of ten Republicans, nine southern Democrats, and all the northern Democrats except three. The three southern Democrats on the House Rules Committee, however, demanded that the NDEA amendment be deleted, citing a *New York Times* editorial that described it as a "cover . . . to slip through large scale federal aid to non-public schools."[22] With the sweetener for the Catholics removed, Catholic Congressman James Delaney, representing a heavily Catholic district in New York, joined with the Republicans and southern Democrats on the Rules Committee to kill the bill in an 8–7 vote. Federal aid to education was effectively dead for the rest of Kennedy's term because a coalition of Republicans who objected to the bill because they opposed any kind of aid to education as fiscally irresponsible and an unwarranted expansion of federal authority killed it. They were joined by southerners concerned about states' rights and fearful that the bill might be used to compel compliance with the *Brown* school desegregation decree. Finally, Congressman Delaney, the northern liberal, joined them because there was nothing in it for the Catholics. A *New York Times* editorial blamed the bill's defeat on "legislative irresponsibility and inept executive leadership," concluding, "The story of the school bill's debacle has been a succession of profiles in lack of courage."[23] Hugh Davis Graham attributes the failure to Kennedy's wish as a Catholic "to do something for the Catholics while appearing not to. As the first Catholic president, he was politically condemned to oppose parochial school aid. . . . But his covert encouragement of the NDEA sweetener backfired on him, and his repeated denials were disingenuous."[24] Hugh Douglas Price also sees the problem as rooted in religion, arguing that Kennedy probably could have got a bill passed in 1962 or 1963, "but only at the cost of disaster for much of the rest of his program, sharpened religious conflict in America and seriously endangering his own re-election."[25]

While Kennedy was disappointed by the defeat of the bill, he blamed it on the conservative coalition on the Rules Committee and not on Congressman Delaney or Catholics generally, telling Sorensen, "That is who really killed the bill, just as they have killed it for fifty years, not the Catholics." But Sorensen goes on to write that the death of the bill had an important positive effect, bringing about "one of the most far-reaching changes in U.S. politics effected during the Kennedy years. To a much greater extent than had been true the previous November, the ban on Catholics in the White House was dead also. John Kennedy had demonstrated that a Catholic could withstand the full pressures of the hierarchy on a bill of real significance to both sides, and he was toasted from Protestant pulpits throughout the land."[26]

Kennedy's failure on federal aid to education illuminates the difficulties of the politics of ethnic avoidance. As a young Catholic Congressman from Boston, Kennedy in 1949 behaved exactly as did Congressman Delaney, the young Catholic Congressman from New York in 1961. In 1949 he cast the decisive vote in committee to kill federal aid to education because it did not have anything in it for his people; nothing for the Catholics. But as president, he was publicly, adamantly opposed to anything for the Catholics, while privately working to do something for his people. In other words, the classic ethnic dilemma; how can one be true to one's own, while at the same time appearing to govern for all the people.

In 1965 the Elementary and Secondary Education Act was passed. President Johnson from the outset insisted that the legislation contain something for the Catholics. He therefore abandoned Kennedy's formula of general aid to education in favor of categorical grants to poor children, based on the poverty of the school district and a state's educational expenditures per child. The act also required school districts to provide special educational services, such as textbooks, to children in private and parochial as well as public schools, which satisfied the Catholic hierarchy. The legislation passed the House 263–153 and the Senate 73–18.[27] Lyndon Johnson was demonstrably a better legislative leader than Kennedy, and he had a larger legislative majority,[28] but on this issue, he was in a better strategic position because he did not have to practice the politics of ethnic avoidance.[29]

The Obama Presidency and Race

In assembling his cabinet and White House staff Obama displayed what Plouffe describes as his "extreme pragmatism."[30] The cabinet was bipartisan and centrist. It included only one African American and no person identified with the left of the Democratic Party. Paraphrasing Kennedy's comment about liberals and Catholics in 1961, no one would mistake Obama's administration for a meeting of Move-On.Org or the NAACP. Like Kennedy also, Obama's economic team comprised people who knew people on Wall Street on a first-name basis. Treasury secretary Timothy Geithner and chief economic advisor Larry Summers were closely associated with individuals and ideas partly responsible for the deregulatory and other policies that helped to bring about the near collapse of the economy.[31] The national security team was headed by Hillary Clinton, appointed secretary of state, and retired general David Jones as national security advisor. Robert Gates, Bush's defense secretary was retained. In addition to Gates, one other Republican—Congressman Ray Lahood—was named to the cabinet as secretary of transportation. During his tenure as president of the Law Review at Harvard Law School, Obama antagonized many liberals and blacks by his tendency to take them for granted while aggressively reaching out to conservatives.[32] This "extreme pragmatism," this wish to reach out to both sides of the ideological spectrum in an effort to forge consensus, characterized not only Obama's appointments but also his proclivities in legislating during the first years of his presidency as well. Obama attributes aspects of this style or presidential character partly to the influence of Hawaii. In an interview with *U.S. News and World Report* during the campaign he said:

> I do think that the multicultural nature of Hawaii helped teach me how to appreciate different cultures. The second

> thing I am certain [of] is that what people call my even temperament I think draws from Hawaii. People in Hawaii generally don't spend a lot of time, you know, yellin' and screamin' at each other. I think there is just a cultural bias toward courtesy and trying to work problems in a way that makes everybody feel like they are listened to and I think that reflects itself in my personality and political style.[33]

This "island style" was reflected at its best and worst in Obama's attempt to name New Hampshire Senator Judd Gregg secretary of commerce. A doctrinaire conservative Republican, Gregg was opposed to each of the priority items on Obama's agenda. He subsequently recognized the virtual impossibility of his being part of a cabinet of a president in which he had such profound disagreements and withdrew his name, but this was an early indication of the pitfalls of island-style character.

Bill Clinton appointed four African Americans to his cabinet, George W. Bush two, but the first black president only one—Eric Holder as attorney general. (African Americans were named U.N. ambassador and special trade representative with cabinet rank.) Meanwhile, he appointed three Latinos (and attempted to appoint a fourth but New Mexico governor Bill Richardson withdrew his nomination for commerce secretary) and two Asian Americans. Overall, the first black president appointed an ethnically diverse cabinet (including four women) but racially it was only a little more diverse than Kennedy's. The core White House staff comprised all white men except Valerie Jarrett, the longtime Chicago friend and associate. He named two persons to the Supreme Court in two years. First, Sonia Sotomayor was the first Latino, replacing Justice David Souter. Second, Elena Kagan, Jewish, the solicitor general and former dean of the Harvard Law School, was Obama's second nominee to the Court, replacing Justice John Paul Stevens. No African Americans appeared on the widely publicized short lists for either vacancy. However, in the first two years a record 25 percent of Obama's lower court appointments were African American (compared to Clinton's 16 percent).

Erwin Hargrove and Michael Nelson categorize Kennedy's first two years as a presidency of "preparation," involving a coherent strategy of presenting legislation to Congress as a form of public education designed to build public support and win reelection in 1964 with congressional majorities sufficient to enact his legislative agenda, thereby transforming his second term into a presidency of "achievement."[34] Using their categories, Obama's first two years would be classified as a presidency of achievement, where he took advantage of his unstable congressional majorities to enact his legislative agenda as quickly as possible before his popular mandate for change and legislative majorities collapsed.

Unlike Kennedy, Obama's first interest and preoccupation was not foreign policy but domestic reform. His major priorities were rejuvenating the economy, reforming the financial system, and enacting national health insurance and energy-climate legislation. But he was a wartime president, commanding wars in Iraq and Afghanistan as well as an amorphous global "war on terror." In addition, he perceived an urgent need to repair the nation's image abroad after eight years of decline under the Bush administration. With the notable exception of Israel, his election was greeted globally with enthusiasm. To the leaders, nations, and peoples of the world, Obama—this talented, charismatic, multicultural son of an African—was the embodiment of hope and change, hope for change in America's relations with the world. Not since John Kennedy had a U.S. president inspired such sentiments.[35] The Nobel committee, in recognition of this hope and in order to encourage it, awarded Obama its peace prize after he was only several months in office. Nations, however, ultimately act on the basis of their interest and not charismatic leaders or their soaring rhetoric. Obama in his first years labored to change the tone and style of U.S. foreign policy, but there was little change in the fundamentals of the nation's imperial globalism.[36]

President Obama's domestic liberal reform agenda was the most expansive, transformative since Kennedy's. Partly as a result of his coattails, he came into office with substantial Democratic majorities in both houses. In 1960 the loss of twenty-one seats in the House and two in the Senate accompanied Kennedy's narrow victory. In 2008 the Democrats expanded their majorities in the House by twenty-four seats and in the Senate by eight, putting them one vote shy of the sixty filibuster-proof majority. (Pennsylvania's Arlen Specter's change of parties in early 2009 provided that sixty-vote majority.) However, as in 1960, the Democratic majority was fractured. It was not a cohesive ideologically liberal bloc. Of the 257 House Democrats, 52 were associated with the centrist "Blue Dog" faction, and in the Senate of the 60 Democrats perhaps 55 were ideologically liberal. Meanwhile the Republicans in both houses were a unified conservative ideological bloc, meaning unlike Kennedy in 1960, Obama could anticipate little bipartisan support for his program. Also unlike 1960, beginning in the late 1990s, the minority party began using the filibuster as a routine parliamentary procedure to delay or defeat virtually all majority party initiatives.

Obama's legislative agenda had four priority items or must-pass bills: (1) a so-called stimulus package or the American Recovery and

Reinvestment Act; (2) energy-climate legislation; (3) financial regulatory reform; and (4) the signature issue of the liberal reform agenda, national health insurance. The administration did not send to Congress draft legislation on any of the bills. Rather, it relied on the speaker, the majority leader, and the chairs of the relevant committees to draft the legislation and work out the necessary compromises. Obama, however, held numerous one-on-one meetings with key members—Republicans and Democrats—on each bill, as well as group sessions with leaders and members at the White House and on Capitol Hill, always making the "intellectual case" for the policy in a "gentle, consensus building style."[37] Obama's island style, his desire to reach out to the Republicans to build bipartisan consensus, failed. Each of the bills passed on near strict party-line votes.

The Recovery Act passed the House on a strict party-line vote, 244–188 (11 Democrats also voted no) and the Senate 60–40 with the votes of 3 "moderate" Republicans including Senator Specter who later switched parties. Many left-liberal economists contended that the $787 billion package was too small and did not focus enough on direct job creation.[38] However, the tax cuts and short- and long-term spending in the legislation are credited with keeping the economy from avoiding a near depression.[39] The legislation also included billions of dollars in long-term investments in education, green technologies, health information technologies, and broadband and wireless Internet access. These long-term investments did little to bring down the unemployment rate. When Obama was elected the unemployment rate was 7.6 percent, and the administration claimed the recovery act would keep unemployment below 8 percent. By the end of 2009, however, the unemployment rate exceeded 10 percent. In its 2010 economic report the administration projected that the unemployment rate would be at 8.2 percent in 2012 and would remain well over 6 percent until 2015.

The American Clean Energy and Security Act passed the House in June 2009, 219–212, with the support of 211 Democrats and 8 Republicans, but failed to come to a vote in the Senate. The financial regulatory reform legislation passed the House later in the year on a strict party-line vote, 232–202, and the Senate in early 2010, 59–39. Twenty-seven House Democrats joined all the Republicans in voting no on what the president described as the second highest priority, after health insurance, on the domestic agenda.

Throughout the yearlong consideration of health insurance Obama engaged in a futile effort to craft a bipartisan consensus bill. This was a predictably futile because since the Truman administration conservatives have been unalterably opposed to national health insurance.[40] Their opposition is based on core conservative values—it is simply not the proper function of government to provide health insurance, and doing so today in light of the looming deficits in Medicare and Medicaid would be fiscally irresponsible. But there was also a strategic, partisan basis to the opposition, clearly articulated for all to know during the debate on Clinton's 1993 health insurance bill. In 1992 in what Haynes Johnson and David Broder call a "celebrated strategy document" William Kristol, the influential neoconservative intellectual and *Fox News* pundit, wrote that Republicans should under no circumstances cooperate in passing any kind of national health insurance. His reasons, Johnson and Broder write, "were Machiavellian": to defeat the Democrats and lay the foundation for an enduring conservative Republican majority.[41] For Kristol national health insurance presented "a clear and present danger to the Republican future; its passage would (as Democrats had earlier advised Clinton) give the Democrats a lock on the crucial middle-class vote. 'It will re-legitimatize middle-class dependence for security on government regulation and spending. It will revive the reputation of the party that spends and regulates, the Democrats, as the generous protector of middle-class interests. And it will at the same time strike a punishing blow against Republican claims to defend the middle class by restraining government.'"[42] For these reasons, regardless of how much Obama embraced his island style, the Republican strategy, for ideological and partisan reasons, required all-out opposition.

The House passed its version of health insurance in November 2009 by the narrowest of margins, 220–215. Thirty-nine Democrats voted no and one Republican, the newly elected Joseph Cao representing the predominantly black New Orleans district, voted aye. The legislation represented a historic milestone in U.S. social policy: the first time a house of Congress had passed a bill that gave *promise* of health insurance for virtually all citizens. Anchored by mandates that individuals and businesses of a certain size purchase insurance, the trillion-dollar House bill also created a government entity that would compete with private, for-profit providers in offering insurance. Although this "public option" was considered crucial to ensure competitiveness and hold down costs, the Senate version passed on Christmas Eve dropped it in order to win the support of several centrist Democrats. The holiday debate in the Senate was acrimonious, tedious, and messy, and several Democratic senators traded their votes in corrupt bargains for special benefits for their states and constituents. Nevertheless, Majority Leader Harry Reid managed to hold together the sixty Democrats and break the Republican filibuster. As the Senate adjourned for the holidays the Democrats celebrated as it appeared likely the sixty-year-old liberal pledge to provide some kind of comprehensive health care to almost all Americans would be signed into law early in the New Year.

In one of the supreme ironies of a book comparing the Kennedy and Obama presidencies, a newly elected senator from Massachusetts, holding a seat first filled by John Kennedy in 1952, was elected and became the decisive vote in killing national health insurance. Edward Kennedy—who passed the symbolic torch of his brother to Obama in the 2008 election and who had made national health insurance "the cause of his life" during his long career in the Senate—died during the summer. He was replaced temporarily by one of his aides until a special election could be held in January. In an astonishing turnabout, the liberal Democratic nominee was decisively defeated by a little-known conservative Republican, Scott Brown. Brown was not only the first conservative elected to the Senate from Massachusetts since Henry Cabot Lodge Sr. defeated John Kennedy's grandfather in 1916, but he also ran explicitly on the pledge that, if elected, he would cast the forty-first vote to defeat the cause of Senator Kennedy's life. Polling after the Massachusetts election indicated that voters were opposed to the Democratic health-care bill and federal government activism generally.[43] In general, by the time of the Senate debate, polls indicated that a majority of Americans did not favor the legislation.[44] Like the Clinton bill in 1993, a summerlong propaganda campaign against the bill with allegations of socialized medicine, government bureaucrats determining patient care, and "death panels" had frightened the majority of the public (which have health insurance) into thinking they would lose under the Democratic plan.[45] But even the minority without health insurance by December was evenly divided on whether the Democratic plan should be adopted.[46] Ironically, then, by December the Republican minority's use of the filibuster was now consistent with the wishes of a near majority of the American people, who wished to see the legislation defeated (although many in this near majority favored a stronger bill, with the public option for example). Polls also indicated that the Democrats were likely to lose seats in both houses of Congress—perhaps even their majority in the House—thus the President and Congressional leaders decided this was their last chance to pass health-care reform in the Obama administration and perhaps for years to come. To avoid sending a House-Senate compromise bill back to the Senate where it would be filibustered, the House adopted the Senate bill and sent it to the President for his signature. In separate legislation passed using the nonfilibusterable "budget reconciliation" process, minor "fixes" were made in the Senate bill (mainly the removal of the corrupt Senate bargains).[47]

The legislation Obama signed—the Patient Protection and Affordability Act—was a remarkably inept piece of legislation, more a compulsory private health insurance scheme than national health insurance. Indeed, the idea of requiring individuals to buy private health insurance—a centerpiece of the legislation—is an idea the conservative Heritage Foundation advanced in the 1990s and that some conservatives offered as an alternative to Clinton's 1993 health insurance plan.[48] With no single payer, no public option, and no enforceable restraints on premium increases, the mandate that millions of individuals purchase health insurance is a vast subsidy to the insurance companies at the expense of working people and the federal Treasury. Yet, this was the best that the President and Democratic leaders of Congress could get; and they barely got this shadow of what real national health insurance would look like. Yet with its generous subsidies to assist individuals in purchasing insurance (up to 400 percent of the poverty level for families or about $90,000 year), the requirement that most employers provide coverage, the expansion of community-based clinics, and access to Medicaid, the act gave *promise* when fully implemented in 2014 of providing coverage for most citizens of the United States. (The estimated 10 to 12 million illegal residents were completely barred from participating in the program.)

The bill was also modestly economically and racially redistributive. Taxes were increased on households earning more than $250,000 and the Medicare payroll tax was expanded to cover dividend, interest, and other unearned income of the wealthy. Meanwhile, the benefits flow mostly to low- and middle-income individuals.[49] Very few African Americans earn more than $250,000 a year, and they are disproportionately low income and more likely than whites not to have health insurance.[50] National health insurance, therefore, is a prime example of an Obama "sweetener" for blacks; doing something for his people while adhering steadfastly to the politics of ethnic avoidance. This is consistent with his emphasis during the campaign and in *The Audacity of Hope* wherein he argued that an emphasis "on universal programs as opposed to race-specific ones isn't just good policy, it is also good politics."[51] Good ethnic politics as well. Obama invoked this mantra frequently when accused of avoiding specific problems plaguing the black community. Regarding health insurance specifically he said, "Spending on health care legislation [will] have a direct impact on African Americans who struggle to afford health insurance. People need to understand that one out of every five African Americans do not have health care. Nobody stands to gain more from this health care bill passing."[52]

Obama signaled this strategy of race avoidance for his presidency at his 100th day in office press conference in the following exchange with Andre Showell of *BET News*:

Showell: Mr. President, as the entire nation tries to climb out of this deep recession, in communities of color the circumstances are far worse. The black unemployment rate, as you know is double digits, and in New York City, for example, the black unemployment rate for men is near 50 percent. My question tonight is, given this unique and desperate circumstance, what specific policies can you point to that target these communities? And what's a timetable for results?

President Obama: Well, keep in mind that every step we've taking [*sic*] is designed to help all people, but folks who are most vulnerable are most likely to be helped. . . . We put in place provisions that would extend unemployment insurance or allow you to keep your health insurance, even if you've lost your job, that probably disproportionately impacted those communities that had lost their jobs. And unfortunately, the African American community and the Latino community are probably overrepresented in those ranks. . . . The Children's Health Insurance program, again, those probably disproportionately impact African American and Latino families. . . . So, my general approach is that if the economy is strong, that will lift all boats as long as it is also supported by, for example, strategies around college affordability and job training, tax cuts for working families as opposed to the wealthiest, that level the playing field and ensure bottom-up growth. And I'm confident it will help the African American community live out the American dream at the same time it is helping communities all across the country.[53]

Later, the President told April Ryan of American Urban Radio, "The only thing I cannot do is, by law, I can't pass laws that say I'm just helping black folks. I'm the president of the entire United States."[54] The African American political scientist Ronald Walters, a former senior advisor to Jesse Jackson, took exception to the contention that it would be unlawful to develop policies specifically designed to deal with race. "There is," Walters wrote:

[a] gross contradiction at the heart of this statement. If it is a mistake to think about ethnic segments of the country in his governance, then why did he sign an executive order mandating the increased participation of Asian and Pacific

> Islanders in federal programs, or say in a speech to the Hispanic Caucus that when their unemployment number reached over 10 percent that was not just a problem for Hispanics, it was a problem for the whole nation. No such statement has been made by the White House about the 15.7 percent rate of the official black unemployment.[55]

The Congressional Black Caucus, the NAACP, and the Urban League also pressed the President to develop targeted, race-specific programs to address the gap in unemployment between blacks and other Americans.[56] The ten black members of the House Financial Services Committee boycotted committee proceedings on the financial regulatory reform legislation until they secured a meeting with the Treasury secretary and White House chief of staff to discuss "more help to African American communities suffering in the economic decline."[57] The African American majority whip in the House, James Clyburn, also called for the development of targeted programs to deal with problems in black communities not because they were black, he said, but because they are suffering disproportionately high rates of joblessness and related economic stresses. The President nevertheless held fast to the politics of ethnic avoidance. Noting the "grumbling," he said, "If you want to line up all the black actors, for example, who support me and put them on one side of the room and a couple who are grumbling on the other, I'm happy to have that. . . ."[58] Equating his support among black entertainers with the "grumbling" of black civil rights and political leaders was perhaps obtuse, but it reflected Obama's understanding of the widespread support he enjoyed in the black community, at both elite and mass levels, based on ties of ethnic kinship and solidarity.[59]At the elite level, *Black Enterprises*, the African American–oriented business magazine, at the end of Obama's first year asked a group of experts (including this writer) to grade the President's performance. Overall, he received a B+.[60] Near the end of his first year his overall approval rating in the black community stood at 91 percent, compared to 39 percent among whites and 70 percent among Latinos.[61]

In an address in February 2009 commemorating the 100th anniversary of the founding of the NAACP, Obama repeatedly invoked the ties of ethnic kinship and solidarity, referring to the organization's leader as "Brother" Jealous and using words like "us," "our folks," "our children," and "the need to do our part ourselves."[62]While acknowledging the "structural inequalities that our legacy of discrimination has left behind," he defended his view that it was his responsibility to lay the "foundation for growth and prosperity" that would "put opportunity within the reach not just of African Americans, but all Americans of every race."[63] At the NAACP, he reaffirmed his blackness—indeed celebrated it—but like Kennedy he understood that as the first of his ethnic group to be president he dare not even give the appearance of ethnic favoritism, of doing anything for the blacks.[64] Like Kennedy—perhaps even more so than Kennedy—he understood that he had to bend over backward to avoid identification with "our folks." To do otherwise would put his presidency at risk. But in spite of Obama's studied practice of the politics of ethnic avoidance, his first year in office saw a threefold increase in the percentage of whites who believed his policies favored blacks, up from between 11 and 13 percent in October 2008 to 37 percent in August 2009.[65]

Obama learned a lesson in the dangers of the appearance of ethnic engagement when at a July 2009 press conference he offhandedly remarked that a white police officer who arrested a black Harvard professor in his house after being called to check out a suspected burglary had acted "stupidly." Overnight his presidency was engulfed in racial controversy and his approval rating among whites dropped precipitously. Obama quickly retreated, declaring that both the professor and the policeman had "probably overreacted," and to make amends invited both men to the White House for what the media described as a "beer summit."[66] After sipping beer with the President, the Vice President, and the policeman, the professor—Henry Louis Gates—issued a statement saying, "I thank God that I live in a country in which police officers put their lives on the line to protect us every day, and more than ever, I've come to understand and appreciate their daily sacrifice on our behalf."[67] Neither the President's apology and quick retreat nor the professor's obsequious statement seemed to matter to most whites. In the days following the incident Obama's personal approval among whites declined, with whites disapproving of his remarks about the professor's arrest from 45 percent to 22 percent.[68] The pitfalls of a politics of ethnic engagement on such a trivial matter as the Gates arrest most likely reinforced in Obama's mind the imperative of the politics of ethnic avoidance. Writing after the incident on the larger problem, the African American *New York Times* columnist Bob Herbert scornfully wrote, "President Obama would rather walk through hell than spend his time dealing with America's racial problems."[69]

Nevertheless Obama seems to have encountered more racially based animus than Kennedy encountered on the basis of religion. An experimental study of white opposition to Obama's health-care plan, for example, found that when it was attributed to Bill Clinton, opposition was substantially less than when it was attributed to Obama. The study concluded that many whites opposed the plan in part because they dislike Obama because he is black.[70] The anchors of race-based animus toward Obama are in the South and among Republicans. For example, the so-called "birthers" (persons who believe the President was not born in the United States) were disproportionately southern and Republican. Only 47 percent of white southerners believed the President is native born—a constitutional requirement to hold the office—compared to 93 percent of Northeast respondents, 90 percent in the Midwest, and 83 percent of white persons living in the West.[71] With regard to party, 93 percent of Democrats and 83 percent of Independents believed he was native born, but only 42 percent of Republicans.[72]

In an unprecedented breach of the dignity, decorum, and deference due a head of state addressing a legislature, South Carolina Congressman Joe Wilson yelled out to the President during an address to Congress, "You lie!" When asked about Wilson's outburst, President Jimmy Carter said he believed "an overwhelming portion of the intensely demonstrated animosity toward President Barack Obama is based on the fact that he is a black man, that he is African American. . . . And I think it's bubbled up to the surface because of the belief among many white people, not just in the South but around the country, that an African American is not qualified to be president."[73] The White House press secretary immediately disavowed Carter's remarks: "The President does not believe it [Wilson's outburst] was based on race."[74]

Tinges of racial animus also surfaced in the so-called Tea Party movement that emerged during the summer of 2009 around opposition to the health-care plan. Largely white and middle class, at the group's opening convention a keynote speaker—Colorado Congressman Tom Tancredo—to enthusiastic applause called for the revival of literacy tests as a qualification for voting because, he said, "people who could not spell the word 'vote' or say it in English put a committed socialist ideologue in the White House—[whose] name is Barack Hussein Obama."[75] Former Republican House Speaker Newt Gingrich and *Fox News* commentators repeatedly invoked the socialist canard. Gingrich, for example, described the Obama administration as "the most radical in American history" and as a "secular socialist machine."[76] Barry Goldwater and others on the right also used the socialist bogeyman to attack John Kennedy, but some polls early in 2010 found a majority of whites believing that Obama, the pragmatic centrist, was a socialist.[77]

Gallup's first poll on President Obama's job performance found a 68 percent approval rating, second only to Kennedy's 78 percent among postwar presidents.[78] At the end of Obama's first year his average monthly approval rating was 57 percent, compared to Kennedy's 76 percent. Coming into office with barely 50 percent of the vote, Kennedy, despite many legislative and foreign policy setbacks at the end of his first year, had won the respect and admiration of the overwhelming majority of his countrymen (his popularity never fell below 59 percent). Obama, with a better legislative record and no foreign policy setbacks, was barely holding on. Indeed, without the overwhelming support of his fellow ethnic blacks, his approval rating would have been less than 50 percent during his first year.

The Elections of 1962 and 2010

In the 1962 midterm elections, the Democratic Party lost four seats in the House and gained two in the Senate. In the 2010 midterm elections, the Democrats lost sixty-three House seats and seven in the Senate. Several factors may account for the different outcomes of Kennedy and Obama's first midterm elections.

In 1962 the Democrats were the majority party, but in the 1960 election Kennedy had won a narrow victory with no coattails. Indeed, he had run fifteen points behind Democratic congressional candidates, doing better in only 134 of the 435 districts. Thus, the so-called withdrawn coattails explanation for the presidential party's loss of seats played little role in 1962 because Kennedy had none in 1960.

The two parties in the early 1960s were not ideologically polarized. The Democratic base included a significant number of conservatives, and the Republican Party included a significant liberal faction.

Although Kennedy had had little success in enacting his liberal reform agenda, he was quite popular in the fall of 1962. His successful handling of the Cuban missile crisis in October had a "rallying around the flag" effect. Between October and Election Day, his Gallup approval rating increased from 61 percent to 73 percent. The economy was in relatively good shape in 1962, with the unemployment rate, for example, having declined from 6.6 percent in January 1961 to 5.7 percent by Election Day. Finally, religion, which had been such a divisive issue two years before, was not an issue at all in 1962.

In 2010 Democrats were not the majority party, the two parties were ideologically polarized, and in 2008 Obama had coattails winning, for example, sixty-five congressional districts Bush won in 2004.[79] The economy was not in good shape, being mired in the worst recession since the Great Depression with unemployment having increased from 7.6 percent on Obama's inauguration to 9.6 percent on Election Day.

Obama, unlike Kennedy, had had major success in enacting his liberal reform agenda, but this did not translate into popular support for him or the Democratic Party (on Election Day his approval rating was in the mid-forties).[80] On the contrary, it may have contributed to their loss of popularity and the size of the party's defeat in the election.[81] This is because Americans generally are less supportive of liberal, reform policies in times of economic decline and distress;[82] concerns about debt and deficits also constrain public support for new government programs.[83] And more than a half century of political science research show that when the economy is in recession the party in the White House loses seats in midterm elections.[84]Finally, although we cannot know now the exact dimensions, race probably played a part in the 2010 election outcomes.

Since World War II, the president in power has lost an average of seventeen House and one Senate seat in his first midterm election. Thus in relationship to the postwar norm, the Democratic losses in 2010 were historic, the largest since 1938 when the Democrats lost eighty-one House seats in Roosevelt's second midterm election.

As Obama prepared for the last two years of his first term, he confronted a Republican-controlled House and a Senate with a diminished Democratic majority. Given the intense partisan and ideological polarization of the parties,[85] Republican control of the House meant the President would most likely not be able to accomplish any further domestic reforms. In effect, the election signaled deadlock of the American democracy and the end of Obama's domestic reform presidency.

This is not unlike what the last two years of Kennedy's term would have been like had he lived. On the week of the President's murder, *Newsweek's* lead story was an analysis of the deadlock between the Senate and the President over his legislative program, including tax cuts, civil rights, foreign aid, and Medicare.[86]

In the 2010 election the electorate was more racially polarized than ever. Obama's approval rating among whites was 39 percent on Election Day, but more than 90 percent of blacks approved of his performance. Democrats won 37 percent of the white vote; the Republicans won 60 percent the party's best congressional showing among whites in the history of modern polling. Meanwhile, 91 percent of blacks voted Democratic. Thus, the first black president, unlike the first Catholic, was not in his first two years in office—notwithstanding his politics of ethnic avoidance—able to transcend the racial divisions of the nation. Indeed, at the end of his first two years, polls indicated Obama had become the most politically, ideologically, and racially polarizing president since polling began.[87]

11

Conclusion

It has been a half century since the first Catholic was elected president. None has been elected since, and only one—John Kerry of Massachusetts—has been a major party nominee (Joseph Biden was elected the first Catholic vice president in 2008). This is not, however, because Catholicism is any kind of bar to the presidency. As indicated in chapter 8, fewer than 5 percent of the electorate in 2008 said they would not vote for a Catholic for president, far below the 25 percent who said so in 1960. When Catholics Eugene McCarthy and Robert Kennedy ran for president in 1968 their religion was rarely mentioned. Since then Jerry Brown, Edmund Muskie, and Edward Kennedy have unsuccessfully sought the Democratic nomination, but no one suggests that religion played *any* role in their defeats. Sorensen writes that this is partly because President Kennedy conducted his "administration free of any bias toward the Catholic church or any other religion. He recommended no aid for religious schools, channeled no funds to faith based programs, created no breaches in the wall between church and state, sent no ambassador to the Vatican, and was not unduly influenced by any clergyman from Catholic or other denominations."[1] In 1965 President Johnson recommended and the Congress enacted aid for students attending religious schools. In 1984 President Reagan sent an ambassador to the Vatican, and in 2002 President George W. Bush channeled public funds to faith-based programs. Thus, virtually all the contentious issues of the 1960 campaign have become nonissues, accepted as part of the broad mainstream of U.S. society and politics. When Kennedy was elected, the Catholic ethnic group was already near full social, economic, cultural, and political incorporation. His selection both symbolized and accelerated the process toward complete incorporation and acceptance. The old Anglo-Saxon Protestant position of superordination was no more.[2]

Catholic observers of post-Kennedy America caution, however, that Kennedy's presidency did not usher in a postnativist America. In the late 1970s Father Andrew Greeley, the prolific sociologist of Catholicism in America, wrote that "anti-Catholic nativism" persisted in the United States. In *The Ugly Little Secret: Anti-Catholicism in North America*, Greeley contended that anti-Catholicism existed among the "nation's intellectual and cultural elites . . . [and] inattention, ignorance and residual bias in about one-fourth of the population."[3] Greeley's principal argument for the persistence of nativism was "the underrepresentation of Catholics in prestigious positions in society and the systematic lack of attention to that underrepresentation."[4] Greeley also questioned why people in the United States consider justice for the people of Israel extremely important, but not "justice for the Catholics in the nasty little colonial regime in the North of Ireland."[5] More recently, Massa called attention to continuing anti-Catholic bigotry, noting that the founder of Bob Jones University (which prohibited Catholics to attend) regularly referred to the Pope as the "Antichrist" and the church as the "mother of Harlots"; and that Jimmy Swaggart, then the most widely televised evangelist in the country, routinely laced his sermons with anti-Catholic messages.[6] Massa also cites as examples AIDs Coalition to Unleash Power (ACTUP), the AIDS activist group's "desecration" of St. Patrick's Cathedral in New York and the popularity of Christopher Hitchen's diatribe against Mother Teresa.[7] And "while most Americans would hardly dare voice any kind of overt prejudice against political candidates, job applicants, or potential spouses for their children on the basis of Catholic affiliation, the press and popular entertainment include regular depictions of Catholic belief and practice that are deeply offensive to practicing Catholics."[8] Massa acknowledges that much of the "reawakening of old prejudices" since Kennedy's election is related to the church hierarchy's controversial positions on abortion, homosexuality, and to the "church culture's" cover-up of sexual abuse of children by Catholic priests. Although survey data indicate that little difference exists between Protestant and Catholic opinion on abortion and gay rights, the media often portray these as primarily Catholic issues.[9] But the Catholic Church hierarchy in the United States since the emergence of these issues has become increasingly aggressive in using its power to influence voting behavior and elections rejecting, in effect, Kennedy's efforts in the 1960s to "privatize" religion. Church leadership certainly has a right—perhaps even a duty—to attempt to have its views on abortion and gay rights become public policy, but then it runs the risk that its opponents will resort to "even . . . sacrilegious, prejudicial and insulting behavior" in order to stop it, thus contributing to the revival of old prejudices.[10]

In his speech to the Houston clergy in 1960, President Kennedy said he believed in a nation where no Catholic prelate would tell a public official how to behave in the public sphere. Increasingly in the abortion controversy, some Catholic prelates have done precisely that, threatening to withhold communion from John Kerry during the 2004 election and in 2008 doing the same thing to Rhode Island Congressman Patrick Kennedy, the President's nephew, because he refused to support an antiabortion provision in the national health insurance bill.[11] One cannot know for sure how President Kennedy would have dealt with these issues. But when the first of the right and wrong, moral or social issues emerged, he embraced the privatization stance he espoused in Houston. Responding to a question asking his reaction to the Supreme Court's decision prohibiting prayer in public schools—a decision under sustained attack from Catholic and Protestant religious leaders—he said, "I think that it is important . . . that we support the Supreme Court decisions even when we may disagree with them. In addition, we have in this case a very easy remedy and that is to pray ourselves. . . . We can pray a good deal more at home, we can attend our churches with a good deal more fidelity, and we can make the true meaning of prayer much more important in the lives of all of our children. That power is very much open to us."[12] One can also perhaps get a sense of the President's likely position on abortion and gay rights by studying the views of his brother Edward. In 1964 Senator Kennedy convened a group of Catholic theologians to discuss how Catholic public officials should deal with abortion. The theologians concluded that Catholic politicians "might tolerate legislation that would permit abortions under certain circumstances if political efforts to repress this moral error led to greater perils to social peace and order."[13] Although Kennedy remained opposed to abortion rights throughout the 1960s and early 1970s, he eventually embraced the position of the theologians by supporting a right to an abortion while remaining personally adverse to the procedure. At his death he received a Catholic burial and his family released a letter he had written to the Pope shortly before his death. He wrote, "I have always tried to be a faithful Catholic."

Religious bigotry and prejudice will most likely always exist in the United States. It is the price of religious conviction and liberty, but fifty years after the election of the first Catholic president, anti-Catholic nativism does not constitute a cultural division of labor, and it is no bar to the presidency. "By the time" the Kennedy years were over Rorabaugh concludes, "the power of the white Anglo-Saxon establishment had been broken . . . the novelty of Catholics and Jews in high places gave way to the possibility of an African American. . . ."[14]

At the conclusion of Barack Obama's presidency scholars will most likely to be able to write that he conducted his administration free of any bias in favor of African Americans or any other ethnic group, that he recommended no special aid for blacks, channeled no funds to black groups or causes, created no breach between the races, and was not unduly influenced by any African American leader or civil rights group. But this constitutes the problem of this book. When John Kennedy was elected, the Catholic ethnic group was well on its way to full incorporation and needed the government to do very little for them. They had made it; they had overcome their decades of subordination in America. Government aid to their schools would be helpful, recognition of the Vatican nice, and assistance to their subordinate kin in the north of Ireland appreciated, but these were largely symbolic aspirations rather than substantive needs. When Obama was elected, blacks had urgent needs rooted in their continued race-based subordination. They had not yet overcome their centuries of oppression; race still constituted a basis for the cultural division of labor. Yet as the first black president, he could do nothing for them; he could not even appear to be doing something about their ethnic-specific needs, doing less or appearing to do less than a liberal reform president like Hillary Clinton might have been able to do. In the long run the election of the first black president in 2008 is most likely to be of little—beyond the symbolic—consequence for black America.[15] Put more starkly, at the end of his presidency, if one asks what difference the first black president made for the material well-being of African Americans, the answer will be none.[16]

As discussed in chapter 6, the persistently high rate of poverty among African Americans is the single best indicator of the continuing race-based cultural division of labor or the semi-incorporated status of the group. Yet during the Obama administration what the Thernstroms described as "the single most depressing fact about black America"—the persistently high poverty rate—saw its highest single-year increase since the government began measuring poverty in 1959.[17] The poverty rate increased among families between 2008 and 2009 from 11.5 percent to 12.5 percent, resulting in a poverty rate of 24.4 percent among blacks compared to 10.5 percent among whites.[18] The first black president, however, did not even consider proposing policies to address this depressing state of affairs. Indeed, in his first two years in office he rarely uttered the word poverty, knowing it was a code word for "blacks." Rather, his mantra was the middle class, the middle class, the middle class; code words for "whites." The imperatives of the politics of ethnic avoidance precluded even the appearance of doing (or even saying) anything about this deepening decline in the well-being of his people. In his history of how past presidents dealt with the problem of the subordination of blacks, Richard Riley concludes that the "incentive structures" of winning the office and governing made it "extremely unlikely" any president would undertake the "controversial enterprise" of trying to achieve racial equality.[19] The imperatives of the politics of ethnic avoidance made this even more so the case for the first black president.[20] Meanwhile, the ephemeral, symbolic incorporation of blacks represented by the election of Obama reinforces the already widespread myth of a "postracist" America, where any black boy can make it—even become president—if he would only abandon the ways of the ghetto and be like Obama.

The ultimate legacy and perhaps tragedy of Obama's presidency in terms of race may be discerned from his own words. Reflecting on Harold Washington's mayoralty in *Dreams* he wrote:

> I wondered whether away from the spotlight, Harold thought about those constraints. . . . Whether like any number of other black officials who now administer inner city life, he felt as trapped as those he served, an inheritor of a sad history, a part of a closed system with few moving parts, a system that was losing heat every day, dropping into low level status. I wondered whether he, too, felt a prisoner of fate.[21]

But tragedy need not be Obama's fate, because even after two terms he will still be a relatively young man with miles to go; promises to keep. In his postpresidency he might return to his roots, the grassroots, because serving as president may serve to reinforce the wisdom he expressed in *Dreams*: "Change won't come from the top; I would say change will come from a mobilized grassroots."[22] Alas, read this as fanciful.

Fancifulness aside, one has to conclude a comparison of the elections and presidencies of the first two ethnic men that it is a manifest defect in America's ethnically plural democracy that the politics of ethnic avoidance appears to be imperative. If the price of ethnic incorporation at the highest level of elective office is ignoring the legitimate needs and aspirations of one's people, then the nation's aspirations to become a truly inclusive, multiethnic democracy has a flaw.

One can only speculate what the implications of the politics of ethnic avoidance might be for the election of the first Latino, Jewish, Muslim, or Mormon president. However, we should not be surprised that Jon Huntsman, a Mormon candidate for the 2012 Republican presidential nomination told an interviewer, "I can't say I am overly religious."[23] One cannot imagine Newt Gingrich, another 2012 candidate for the Republican nomination, declaring he was not overly religious, or Richard Nixon declaring in 1960 that he was not overly Protestant, or John McCain in 2008 disavowing his whiteness.

The politics of ethnic avoidance that Kennedy and Obama practiced suggests an imperfect social contract, one where the terms and conditions are not set by all of the people but by a majority unwilling to accept the religions, cultures, needs, or aspirations, however legitimate, of minorities. The cost of the politics of ethnic avoidance for these minorities is that they are unable to participate in the selection of national leadership in a manner reflective of their interests. Thus, the politics of ethnic avoidance not only raises questions about the viability of America's multiethnic democracy, but also about the equalitarian foundations of the society.

Notes

Introduction

1. Andrew Greeley, *That Most Distressful Nation: The Taming of the American Irish* (Chicago: Quadrangle Books, 1972), p. 121.

2. Ibid., p. 123.

3. Daniel Levine, *The Irish and Irish Politicians* (Notre Dame, IN: University of Notre Dame Press, 1966), p. x.

4. Daniel P. Moynihan, "Forward" to *That Most Distressful Nation*, p. xvi.

5. Robert C. Smith, *We Have No Leaders: African Americans in the Post–Civil Rights Era* (Albany, NY: SUNY Press, 1996), p. 279.

6. Michael Dawson explores this idea of this strong tie with the concept of "linked fate." See *Behind the Mule: Race and Class in African American Politics* (Princeton, NJ: Princeton University Press, 1994), pp. 71–88.

7. See Caroline Kennedy, "A President Like My Father," *New York Times*, Jan. 27, 2008; and Jeff Zeleny "Kennedy Calls Obama New Generation of Leadership," *New York Times*, Jan. 28, 2008.

8. See as examples, Greeley, *That Most Distressful Nation*; Nathan Glazer and Daniel P. Moynihan, *Beyond the Melting Pot* (Cambridge, MA: MIT Press, 1963, 1970); Oscar Handlin, *Boston's Immigrants* (Cambridge, MA: Harvard University Press, 1979); Steven Erie, "Two Faces of Ethnic Power: Comparing the Irish and Black Experience," *Polity* 13 (1980): 261–84; Michael Hecter, *Internal Colonialism: The Celtic Fringe in British National Development, 1536–1966* (Berkeley: University of California Press, 1975); Peter Linebaugh and Marcus Rediker, *The Many-Headed Hydra: Sailors, Slaves and Commoners and the Hidden History of the Revolutionary Atlantic* (Boston: Beacon Press, 2000); Theodore Allen, *The Invention of the White Race*, vol. 1 (London: Verso, 1994); and Noel Ignatiev, *How the Irish became White* (New York: Routledge, 1995). For an in-depth examination of the relationship generally between Catholics and blacks in twentieth-century American cities including Boston and Chicago, see John T. McGreevy, *Parish Boundaries: The Catholic Encounter with Race in the Twentieth Century Urban North* (Chicago: University of Chicago Press, 1998). Finally, for a brief comparison specifically of the Kennedy and Obama

elections focusing on religion and race, see Randall Kennedy, *The Persistence of the Color Line: Racial Politics and the Obama Presidency* (New York: Pantheon, 2011), pp. 125–32.

9. Moynihan, "Forward," p. xi.

10. Greeley, *That Most Distressful Nation*, p. 41.

11. Thomas O'Connor, *The Boston Irish: A Political History* (Boston: Northwestern University Press, 1995), p. x.

Chapter 1. Understanding Ethnicity and Ethnic Incorporation in the United States

1. Michael Hechter, *Internal Colonialism: The Celtic Fringe in British National Development, 1536–1966* (Berkeley: University of California Press, 1975), p. 9.

2. Ibid, p. 270.

3. Joseph Curran, *Hibernian Green on the Silver Screen: The Irish and American Movies* (New York: Greenwood Press, 1989), p. 2. On the incorporation of the Scotch-Irish during the early years of the Republic, see Forrest McDonald, *The Presidency of Thomas Jefferson* (Lawrence: University Press of Kansas, 1976), pp. 6–12.

4. Ibid. See also Frederick Wittke, *The Irish in America* (Baton Rouge: Louisiana State University Press, 1956), pp. vi, vii; and Noel Ignatiev, *How the Irish became White* (New York: Routledge, 1995).

5. Arthur Mitchell, *JFK and His Irish Heritage* (Dublin, Ireland: Moytura Press, 1993), p. 11.

6. Phillip Converse, "Religion and Politics: The 1960 Election," in *Elections and the Political Order*, ed. Angus Campbell et al. (New York: Wiley, 1966), p. 104.

7. The persistence of Jewish solidarity or nationalism may be traced to religiosity, identification with Israel, and continuing although varying degrees of anti-Semitism. We should note that since Kennedy's election no Jew has been among the serious candidates for the presidential nomination of either major party and only one (Joe Lieberman in 2000) has been nominated for vice president. This is noteworthy because Jews are the most incorporated and politically engaged of all American ethnic groups.

8. Ignatiev, *How the Irish became White*, p. 112.

9. Matthew Holden Jr., *The Politics of the Black Nation* (New York: Chandler, 1973), pp. 209–10.

10. Wsevolod Isajiw, "Definitions of Ethnicity," *Ethnicity* 1 (1944): 111–24.

11. Max Weber, "The Ethnic Group," in *Theories of Society*, ed. Talcott Parsons (Glencoe, IL: Free Press, 1961), p. 212.

12. Robert Schermerhorn, *Comparative Ethnic Relations: A Framework for Theory and Research* (New York: Random House, 1970), p. 23.

13. See also in addition to Hechter James Nagel and Susan Olzak, "Ethnic Mobilization in New and Old States: An Extension of the Competitive Model," *Social Problems* 30 (1982): 127–43; and Robert C. Smith, "Sources of

Urban Ethnic Politics: A Comparison of Alternative Explanations," in *Research in Race and Ethnic Relations*, vol. 5, ed. Cora Bagley Marrett and Cheryl Leggon (Greenwich, CT: JAI Press, 1988), pp. 159–92.

14. Wsevolod Isajiw, "Definition and Theoretical Dimensions of Ethnicity: A Theoretical Framework," paper prepared for presentation at the Joint Canada–United States Conference on the Measurement of Ethnicity, Ottawa, Canada, April 2, 1992, p. 13.

15. Leslie Burl McLemore, "Toward a Theory of Black Politics: The Black and Ethnic Models Revisited," *Journal of Black Studies* 2 (1972): 323. See also Dianne Pinderhughes, *Race and Ethnicity in Chicago Politics: A Reexamination of Pluralist Theory* (Urbana: University of Illinois Press, 1987), p. 258; Marguerite Ross Barnett, "A Theoretical Perspective on American Racial Public Policy," in *Public Policy for the Black Community*, ed. Barnett and James Hefner (New York: Alfred Publishers, 1976), pp. 1–54; and Pierre L. Van den Berghe, *Race and Ethnicity: Essays in Comparative Sociology* (New York: Basic Books, 1970), p. 10.

16. Barnett, "A Theoretical Perspective on American Racial Public Policy," p. 14.

17. Ralph Bunche, *A Brief and Tentative Analysis of Negro Leadership*, ed. Jonathan Holloway (New York: New York University Press, 2005), p. 36.

18. Isajiw, "Definition and Dimensions of Ethnicity," p. 21.

19. Milton Gordon, "Toward a General Theory of Racial and Ethnic Group Relations," in *Ethnicity: Theory and Experience*, ed. Nathan Glazer and Daniel P. Moynihan (Cambridge, MA: Harvard University Press, 1975). Radical adherents of Marx and liberal adherents of Weber share this idea of the declining significance of ethnicity over time. On these liberal and radical "expectancies" regarding ethnicity, see Glazer and Moynihan "Introduction," in *Ethnicity: Theory and Experience*, pp. 6–7.

20. Hechter, *Internal Colonialism*, pp. 18–20.

21. E. Digby Baltzell, *The Protestant Establishment: Aristocracy and Caste in America* (New York: Vintage Books, 1964), p. 12.

22. William Domhoff, *The Power Elite and the State* (New York: Aldine de Gruyter, 1990), p. 113.

23. Hechter, *Internal Colonialism*, p. 42.

24. Ibid., pp. xiv–xvi.

25. Robert Dahl, *Who Governs? Democracy and Power in an American City* (New Haven, CT: Yale University Press, 1961).

26. Ibid., p. 35.

27. Ibid., pp. 35–36.

28. The Germans took eighty years to move from stage one to three, the "Russians" (largely Jews) sixty, and the Italians seventy. By 1950 all ethnic groups in New Haven were fully incorporated except blacks.

29. Martin Kilson, "Political Change in the Negro Ghetto, 1900–1940s," in *Key Issues in the Afro-American Experience*, ed. Nathan Huggins, Martin Kilson, and Daniel Fox (New York: Harcourt Brace Jovanovich, 1971), p. 182.

30. Mary Summers and Phillip Klinkner, "The Election of John Daniels as Mayor of New Haven," *PS: Political Science and Politics* 23 (1990): 142–44.

31. Ibid., p. 144.

Chapter 2. The Subordination of Irish Catholics and African Americans

1. Michael Hechter, *Internal Colonialism: The Celtic Fringe in British National Development, 1536–1966* (Berkeley: University of California Press, 1975), p. 73.

2. David Brion Davis, *Problem of Slavery in Western Culture* (Ithaca, NY: Cornell University Press, 1966), pp. 48–49.

3. Hechter, *Internal Colonialism*, pp. xvi–xvii.

4. Quoted in Cecil Woodham-Smith, *The Great Hunger: Ireland 1845–1849* (New York: Harper and Row, 1962), p. 23.

5. Theodore Allen explicitly compares the Penal Laws and the Slave Codes with respect to property, civil rights, criminalization of literacy, and the displacement of family rights. See *The Invention of the White Race* (New York: Verso, 1994), pp. 82–90.

6. Edward Levine, *The Irish and the Irish Politician* (Notre Dame, IN: University of Notre Dame Press, 1966), p. 16.

7. Ibid.

8. Noel Ignatiev, *How the Irish became White* (New York: Routledge, 1995), p. 35.

9. Woodham-Smith, *The Great Hunger.* In 1841 the population of Ireland, Woodham-Smith estimates, "was 8,175,124; in 1851 after the famine it had dropped to 6,552,385. The census commissioners calculated that at the normal rate of increase, the total should have been 9,018,799, so that a loss of at least 2-1/2 million persons had taken place. Between 1846 and 1851 nearly a million persons emigrated, and it therefore appears that roughly about a million and a half perished during the famine of hunger and of diseases brought on by hunger and fever" (p. 411).

10. Ignatiev, *How the Irish Became White*, p. 140. See also Woodham-Smith, *The Great Hunger*, p. 75.

11. Carl Wittke, *The Irish in America* (Baton Rouge: Louisiana State University Press, 1956), p. 8.

12. Woodham-Smith, *The Great Hunger*, p. 407.

13. Wittke, *The Irish in America*, pp. 23–24.

14. Richard Whalen, *The Founding Father: The Story of Joseph P. Kennedy* (New York: American Library, 1964), p. 7.

15. Ibid., p. 8.

16. Tip O'Neill with William Novak, *Man of the House: The Life and Political Memoirs of Speaker O'Neill* (New York: Random House, 1989), p. 7.

17. Adam Hochshild, *King Leopold's Ghost: A Story of Greed, Terror and Heroism in Colonial Africa* (New York: Mariner, 1998), p. 233.

18. Ibid., p. 87. In the United States there was a "conspiracy of silence" about Leopold's crimes. The administrations tacitly supported the regime; the newspapers generally did not report the activities of the regime; little was said in Congress; and major U.S. businessmen (including John D. Rockefeller and

J. P. Morgan) had investments in the Congo. See Stefan Heyn's "Introduction" to Mark Twain's *King Leopold's Soliloquy* (New York: Seven Seas Books, 1970), pp. 12–13. Although the U.S. media generally ignored Twain's 1903 pamphlet, it was a devastating attack on what he called Leopold's "Monument of Skulls." African American leaders also attempted to call attention to the atrocities. See Booker T. Washington, "Cruelty in the Congo," *Outlook* 78 (1904): 375–77; and John Hope Franklin, *George Washington Williams* (Chicago: University of Chicago 1985), pp. 201–21. Williams, the historian and diplomat, visited the Congo and was appalled by what he saw. His open letter to the King protesting the treatment of the Congolese people and his report to President Benjamin Harrison on the subject are reprinted in Franklin's *George Washington Williams.*

19. Ibid., p. 122.

20. Ibid., p. 165.

21. Ibid., p. 283.The British colonialization of Kenya followed the pattern employed in Ireland and North America: expropriation of native lands, forced labor, cultural and religious subjugation, and a rigid order of apartheid based on racism and a virulent ideology of Anglo-Saxon superiority. However, once the Mau Mau resistance emerged in the 1950s, Caroline Elkins writes that the process began to resemble Leopold's Congo, including a "campaign of terror, dehumanizing torture and genocide" and the detention of "some 1.5 million people, or nearly the entire Kikuyu population." See *The Imperial Reckoning: The Untold Story of Britain's Gulag in Kenya* (New York: Holt, 2005), pp. xiv, 90. In his memoir Obama writes that his grandfather—Hussein Onyango Obama—was among the detained, returning home a beaten and broken man. See *Dreams of My Father* (New York: Crown, 1995), pp. 380–81.

22. Ibid., p. 11.

23. Ibid., p. 268.

24. Ignatiev, *How the Irish became White.*

25. John Higham, *Strangers in the Land: Patterns of American Nativism, 1860–1925* (New Brunswick, NJ: Rutgers University Press, 1955, 1968), p. 5. In addition to anti-Catholicism Higham identified the anti-(foreign) radical and "Anglo-Saxonism" as the two other basic patterns of nativism.

26. Thomas Carty, *A Catholic in the White House? Religion, Politics and John F. Kennedy's Campaign* (New York: Palgrave Macmillan, 2004), p. 13.

27. Lawrence Fuchs, *John F. Kennedy and American Catholicism* (New York: Meredith Press, 1967), p. 34.

28. Mark S. Massa, *Anti-Catholicism in America: The Last Acceptable Prejudice* (New York: Crossroads Publishing, 2003), p. 19.

29. Fuchs, *John F. Kennedy and American Catholicism*, p. 34. Levine avers that many of these colonial laws were "very similar to the penal codes." See *The Irish and the Irish Politician*, p. 61.

30. Fuchs, *John F. Kennedy and American Catholicism*, p. 37.

31. Ibid., p. 30.

32. Wittke, *The Irish in America*, p. 120.

33. Massa, *Anti-Catholicism in America.*

34. William Shannon, *The American Irish: A Political and Social Portrait* (Amherst: University of Massachusetts Press, 1989), p. 25.

35. Joseph Curran, *Hibernian Green on the Silver Screen: The Irish in American Movies* (New York: Greenwood Press, 1989), p. 5.

36. Higham, *Strangers in the Land*, p. 29.

37. Massa, *Anti-Catholicism in America*, p. 28.

38. Wittke, *The Irish in America*, p. 122.

39. For a detailed study of the APA see Donald Kinzer, *An Episode in Anti-Catholicism: The American Protective Association* (Seattle: University of Washington Press, 1964).

40. Higham, *Strangers in the Land*, p. 291. See also Massa, *Anti-Catholicism in America*, p. 32; and Nancy MacLean, *Behind the Mask of Chivalry: The Making of the Second Ku Klux Klan* (New York: Oxford University Press, 1994).

41. Ibid., p. 132.

42. Ibid.

43. Quoted in Leon Kamin, *The Science and Politics of IQ* (Potomac, MD: Lawrence Erlbaum, 1974), pp. 350–51.

44. Senator John F. Kennedy wrote a book calling for repeal or liberalization of the 1924 law. See *A Nation of Immigrants* (New York: Harper and Row, 1958, 1964). Although because President Kennedy did not make immigration reform a legislative priority, in 1965 the 1924 act was repealed. The reforms of 1965 ending racism in immigration law came about partly as a result of the civil rights movement. As Briggs writes, "It was the passage of the Civil Rights Act of 1964 . . . that created the national climate needed to legislatively end the discriminatory national origins system the following year with the adoption of the Immigration Act of 1965." See Vernon Griggs, "The Economic Well Being of Black Americans: The Overarching Influence of U.S. Immigration Policies," in *The Impact of Immigration on African Americans*, ed. Steven Shulman (New Brunswick, NJ: Transaction, 2004), p. 12.

45. In addition to the nativists, Okrent indicates racists and white supremacists were part of the broad prohibition coalition. He writes that in many southern states the "prohibition laws [were] often congenitally linked to Jim Crow voting laws." In the South and elsewhere images were constructed of the black man "with a bottle of whiskey in one hand and a ballot in the other . . . intensifying the constant threat of plunder and rape." See Daniel Okrent, *Last Call: The Rise and Fall of Prohibition* (New York: Scribner, 2010), pp. 43, 44.

46. James Melton, *Bullwhip Days: The Slaves Remember* (New York: Widenfeld Nickerson, 1988), p. xii.

47. Kenneth Stamp, *The Peculiar Institution: Slavery in the Ante-Bellum South* (New York: Vintage Books, 1965).

48. W. E. B. Du Bois, "Introduction" by Saidiya Hartman, *The Suppression of the African Slave Trade to the United States of America, 1638–1870* (New York: Oxford University Press, 2007).

49. Philip Curtin, *The Atlantic Slave Trade: A Census* (Madison: University of Wisconsin Press, 1969).

50. Stamp, *The Peculiar Institution*, p. 28.

51. Melton, *Bullwhip Days*, p. 59

52. W. E. B. Du Bois, "Introduction" by E. Digby Baltzell, *The Philadelphia Negro: A Social Study* (New York: Schocken Books, 1967).

53. Theodore Hershberg, Alan Burnstein, Eugene Erickson, Stephanie Greenberg, and William Yancey, "A Tale of Three Cities: Blacks and Immigrants in Philadelphia, 1850–1880, 1930 and 1970," in *Annals of the American Academy of Political and Social Science* 441 (1979):55–81.

54. Ignatiev, *How the Irish became White*, p. 125.

55. Ibid., p. 136.

56. Curran, *Hibernian Green*, p. 8. See also Thomas O'Connor, *The Boston Irish: A Political History* (Boston: Northeastern University Press, 1995), pp. 82–92. The Catholic Church did not take an official position on the enslavement of Africans but, according to Wittke, under Catholic doctrine "slavery was an evil to be borne, but not extended or expanded; the fugitive slave law was to be obeyed out of respect for property rights but the African slave trade was to be condemned and remain closed." *The Irish in America*, p. 129. In his 1845 visit, Irish nationalists welcomed Frederick Douglass as a kindred spirit in resistance to oppression, and he developed an especially close relationship with Daniel O'Connell, a leading figure in the Irish liberation movement. See Lee Jenkins, "Beyond the Pale: Frederick Douglass in Cork," *Irish Review* 24 (1999): pp. 29–47.

57. See the discussion of Lincoln's support for the first Thirteenth Amendment passed by Congress on the eve of the Civil War. This amendment would have prohibited any future amendment to the Constitution interfering with slavery in any state where it then existed. Adopted by Congress in order to persuade the southern states to remain in the Union, it was not ratified because most southern states had already seceded. Mark Brandon, "The 'Original' Thirteenth Amendment and the Limits of Formal Constitutional Change," in *Responding to Imperfection: The Theory and Practice of Constitutional Amendment*, ed. Sanford Levinson (Princeton, NJ: Princeton University Press, 1995). Lincoln's "preliminary" Emancipation Proclamation issued on September 22, 1862, told the southern states that if they returned to the union by January 1, 1863, he would ask Congress to compensate them if they promised to gradually free the enslaved.

58. Abraham Lincoln, "Letter to Albert C. Hodges, April 4, 1864," in *Classics of the American Presidency*, ed. Harry Bailey (Oak Park, IL: Moore Publishing, 1980), p. 34.

59. Hofstadter and the *London Spectator* are quoted from Robert C. Smith, "Emancipation Proclamation," in *Encyclopedia of African American Politics* (New York: Facts on File, 2003), p. 129.

60. W. E. B. Du Bois, *Black Reconstruction* (New York: Atheneum, 1935, 1969), p. 312.

61. Patricia Sullivan, *Lift Every Voice: The* NAACP *and the Making of the Civil Rights Movement* (New York: Free Press, 2009).

62. President Lyndon B. Johnson's Commencement Address at Howard University, June 4, 1965, as reprinted in Ira Katznelson, *When Affirmative Action Was White* (New York: Norton, 2005), p. 175.

63. Robert C. Smith, *Conservatism and Racism, and Why in America They Are the Same* (Albany, NY: SUNY Press, 2010).

Chapter 3. Identity, Consciousness, Solidarity, and Culture: Irish Catholics and African Americans

1. Here I am slightly modifying William Gamson's concept of solidary groups. See "Stable Unrepresentation in American Society," *The American Behaviorist* 12 (1968): 15–21. Although he does not refer to Gamson, Michael Dawson's use of the concept "linked fate" to explain black ethnic solidarity in the post–civil rights era is related to Gamson's concept. See *Beyond the Mule: Race and Class in African American Politics* (Princeton, NJ: Princeton University Press, 1994), pp. 71–88.

2. In its extreme, "institutional completeness" would be "when an ethnic community could perform all the services required by its members. Members would never have to make use of native institutions for the satisfaction of any of their needs, such as education, work, food and clothing, medical care, or social assistance." Raymond Briton, "Institutional Completeness of Ethnic Communities and the Personal Relations of Immigrants," in *The Ethnic Factor in American Politics*, ed. Brett Hawkins and Robert Lorinskas (Columbus, OH: Merrill, 1970).

3. Oscar Handlin, *Boston's Immigrants: A Study in Acculturation* (Cambridge, MA: Harvard University Press, 1959), p. 175.

4. Ibid., p. 176.

5. August Meier, *Negro Thought in America, 1880–1915* (Ann Arbor: University of Michigan Press, 1968), pp. 13–14.

6. Handlin, *Boston's Immigrants*, p. 176.

7. Ibid., p. 6.

8. These terms are from Matthew Holden Jr., *The Politics of the Black "Nation"* (New York: Chandler, 1973), pp. 26–34.

9. Ibid., p. 17.

10. Carl Wittke, *The Irish in America* (Baton Rouge, Louisiana State University Press, 1956), p. 89.

11. Ibid., p. 25; E. Franklin Frazier, *The Negro Church in America* (New York: Schocken Books, 1964), p. 43.

12. Wittke, *The Irish in America*, p. 103; William Shannon, *The American Irish: A Political and Social Portrait* (Amherst: University of Massachusetts Press, 1989), p. 9; and Thomas O'Connor, *The Boston Irish: A Political History* (Boston: Northeastern University Press, 1995), p. 22.

13. Holden, *The Politics of the Black "Nation,"* p. 21.

14. Edward Levine, *The Irish and the Irish Politician* (Notre Dame, IN: University of Notre Dame Press, 1966), p. 139. On the centrality of politics to the Catholic Irish experience, see also Nathan Glazer and Daniel P. Moynihan, *Beyond the Melting Pot* (Cambridge, MA: MIT Press, 1963, 1970), p. 139; and Wittke, *The Irish in America*, chap. 10, "The Lure of Politics."

15. On the lure of politics see Eric Foner, *Reconstruction: America's Unfinished Revolution, 1863–1877* (New York: Harper and Row, 1988), pp. 282, 291; and Robert Dahl, *Who Governs* (New Haven, CT: Yale University Press, 1961), pp. 294–95.

16. Dahl, *Who Governs*; Elmer Cornwell, "Party Absorption of Ethnic Groups," *Social Forces* 38 (1960): 205–10.

17. Steven Eric writes, "The economic disadvantages suffered by the Irish could not be readily overcome by politics, they may have even aggravated them. Celtic economic success came after the machine's heyday." See *Rainbow's End: Irish Americans and the Dilemmas of Urban Machine Politics* (Berkeley: University of California Press, 1988), p. 244.

18. Doris Kearns Goodwin, *The Fitzgeralds and Kennedys* (New York: Simon and Schuster, 1987), p. 30.

19. Ibid., p. 62.

20. Paul Blanchard, *American Freedom and Catholic Power* (Boston: Beacon Press, 1958), p. 82.

21. Levine, *The Irish and Irish Politicians*, p. 84.

22. Wittke, *The Irish in America*, p. 48; O'Connor, *The Boston Irish*, p. 65; and Richard Whalen, *The Founding Father: The Story of Joseph P. Kennedy* (New York: New American Library, 1964), p. 14.

23. O'Connor, *The Boston Irish*, p. 64.

24. Glazer and Moynihan, *Beyond the Melting Pot*, p. 257. Moynihan's career itself was affected by drink. See Godfrey Hodgson, *The Gentleman from New York: A Biography of Daniel Patrick Moynihan* (Boston: Houghton Mifflin, 2000), pp. 293–94.

25. In African American culture, see Ulf Hannerz, *Soulside: Studies in Ghetto Culture and Community* (New York: Columbia University Press, 1969). A high rate of alcohol consumption characterizes native cultures in the United States.

26. Joseph Curran, *Hibernian Green on the Silver Screen: The Irish in American Movies* (New York: Greenwood Press, 1995), p. 6. See also O'Connor, *The Boston Irish*, pp. 64–65.

27. Levine, *The Irish and Irish Politicians*, p. 103.

28. Handlin, *Boston's Immigrants*, p. 222.

29. Randall Kennedy, *Sellout: The Politics of Racial Betrayal* (New York: Pantheon, 2008), p. 3.

30. Sinclair Drake and Horace Cayton, *Black Metropolis* (New York: Harcourt Brace, 1945), pp. 720–22.

31. Holden, *The Politics of the Black "Nation,"* pp. 27–28; and Gunnar Myrdal, *An American Dilemma: The Negro Problem and Modern Democracy* (New York: Harper and Row, 1944, 1962), p. 697.

32. Handlin, *Boston Immigrants*, p. 177.

33. Kearns-Goodwin, *The Fitzgeralds and Kennedys*, p. 666.

34. Ibid. p. 677; Kearns-Goodwin reports that letters from priests and nuns from throughout the country were sent to the Kennedys commiserating with them on their "great misfortune" (p. 679).

35. Arthur Mitchell, *JFK and His Irish Heritage* (Dublin, Ireland: Moytura Press, 1993), p. 39.

36. Randall Kennedy, *Interracial Intimacies: Sex, Marriage, Identity and Adoption* (New York: Pantheon, 2003).

37. Donald McCormack, "Stokely Carmichael and Pan Africanism: Back to Black Power," *Journal of Politics* 35 (1973), pp. 386–409; Paul Peterson, "Organizational Imperatives and Ideological Change: The Case of Black Power," *Urban Affairs Quarterly* 14 (1979), pp. 465–84; and Robert C. Smith, "Black Power and the Transformation from Protest to Politics," *Political Science Quarterly* 96 (1981): 431–45. For a history see Peniel Joseph, *Waiting 'til the Midnight Hour: A Narrative History of Black Power* (New York: Henry Holt, 2006). Politically, between 1966 and the early 1970s, the black power movement evolved into two factions: a radical revolutionary one that challenged capitalism, American imperialism as well as racism and white supremacy, and a reformist faction that challenged only racism and white supremacy. The radical revolutionary faction succumbed to factionalism, utopianism, and state repression. The reformist, ethnic group pluralism faction was incorporated.

38. Stokely Carmichael and Charles Hamilton, *Black Power: Politics of Liberation in America* (New York: Vintage Books, 1967), p. 44.

39. Paul Hagner and John Pierce, "Racial Differences in Political Conceptualization," *Western Political Quarterly* 37 (1984): 215.

40. Robert Washington, *The Ideologies of African American Literature: From the Harlem Renaissance to the Black Nationalist Revolt* (Lanham, MD: Rowman and Littlefield, 2001), chap. 5.

41. Joel Aberbach and Jack Walker, "The Meaning of Black Power: A Comparison of White and Black Interpretations of a Political Slogan," *American Political Science Review* 64 (1970): 380.

42. Ronald Walters, "Barack Obama and the Politics of Blackness," *Journal of Black Studies* 38 (2007): 27.

Chapter 4. Boston, Chicago, and the Rise of Kennedy and Obama

1. Stephan Thernstrom, *The Other Bostonians: Poverty and Progress in the American Metropolis, 1880–1970* (Cambridge, MA: Harvard University Press, 1973), p. 5; and Thomas O'Connor, *The Boston Irish: A Political History* (Boston: Northeastern University Press, 1995), p. 5.

2. Oscar Handlin, *Boston's Immigrants: A Study in Acculturation* (Cambridge, MA: Harvard University Press, 1979), p. 70.

3. Ibid.

4. Ibid.

5. Ibid., p. 161.

6. Tip O'Neill with William Novak, *The Life and Political Memoir of Speaker Tip O'Neill* (New York: Random House, 1987), p. 8.

7. Nancy Lusignan Schultz, *Fire and Roses: The Burning of the Charlestown Convent* (New York: Free Press, 2000), p. 1.

8. Ibid., p. 166.

9. O'Neill, *The Life and Political Memoir*, p. 8.

10. Thernstrom, *The Other Bostonians*, pp. 161–68.

11. Ibid., p. 187.

12. Ibid., p. 194.

13. Ibid.

14. Ibid., p. 218.

15. Ibid.

16. Partly because of the violence in 1974 surrounding the desegregation of Boston's schools (when riot police were dispatched to largely Catholic Irish South Boston), the city is viewed today as one of the least hospitable to African Americans. See Associated Press, "At 100, Boston NAACP Confronts City's Mixed Past," *New York Times*, Jan. 15, 2011. Some scholars have suggested that historic Catholic Irish resentment of their "Yankee Overlords" who in their view were, as they always had, oppressing the Irish while catering to the blacks to some extent fueled the desegregation conflict. See Steven J. L. Taylor, *Desegregation in Boston and Buffalo: The Influence of Local Leaders* (Albany, NY: SUNY Press, 1998), pp. 172–73; and Ronald Formisano, *Boston against Busing: Race, Class and Ethnicity in the 1960s and 1970s* (Chapel Hill: University of North Carolina Press, 1991), p. 10.

17. Peter Eisinger, *The Politics of Displacement: Racial and Ethnic Transition in Three American Cities* (New York: Academic Press, 1980), p. 33.

18. Ibid., p. 30.

19. Ibid., p. 36.

20. Ibid.

21. Doris Kearns-Goodwin, *The Fitzgeralds and Kennedys* (New York: Simon and Schuster, 1987), p. 230.

22. William Shannon, *The American Irish: A Political and Social Portrait* (Amherst: University of Massachusetts Press, 1989), p. 214–15.

23. Ibid., p. 229.

24. Richard Whalen, *The Founding Father: The Story of Joseph P. Kennedy* (New York: New American Library, 1964), p. 32. For a brilliantly written account of Curley's career see Jack Beatty, *The Rascal King: The Life and Times of James Michael Curley, 1874–1958* (Reading, MA: Addison-Wesley, 1993).

25. O'Neill, *The Life and Political Memoir*, p. 28.

26. Whalen, *The Founding Father*, p. 422.

27. Eisinger, *The Politics of Displacement*, p. 45.

28. Ibid., p. 42. Lodge's views are indicative of what Okrent calls the "race hatred" that characterized Anglo-Saxon elite attitudes toward the Catholic Irish. Another indicator: In 1882 Theodore Roosevelt referred to his Catholic Irish colleagues in the New York state legislature as a "stupid, sodden, vicious lot, most of them being equally deficient in brains and virtue, . . . a low, venal, corrupt and unintelligent brute." Daniel Okrent, *Last Call: The Rise and Fall of Prohibition* (New York: Scribner, 2010), p. 46.

29. Ibid.

30. Kearns-Goodwin, *The Fitzgeralds and Kennedys*, p. 407.

31. In 1919 Fitzgerald was expelled from the House for vote fraud in the 1918 election, but the circumstances surrounding the expulsion remain obscure. See Seymour Hersh, *The Dark Side of Camelot* (Boston: Little, Brown, 1997), pp. 36–37; Victor Lasky, *J.F.K.: The Man and the Myth* (New York: Macmillan, 1963), p. 63; and John Henry Cutler, *"Honey Fitz": Three Steps to the White House: The Colorful Life and Times of John F. Fitzgerald* (Indianapolis: Bobbs-Merrill, 1962), pp. 225–29.

32. Cutler, "*Honey Fitz,*" pp. 63–64.

33. Whalen, *The Founding Father*, p. 31.

34. Ibid.

35. Kearns-Goodwin, *The Fitzgeralds and Kennedys*, p. 104.

36. Ibid., p. 504.

37. Ibid., p. 504.

38. Ibid., p. 104.

39. Ibid., p. 395. Years later Kennedy was still angry: "those narrow minded bigoted sons of bitches barred me because I was Irish Catholic and son of a barkeep. You can go to Harvard and it doesn't mean a damned thing. The only thing these people understand is money." Quoted in Thomas Reeves, *A Question of Character: A Life of John F. Kennedy* (New York: Free Press, 1991), p. 28.

40. Ibid.

41. Ibid., p. 302.

42. Whalen, *The Founding Father*, p. 166.

43. Ibid.

44. Ibid., p. 391.

45. Ibid.

46. Hersh, *The Dark Side of Camelot*, p. 71. Nigel Hamilton writes, "For years the ex-ambassador had bribed a veritable corps of Washington, New York and Boston newspapers with lavish gifts to write up the Kennedys." See *JFK: Restless Youth* (New York: Random House, 1992), p. 663.

47. Kearns-Goodwin, *The Fitzgeralds and Kennedys*, p. 498.

48. Whalen, *The Founding Father*, p. 203.

49. Robert Dallek, *An Unfinished Life: John F. Kennedy, 1917–1963* (Boston: Little, Brown, 2003), p. 235. In 1944 Joe Kennedy reportedly told Truman, "Harry, what are you doing campaigning for that crippled son of bitch that killed my son Joe. Truman was stunned by Kennedy's rancor and never forgot it." See Hamilton, *JFK: Reckless Youth*, p. 669.

50. Lasky, *J.F.K.*, p. 395.

51. Whalen, *The Founding Father*, chaps. 15–16.

52. Kearns-Goodwin, *The Fitzgeralds and Kennedys*, p. 530.

53. Hersh, *The Dark Side of Camelot*, p. 66.

54. Several students of the Kennedy family—journalists and academics—have concluded that Joe Kennedy was probably a bootlegger during prohibition. But Okrent's recent and comprehensive study of prohibition concludes that the rumors and gossip notwithstanding, "there is really no reason to believe he was one." Even the reputable investigators, Okrent concludes, have been unable to

find evidence sufficient to conclude that Kennedy was involved in the illegal liquor trade. See *Last Call*, pp. 368, 370–71.

55. C. Wright Mills, *The Power Elite* (New York: Oxford, 1956), p. 60.

56. Ibid., p. 52.

57. Whalen, *The Founding Father*, p. 166.

58. Ibid., p. 392.

59. Ibid.

60. Ibid., p. 135.

61. Quoted in Garry Wills, *The Kennedy Imprisonment: A Meditation on Power* (New York: Pocket Books, 1982), p. 134.

62. Ibid. Reading the book more than a half century later, I found it an intelligently written, well-documented inquiry, and one that should have easily satisfied the requirements for even a graduate thesis at Harvard.

63. Ibid.

64. While Kennedy was undoubtedly a hero and acted with extraordinary courage during the PT 109 incident, his behavior as commander was clearly negligent and reckless and likely precipitated the incident. See Hamilton, *JFK: Restless Youth*, pp. 528–34; and Thomas Reeves, *A Question of Character: A Life of John F. Kennedy* (New York: Free Press, 1991), pp. 64, 68.

65. Hamilton even suggests that Joe Kennedy used his influence to get his son assigned to a PT boat because he thought it would be good for his presidential aspirations. See *JFK: Restless Youth*, pp. 652–53.

66. Whalen writes, "It was understood the candidate . . . would make the final decisions but the alternatives set before him were usually framed by his father's handpicked brain trust," *The Founding Father*, p. 422.

67. Hamilton and Dallek estimate at least $250,000, which Dallek qualifies by noting, "The precise amount will never be known since so much of it was handed out in cash." See Hamilton, *JFK: Reckless Youth*, p. 754; and Dallek, *An Unfinished Life*, p. 130.

68. Hamilton, *JFK: Reckless Youth*, p. 674.

69. Dallek, *An Unfinished Life*, p. 172. Always sensitive about the role of his father's money in his successes, years later John Kennedy told a reporter, "people say Kennedy bought the elections. Kennedy could never have been elected if his father had not been a millionaire. Well, it wasn't the Kennedy name and the Kennedy money that won that election. I beat Lodge because I hustled for three years. I worked for what I got." Quoted in Whalen, *The Founding Father*, p. 419.

70. Cutler, "*Honey Fitz*," p. 309.

71. Ibid., p. 413.

72. Ibid.

73. Whalen, *The Founding Father*, p. 422. The saga of the Lodges and Kennedys continued. In 1960 Nixon's running mate was Henry Cabot Lodge; in 1962 Edward Kennedy ran to succeed his brother in the Senate against George Lodge, the son of Henry Cabot; and in 1962 President Kennedy appointed Henry Cabot ambassador to South Vietnam.

74. Quoted from Doris Kearns Goodwin, *A Team of Rivals: The Political Genius of Abraham Lincoln* (New York: Simon & Schuster, 2005), p. 204.

75. Alan Spear, *Black Chicago: The Making of a Ghetto, 1890–1920* (Chicago: University of Chicago Press, 1967).

76. Ibid., p. 11.

77. As in Philadelphia, Irish Catholic hooligans were often in the forefront of the mob violence against the African American community, most likely including a teenage Richard J. Daley. See Edward McClelland, *Young Mr. Obama: Chicago and the Making of a Black President* (New York: Bloomsbury Press, 2010), pp. 28–29.

78. Ibid., p. 26. Diane Pinderhughes writes, "For much of Chicago's history . . . blacks were highly segregated, restricted from home ownership, overcrowded, economically disadvantaged, overcharged for housing, and subject to violent attack by mobs"; see *Race and Ethnicity in Chicago: A Reexamination of Pluralist Theory* (Urbana: University of Illinois Press, 1987), p. 35.

79. Studs Terkel, "Foreword," in *Bridges of Memory: Chicago's First Wave of Black Migration*, by Timuel Black (Evanston, IL: Northwestern University Press, 2003), p. ix. Black's memoir is a moving account of early migrants to Chicago. See also James Grossman, *Land of Hope: Chicago, Black Southerners and the Great Migration* (Chicago: University of Chicago Press, 1989).

80. David Levering Lewis, *When Harlem Was in Vogue* (New York: Oxford, 1981), p. 216.

81. Ibid., pp. 171–72. See also Mike Rowe, *Breakdown* (New York: Drake Publishers, 1975); and for an evocative account of the incorporation and commodification of the blues in contemporary Chicago, see David Grazian, *Blue Chicago: The Search for Authenticity in Urban Blues* (Chicago: University of Chicago Press, 2003).

82. St. Clair Drake and Horace Cayton, *Black Metropolis: A Study of Negro Life in a Northern City* (Chicago: University of Chicago Press, 1945, 1993), p. 412.

83. Harold Gosnell, *Negro Politicians: The Rise of Negro Politics in Chicago* (Chicago: University of Chicago Press, 1967), p. 2. Adam Green, in his study of postwar Chicago, indicates how the commercialization of the city's music, the influence of *Ebony* and *Jet* magazines (founded by Chicago's John Johnson), and the mobilization of local and national outrage after the brutal Mississippi murder of the city's native son Emmett Till shaped "Chicago's pivotal role" in the national articulation of ideas of racial community and solidarity. See *Selling the Race: Culture, Community and Black Chicago, 1940–1955* (Chicago: University of Chicago Press, 2007). On Chicago as an incubator of modern black politics see also James Lance Taylor, *Black Nationalism in the United States: From Malcolm X to Barack Obama* (Boulder, CO: Lynne Rienner, 2011), chap. 9.

84. Richard Wright, "Introduction" to *Black Metropolis*, by Drake and Cayton, p. viii.

85. James Ralph Jr., *Northern Protest: Martin Luther King, Jr., Chicago and the Civil Rights Movement* (Cambridge, MA: Harvard University Press, 1993).

86. Martin Dupuis and Keith Boeckelman, *Barack Obama and the New Face of American Politics* (Westport, CT: Praeger, 2008), p. 78. See also Pin-

derhughes, *Race and Ethnicity in Chicago*, p. 60. For a somewhat personal narrative history of black politics in Chicago from the earliest days until the Harold Washington years, see Dempsey Travis, *An Autobiography of Black Politics* (Chicago: Urban Research Service, 1987).

87. William Grimshaw, *Bitter Fruit: Black Politics and the Chicago Machine, 1931–1990* (Chicago: University of Chicago Press, 1992), p. 117.

88. The Catholic Irish in Chicago have not been studied as extensively as in Boston, but see Lawrence McCaffery et al., *The Irish in Chicago* (Urbana: University of Illinois Press, 1990).

89. Milton Rakove, *Don't Make No Waves, Don't Back No Losers* (Bloomington: Indiana University Press, 1975), p. 33.

90. Ibid.

91. Ibid., pp. 32–33.

92. Ibid., p. 45.

93. Ibid., p. 57.

94. Grimshaw, *Bitter Fruit*, p. 118.

95. Adam Cohen and Elizabeth Taylor present a thorough and engaging account of Daley's life and career with extensive focus on his religiosity and racial attitudes in *American Pharaoh: Mayor Richard J. Daley and His Battle for Chicago and the Nation* (Boston: Little, Brown, 2000).

96. Grimshaw, *Bitter Fruit*, p. 20.

97. For alternative perspectives on urban machines, see Harold Gosnell, *Machine Politics: Chicago Model* (Chicago: University of Chicago Press, 1937); Martin Shafter, "The Emergence of the Political Machine: An Alternative View," in *Theoretical Perspectives on Urban Politics*, ed. Willis Hawley et al. (Englewood Cliffs, NJ: Prentice-Hall, 1976); and Theodore Lowi, "Machine Politics: Old and New," *Public Interest* 9 (1967): 83–92.

98. Pinderhughes, *Race and Ethnicity in Chicago*, p. 9.

99. Ibid., pp. 248–49.

100. Marshall Frady, *Jesse: The Life and Pilgrimage of Jesse Jackson* (New York: Random House, 1996), p. 189.

101. Ibid., pp. 192–93.

102. Ibid., p. 299.

103. Quoted in Robert C. Smith, "The Black Congressional Delegation," *Western Political Quarterly* 34 (1981): 221. The 1969 murder of Illinois Black Panther leaders Fred Hampton and Mark Clark by the Chicago police, and the Daley and the machine's cover-up also eroded support for the machine in the black community.

104. Grimshaw, *Bitter Fruit*, p. 151.

105. Ibid., p. 167.

106. Ibid., p. 173. See also Abdul Alkalimat and Doug Gills, "Black Power vs. Racism," in *The New Black Vote*, ed. Rod Bush (San Francisco: Synthesis Publications, 1984).

107. Ibid., p. 164.

108. The 1983 Chicago mayoral election is one of the most thoroughly studied in urban history. In addition to the works by Pinderhughes, Grimshaw,

and Alkalimat and Gill cited earlier, see Gary Rivlin, *Fire on the Prairie: Chicago's Harold Washington and the Politics of Race* (New York: Henry Holt, 1992); and Paul Kleppner, *Chicago: The Making of a Black Mayor* (DeKalb: Northern Illinois University Press, 1985).

109. Grimshaw, *Bitter Fruit.*

110. Ibid., p. 220

111. Paul Street, *Barack Obama and the Future of American Politics* (Boulder, CO: Paradigm Publishers, 2009), p. 79

112. Barack Obama, *Dreams from My Father* (New York: Crown, 1995), p. 212. Obama in 2008 told the Congressional Black Caucus as he was receiving its Harold Washington award that he "originally moved to Chicago in part because of the inspiration of Mayor Washington's campaign." Quoted in McClelland, *Young Mr. Obama*, p. 26.

113. Robert Starks and Michael Preston, "The Political Legacy of Harold Washington," *National Political Science Review*, 2 (1990): 164. Twenty years later Starks writes, "The most important problem facing Black people in Chicago since the death of Harold Washington is the lack of unity within the leadership and the factionalism that allowed Mayor Daley to retain control for the last 21 years. Mayor Daley was able to play the Black middle class against the Black poor, the Black elected officials were co–opted and made to play by the rules laid down by the mayor, and the Black ministers were brought into the Daley camp with the promise of access and offers of city land and grants" (Personal communication, Oct. 17, 2010). In the 2011 election to succeed Daley, the former Congressman and Obama White House chief of staff Rahm Emanuel was easily elected. Carol Mosley Braun, the African American candidate, received less than 10 percent of the vote.

114. "Interview: Jesse Jackson," *Playboy*, July 1984, p. 74.

115. Project for Excellence in Journalism, "Character and the Primaries of 2008: What Were the Media Narratives about the Candidates during the Primary Season," (Boston, MA: Joan Shorenstein Center for the Press and Politics, Harvard University, 2008), pp. 6–7.

116. This is the title of Liz Mundy's article dealing mainly with Obama's career at Harvard. See "A Series of Fortunate Events," *Washington Post Magazine*, Aug. 12, 2007.

117. Obama, *Dreams from My Father*, p. 215.

118. Ibid., p. 208.

119. Mundy, "A Series of Fortunate Events."

120. David Mendel, *Obama: From Promise to Power* (New York: Amistad/ Harper/ Collins Imprint, 2007), p. 104.

121. Dupuis and Boeckelman, *Barack Obama and the New Face of American Politics*, p. 8; and Randolph Burnside and Kami Whitehurst, "From the Statehouse to the White House? Barack Obama's Bid to become the Next President," *Journal of Black Studies* 38 (2007): 75–89.

122. McClelland, *Young Mr. Obama*, pp. 182–83, 188–89, 193.

123. Barack Obama, *The Audacity of Hope* (New York: Crown, 2006), p. 3.

124. Alan Gerber, "African American Careers and the House Delegation," *Journal of Politics* 58 (1996): 831–45.

125. Quoted in Street, *Barack Obama and the Future of American Politics*, p. 107.

126. Mendel, *Obama: From Promise to Power*, p. 224.

127. Michael Eric Dyson, "His Way with Words Begins at the Pulpit," *Washington Post*, Jan. 18, 2010.

128. Mendel, *Obama: From Promise to Power*, p. 190.

129. In 1992 Moseley–Braun, the Chicago recorder of deeds, became the second African American popularly elected to the Senate. In a three-way primary contest on the strength of the black and feminist support she won 38 percent of the vote and defeated her Republican opponent 53 percent to 47 percent. She was defeated for reelection after a tumultuous tenure marked by constant allegations of ethical misconduct.

130. Mendel, *Obama: From Promise to Power*, pp. 158–59.

131. Ibid.

132. The remnants of the Daley Machine supported Obama's remaining primary opponent, Dan Hynes. As an "unadulterated Irish Catholic," Obama's defeat of Hynes was symbolic of one last triumph of African Americans over Catholic Irish machine politics. See McClelland, *Young Mr. Obama*, pp. 255–56.

133. For an analysis of the collapse of the Hull and Ryan campaigns see Mendel, *From Promise to Power*, chaps. 15, 19.

134. Lorrie Frasure, "The Burden of Jekyll and Hyde: Barack Obama, Racial Identity and Black Political Behavior," in *Whose Black Politics?* ed. Andra Gillespie (New York: Routledge, 2010), pp. 144–48.

135. Mendel, *Obama: From Promise to Power*, p. 301.

136. Kerry apparently decided to ask Obama to deliver the address after being impressed with his performance at a joint appearance at a Chicago campaign rally.

137. Ibid., p. 144, and Obama, *Audacity of Hope*, p. 355.

138. Michael Barone, *The Almanac of American Politics, 2006* (Washington, DC: National Journal, 2006), p. 560.

139. Street, *Barack Obama and the Future of American Politics*, p. xxxv.

140. Ibid., p. 2.

Chapter 5. Ethnic Men: The Al Smith and Jesse Jackson Campaigns

1. The concept of independent leverage discussed later in the chapter was developed by Ronald Walters, *Black Presidential Politics: A Strategic Approach* (Albany, NY: SUNY Press, 1988), pp. 110–38.

2. James MacGregor Burns, *John Kennedy: A Political Profile* (New York: Harcourt Brace, 1960), p. 252.

3. Oscar Handlin, *Al Smith and His America* (Boston: Little, Brown, 1958), p. 30.

4. Lawrence Fuchs, *John F. Kennedy and American Catholicism* (New York: Meredith Press, 1967), p. 66.

5. Christopher Finan, *Alfred E. Smith: The Happy Warrior* (New York: Hill and Wang, 2002), p. 4.

6. Ibid., p. 176.

7. Ibid.

8. Andrew Sinclair, *Prohibition: The Age of Excess* (Boston: Little, Brown, 1962). See also Daniel Okrent, *Last Call: The Rise and Fall of Prohibition* (New York: Scribner's, 2010).

9. Finan, *Alfred E. Smith*, p. 162.

10. Ibid., p. 56.

11. Edmund Moore, *A Catholic for President: The Campaign of 1928* (New York: Ronald Press, 1956), pp. 92–96.

12. Quoted in Thomas Carty, *A Catholic in the White House? Religion, Politics and John F. Kennedy's Presidential Campaign* (New York: Palgrave Macmillan, 2004), p. 35.

13. Alan Lichtman, *Prejudice and the Old Politics: The Presidential Election of 1928* (Chapel Hill: University of North Carolina Press, 1979), p. 10.

14. Finan suggests that one indicator of Smith's fidelity to his faith was his fidelity to his wife. See *Alfred E. Smith*, p. 58.

15. Moore, *A Catholic for President*, p. 57.

16. Carty, *A Catholic in the White House?* p. 37.

17. William Shannon, *The American Irish: A Political and Social Portrait* (Amherst: University of Massachusetts Press, 1989), p. 156.

18. Moore, *A Catholic for President*, p. 116.

19. Lichtman, *Prejudice and the Old Politics*, p. 108; and Finan, *Alfred E. Smith*, pp. 208–09.

20. On Smith's liberalism see Donn Neal, "What If Al Smith Won," *Presidential Studies Quarterly*, 14 (1984): 242–48.

21. Finan, *Alfred E. Smith*, p. 221. See also Handlin, *Al Smith and His America*, p. 130.

22. Patricia Sullivan, *Lift Every Voice: The NAACP and the Making of the Civil Rights Movement* (New York: Free Press, 2009), p. 134.

23. Robert Slayton, *Empire Statesman: The Rise and Redemption of Al Smith* (New York: Free Press, 2001): 314–15.

24. Sullivan, *Lift Every Voice*, p. 134.

25. Lichtman, *Prejudice and the Old Politics*, pp. 58–59. See also Finan, *Alfred E. Smith*, pp. 210–11.

26. Moore, *A Catholic for President*, p. 69; and, *A Catholic in the White House?* pp. 29, 34.

27. Finan, *Alfred E. Smith*, p. 234; and Lichtman, *Prejudice and the Old Politics*, p. 67.

28. Lichtman, *Prejudice and the Old Politics*, p. 58.

29. Quoted in Moore, *A Catholic for President*, p. 184.

30. Ibid.

31. Finan, *Alfred E. Smith*, p. 303.

32. Carty, *A Catholic in the White House?* pp. 189–94.

33. Ibid.

34. Finan, *Alfred E. Smith*, p. 207; and Carty, *A Catholic in the White House?* pp. 127, 152.

35. Finan, *Alfred E. Smith*, p. 320.

36. Ibid.

37. Lichtman, *Prejudice and the Old Politics*, p. 117.

38. Ibid., p. 89.

39. Ibid.

40. Kristi Anderson, *The Creation of a Democratic Majority: 1928–1936* (Chicago: University of Chicago Press, 1979), pp. 3–10; and V. O. Key, "A Theory of Critical Elections," *Journal of Politics* 17 (1955): 2–13.

41. Carty, *A Catholic in the White House?* p. 120.

42. In a memoir published a year after the campaign, Smith hinted that he thought he lost because of a whispering campaign that was rooted in anti-Catholicism. See Al Smith, *Up to Now: An Autobiography* (New York: Viking Press, 1929), pp. 410–16.

43. Richard Whalen, *The Founding Father: The Story of Joseph P. Kennedy* (New York: New American Library, 1964), p. 119.

44. Arthur Schlesinger Jr., *The Age of Roosevelt: The Politics of Upheaval* (Boston: Houghton Mifflin, 1960), p. 519.

45. At the 1932 convention Smith came in a distance second to Franklin Roosevelt, but refused to make the nomination unanimous. Arthur Schlesinger Jr. writes, Smith "left the hall with bitterness on his face. . . . [And] that night Smith irreconcilables ripped posters of Roosevelt to pieces in the hotels." See *The Age of Roosevelt: The Crisis of the Old Order* (Boston: Houghton Mifflin, 1957), p. 311.

46. Only two biographies of Smith have been written and four books on the campaign.

47. Marshall Frady's *Jesse: The Life and Pilgrimage of Jesse Jackson* (New York: Random House, 1996), pp. 228–34, provides the most detailed account of the dispute about Jackson's behavior at the time of King's death.

48. On Jackson's media savvy see ibid.

49. One month after King's death the *New York Times* referred to Jackson as "probably the most persuasive black leader on the scene"; in a 1969 *Playboy* interview he was declared King's "fiery heir apparent," and in 1970 he appeared for the first time on the cover of *Time* magazine; see ibid., p. 247.

50. Quoted in Robert C. Smith, *We Have No Leaders: African Americans in the Post–Civil Rights Era* (Albany, NY: SUNY Press, 1996), p. 48.

51. Karen Stanford, *Beyond the Boundaries: Reverend Jesse Jackson in International Affairs* (Albany, NY: SUNY Press 1997).

52. In 2000 a panel of African American political scientists declared Jackson one of the greatest black leaders of all time, ranking him number seven on a list of twelve. See Robert C. Smith, "Rating Black Leaders," *National Political Science Review* 8 (2001): 124–38.

53. Frady, *Jesse*, pp. 100–01.

54. Ibid., p. 104.

55. Ibid.

56. Joseph McCormack and Robert C. Smith, "Through the Prism of Afro-American Culture: An Interpretation of the Jackson Campaign Style," in *Jesse Jackson's 1984 Presidential Campaign*, ed. Lucius Barker and Ronald Walters (Urbana: University of Illinois Press, 1989).

57. Frady, *Jesse*, p. 32.

58. Lucius Barker, "Jesse Jackson's Candidacy in Political-Social Perspective," in *Jesse Jackson's 1984 Presidential Campaign*, ed. Barker and Walters, p. 11.

59. Walters, *Black Presidential Politics*.

60. Frady, *Jesse*, p. 52.

61. Address to the 1984 Democratic Party Convention, San Francisco, July 17, as reprinted in the *Urban League Review*, 9 (1985): 123–32.

62. Lorn Foster, "Avenues for Black Political Mobilization: The Presidential Campaign of Rev. Jesse Jackson," in *The Social and Political Implications of the 1984 Jesse Jackson Presidential Campaign*, ed. Lorenzo Morris (New York: Praeger, 1990).

63. Robert C. Smith, "From Insurgency to Inclusion: The Jackson Campaigns of 1984 and 1988," in ibid.

64. Among the key party insiders that joined the campaign in 1988 were Jimmy Carter aides Bert Lance and Ann Lewis. See ibid.

65. Frady, *Jesse*, p. 269. This fantasy continued in 1992, when Jackson prepared a long memorandum to Bill Clinton outlining the strengths he would bring to the ticket as the vice presidential nominee. Clinton apparently would not engage the fantasy, reportedly telling Jackson, "I'm not going to put you through what Fritz Mondale and Mike Dukakis did" (referring to Mondale and Dukakis's telling Jackson that he was on the lists of possible running mates when they had no intention of choosing him). See Bob Woodward, *The Agenda* (New York: Simon and Schuster, 1995), pp. 29–33.

66. Frady, *Jesse*, p. 368.

67. Dan T. Carter, *From George Wallace to Newt Gingrich: Race and the Conservative Counterrevolution, 1963–1994* (Baton Rouge: Louisiana State University Press, 1996).

68. Thomas Cavanagh and Lorn Foster, *Jesse Jackson's Campaign: Primaries and Caucuses* (Washington, DC: Joint Center for Political and Economic Studies, 1984), p. 17.

69. Smith, "From Insurgency to Inclusion," p. 226.

70. Lorenzo Morris and Linda Williams, "The Coalition at the End of the Rainbow," in *Jesse Jackson's 1984 Presidential Campaign*, ed. Barker and Walters, p. 234.

71. Linda Williams, "White/Black Perceptions of the Electability of Black Political Candidates," *National Political Science Review*, 2 (1990): 51.

72. Frady, *Jesse*, p. 411.

73. See Robert C. Smith, "In the Shadows of Ronald Reagan: Civil Rights Policy Making in the Clinton Administration," in *Winning While Losing? Civil Rights, the Conservative Movement, and the Presidency from Nixon to*

Obama, ed. Kenneth Osgood and Derrick White (Gainesville: University Press of Florida, forthcoming).

74. Williams, "White/Black Perceptions of Electability," p. 62.

75. Frady, *Jesse*, p. 417.

76. See the text of the speech in *Chicago Sun-Times*, Mar. 5, 2007. Interestingly, in this speech Obama compared his father's experience with British colonizers in Kenya to the black experience in the Jim Crow South.

Chapter 6. The Incorporation of the Catholic Irish and the Semi-Incorporation of African Americans

1. Andrew Greeley, *That Most Distressful Nation: The Taming of the American Irish* (Chicago: Quadrangle Books, 1972), p. 120.

2. National Conference on Inter-Group Relations, *Taking America's Pulse: The Full Report of the National Conference Survey on Inter-Group Relations* (New York, 1994).

3. Ibid., p. 12.

4. Ibid., p. 13.

5. Ibid., p. 6.

6. Ibid.

7. Ibid., p. 7.

8. Richard Alba, *Ethnic Identity: The Transformation of White America* (New Haven, CT: Yale University Press, 1990), p. 42.

9. Cited in Robert C. Smith, *Racism in the Post-Civil Rights Era* (Albany, NY: SUNY Press, 1995), p. 39.

10. Jonathan Darman, "The White Stuff," *Newsweek* http://www.newsweek.com/id/138456output/print, and Jon Cohen and Jennifer Agiesta "3 in 10 Americans Admit to Race Bias," *Washington Post*, June 22, 2008.

11. Joseph Curran, *Hibernian Green on the Silver Screen: The Irish in American Movies* (New York: Greenwood Press, 1989), p. xvi.

12. Tracy Mislkin, *The Harlem and Irish Renaissances: Language, Identity and Representation* (Gainesville: University Press of Florida, 1998).

13. Carl Wittke, *The Irish in America* (Baton Rouge: Louisiana State University Press, 1956), p. 263.

14. Curran, *Hibernian Green*, p. 11.

15. Ibid., p. 12, and Wittke, *The Irish in America*, p. 263.

16. Ibid., p. 24.

17. Ibid., p. 41.

18. Ibid., p. 71.

19. Ibid., p. 106.

20. Ibid.

21. William Shannon, *The American Irish: A Political and Social Portrait* (Amherst: University of Massachusetts Press, 1989), p. 233.

22. Ibid., p. 255.

23. Ibid., p. 255.

24. Mark Dyreson, *Making the American Team: Sport, Culture, and the Olympic Experience* (Urbana: University of Illinois Press, 1998), p. 125.

25. John Schaefer, "The Irish American Athletic Club: Redefining Americanism at the 1908 Olympics Games" (New York: Archives of Irish America, New York University, 2001). Accessed at http://www.nyc.edu/library/bcbst/research/aia/newresearch/schaeferold.pdf.

26. Ibid., p. 3.

27. Ibid., p. 9.

28. Joseph O'Grady, *How the Irish became Americans* (New York: Twayne, 1973), pp. 115–16.

29. Wittke writes that the reputation of Irish ballplayers was so great that members of other ethnic groups used Irish names to help the advance of their careers. See *The Irish in America*, p. 279.

30. Lawrence Fuchs, *John F. Kennedy and American Catholicism* (New York: Meredith Press, 1967), p. 63.

31. Greeley, *That Most Distressful Nation*, p. 121; Edward Levine, *The Irish and the Irish Politicians* (Notre Dame, IN: University of Notre Dame Press, 1966), p. 216; and Thomas O'Connor, *The Boston Irish: A Political Portrait* (Boston: Northeastern University Press, 1995), p. 142.

32. Levine, *The Irish and Irish Politicians*, p. 142.

33. Garry Wills, *The Kennedy Imprisonment: A Meditation on Power* (New York: Simon & Schuster, 1982), p. 65.

34. Alba, *Ethnic Identity*, p. 291.

35. Herbert Gans, "Symbolic Ethnicity: The Future of Ethnic Groups and Cultures in America," *Ethnic and Racial Studies* 2 (1979): 1–20.

36. Levine, *The Irish and Irish Politicians*, p. 142.

37. O'Connor, *The Boston Irish*, p. 216.

38. Greeley, *That Most Distressful Nation*, pp. 126–27.

39. Ibid., p. 85.

40. Andrew Greeley, *Ethnicity in the United States: A Preliminary Reconnaissance* (New York: Wiley, 1974), p. 87.

41. Shannon, *The American Irish*, p. 327.

42. Ibid., p. 331.

43. Nathan Glazer and Daniel P. Moynihan, *Beyond the Melting Pot* (Cambridge, MA: MIT Press, 1963, 1970), p. 272.

44. Associated Press Video, "Obama and Willie Mays Aboard *Air Force One*," *Newsday*, July 15, 2009.

45. Orlando Patterson, *The Ordeal of Integration* (Washington, DC: Civitas Counterpoint, 1997), pp. 17–19.

46. Ibid., p. 18.

47. Jabrani Asim, *What Obama Means for Our Culture, Our Politics, Our Future* (New York: Morrow, 2009).

48. Robert Washington, *The Ideologies of African American Literature* (Lanham, MD: Rowman and Littlefield, 2001), pp. 326–30.

49. Daniel Leab, *From Sambo to Superspade: The Black Experience in Motion Pictures* (Boston: Houghton Mifflin, 1975), pp. 22, 29; and Donald

Bogle, *Bright Boulevards, Bold Dreams: The Story of Black Hollywood* (New York: One World Ballantine Books, 2005), p. 13.

50. Quoting the novelist John Oliver Killan as cited in Leab, *From Sambo to Superspade*, p. 22.

51. Ibid., p. 129.

52. Melvin Patrick, *The Adventures of Amos 'n Andy: A Social History of an American Phenomenon* (New York: Free Press, 1991).

53. Leab, *From Sambo to Superspade.*

54. Washington, *The Ideologies of African American Literature*, p. 198.

55. Leab, *From Sambo to Superspade*, pp. 163–64. Cripps is quoted in *Split Images: African Americans in Mass Media*, ed. Janette Dates and William Barlow (Washington, DC: Howard University Press, 1993), p. 155.

56. Janice Peck, "Talk about Racism: Framing a Popular Discourse on Race on Oprah Winfrey," *Cultural Critique* 27 (1994): 91. Peck's book is an incisive treatment of Winfrey's role as a subtle advocate of neoconservative postures on race, poverty, and the imperatives of "personal responsibility" and a limited role for the government. See *Oprah: Cultural Icon for the Neoliberal Era* (Boulder, CO: Paradigm, 2008).

57. The *Washington Post* film critic referred to Lee's early works as "radical filmmaking at its best." But John Howard writes, "In the years after 'Malcolm X' there were no more references to 'radical film making.' The meaning of race in America was changing, and Lee, to survive as a presence in the industry, had to change with them." See *Faces in the Mirror: Oscar Micheaux and Spike Lee* (Lady Lake, FL: Fireside Press, 2009), p. 240.

58. Brian Stetler, "Endorsement from Winfrey Quantified: A Million Votes," *New York Times*, Aug. 11, 2008.

59. Charles Henry, *Culture and African American Politics* (Bloomington: Indiana University Press, 1990).

60. Robert O'Meally, ed., *The Jazz Cadence of American Culture* (New York: Columbia University Press, 1998).

61. Gerald Early, *One Nation under a Groove: Motown and American Culture* (Ann Arbor: University of Michigan Press, 2004). Motown's cultural impact is also discussed in Nelson George, *Blackface: Reflections on African Americans and the Movies* (New York: Harper/Collins, 1994).

62. Brian Ward, *Just My Soul Responding: Rhythm and Blues, Black Consciousness and Race Relations* (Berkeley: University of California Press, 1998).

63. Nelson George, *The Death of Rhythm and Blues* (New York: Dutton, 1989), p. xii. George's concern is a major concern of this book, which I raised twenty years ago in the short essay, "Recent Elections and Black Politics: The Maturation or Death of Black Politics?" *Political Science and Politics* 23 (1990): 160–62.

64. Matt Bai, "Is Obama the End of Black Politics," *New York Times Magazine*, Aug. 6, 2008. See also Andra Gillespie, ed., *Whose Black Politics? Cases in Post-Racial Black Leadership* (New York: Routledge, 2010).

65. Kimberly McLeod, "Authenticity within Hip-Hop and Other Cultures Threatened with Assimilation," *Journal of Communications* 49 (1999): 134–50.

66. Shaun Ossei-Owasu, "The Hip-Hop Community and Barack Obama," in *The Obama Phenomenon: Toward a Multiracial Democracy*, ed. Charles Henry, Robert Allen, and Robert Chrisman (Urbana: University of Illinois Press, 2011).

67. Dyreson, *Making the American Team*, p. 115.

68. Ibid.

69. Ibid.

70. Geoffrey Ward, *Unforgivable Blackness: The Rise and Fall of Jack Johnson* (New York: Knopf, 2004).

71. Lauren Rebecca Sklaroff, "Constructing G. I. Joe: Joe Louis, Cultural Solutions to the 'Negro Problem' during World War II," *Journal of American History* 89 (2002): 958–83; and Dominic Capreci and Martha Wilkerson, "Multifarious Hero: Joe Louis and Race Relations during World War II," *Journal of Sport History* 10 (1983): 5–25.

72. Richard Hoffer, *Something in the Air: American Passion and Defiance in the 1968 Mexico City Olympics* (New York: Free Press, 2009).

73. Early, *One Nation under a Groove*, p. 94. See also Jules Tygiel, *Baseball's Great Experiment: Jackie Robinson and His Legacy* (New York: Oxford, 1983).

74. William C. Rhoden, *Forty Million Dollar Slaves: The Rise, Fall and Redemption of the Black Athlete* (New York: Crown, 2006), p. 215.

75. John Underwood, "On the Playground," *Life*, Spring 1998, pp. 102–08.

76. Ira Berkow, "Black Quarterbacks Bloom," *New York Times*, Jan. 15, 1989.

77. Richard Lapchick, "Pseudo-Scientific Prattle about Black Athletes," *New York Times*, Apr. 29, 1989.

78. C. Wright Mills, *The Power Elite* (New York: Oxford, 1956), p. 74.

79. Kerry Ann Rockque, "Deconstructing Tiger Woods: The Promises and Pitfalls of Multiracial Identity," in *The Politics of Multiracialism: Challenging Racial Thinking*, ed. Heather Dalmaze (Albany, NY: SUNY Press, 2004); and Habiba Ibrahm, "Toward Black and Multiracial 'Kinship' after 1997, or How a Race Man became 'Cablinasian,'" *Black Scholar* 39 (2009): 23–31.

80. David Levring Lewis, *When Harlem Was in Vogue* (New York: Oxford, 1981), p. 149.

81. On the pervasiveness of racist and white supremacist stereotypes in the media during this period, see Rayford Logan, *The Betrayal of the Negro* (New York: 1965), chaps. 10–13. The phrase "civil rights" by copyright is from Lewis, *When Harlem Was in Vogue*, p. xvi.

82. In his fine study of the political and cultural implications of black literature, Washington identifies five "schools" of black literature: the primitivist school of the Harlem Renaissance, the naturalistic school of Richard Wright, the existentialist school represented by Ralph Ellison, the moral suasionist school of James Baldwin, and the Black Nationalist school represented by Amiri Baraka. Each of these schools except the last were sponsored by the white literary establishment and were broadly integrationists or incorporationist. Baraka's school was autonomous and defiantly ethnic, and it was repressed and then ignored

by the literary establishment, although it had a major impact on the internal cultural politics of the black community. See *The Ideologies of African American Literature.*

83. Ibid., p. 69.

84. Ibid., p. 41.

85. Langston Hughes, "The Negro Artist and the Racial Mountain," *The Nation*, June 23, 1926.

86. Washington, *The Ideologies of African American Literature*, p. 223.

87. Ibid., p. 336.

88. Michael Berube, "Public Academy," *New Yorker*, Jan. 9, 1995.

89. Patterson, *The Ordeal of Integration*, p. 16.

90. Ricky Hill, "The New Custodians of the Black Experience: A Critique of Black Public Intellectuals," paper prepared for presentation at the nineteenth annual Olive-Harvey Black Studies Conference, Chicago, April 1996. Houston Baker suggests that this group of black intellectuals has betrayed the interests of the community with respect to the problem of the incorporation of the ghettoized poor. See *Betrayal: How Black Intellectuals Have Abandoned the Ideals of the Civil Rights Movement* (New York: Columbia, 2008).

91. Vincent Harding, *MLK: An Inconvenient Hero*, rev. ed. (Maryknoll, NY: Orbis, 2008), p. 13.

92. Stephan and Abigail Thernstrom, *America in Black and White* (New York: Simon and Schuster, 1997), p. 524.

93. Patterson, *The Ordeal of Integration*, p. 197.

94. Ibid., p. 196.

95. Thernstroms, *America in Black and White*, p. 526. In 2010 about 8 percent of marriages in the United States were interracial. About 14.5 percent of black men and 6.5 percent of women were in mixed marriages in 2010. See Hope Yen, "Interracial Marriages Still Rising, But Not Fast," *Washington Post*, May 26, 2010.

96. African Americans generally are less willing to date across ethnic lines and are especially less willing to date whites. See George Yancey, "Crossracial Differences in the Racial Preferences of Potential Dating Partners," *Sociological Quarterly* 50 (2009): 121–43. The vitriol directed at Tiger Woods on black talk radio and other media when it was reported that he had a series of affairs—all with white women—revealed the continuing hostility to interracial intimacies among blacks. See Jesse Washington, "Race Issue Arises in Woods Saga: Criticisms from Black Community follows News of 'Transgressions,'" *Contra Costa Times*, Dec. 6, 2009.

97. Michael Dawson, *Behind the Mule: Race and Class in African American Politics* (Princeton, NJ: Princeton University Press, 1994), pp. 45–68.

98. The data on black and white opinion on AIDS and drugs are analyzed in detail in Robert C. Smith and Richard Seltzer, *Contemporary Controversies and the American Racial Divide* (Lanham, MD: Rowman and Littlefield, 2000).

99. Randall Robinson, *The Debt: What America Owes to Blacks* (New York: Dutton, 2000); Ronald Walters, *The Price of Racial Reconciliation* (Ann Arbor:

University of Michigan Press, 2008); and Charles Henry, *Long Overdue: The Politics of Reparations* (New York: New York University Press, 2007).

100. Michael Dawson and Rovana Popoff, "Reparations: Justice and Greed in Black and White," *Du Bois Review* 1 (2004): 61–66.

101. There are no strata of black Brahmin wealthy entrepreneurs like Joe Kennedy. Black wealth, to the extent it exists, is usually held by athletes or entertainers. For example, three blacks are noted as billionaires: Oprah Winfrey, Tiger Woods, and Robert Johnson, the founder of Black Entertainment Television (BET).

102. Thernstroms, *America in Black and White*, p. 234. The ghettos and the persistently high poverty rate among African Americans are the most glaring indicators of the absence of economic incorporation. But when Obama took office, black per capita income was $17,902, 58.8 percent of the $30,431 white per capital income. The wealth (total assets minus liabilities) gap was even larger than the income gap; $88,651 for whites compared to $5,998 for blacks. These data are from Sundiata Keita Cha-Jua, "The New Nadir: The Contemporary Black Racial Formation," *Black Scholar* 40 (2010): 38–58. Cha-Jua's article is a cogent analysis of the deteriorating social and economic status of blacks as Obama assumed office.

103. Clarence Lusane, *Colin Powell, Condoleezza Rice and the New American Century* (New York: Praeger, 2006).

104. The Gallup data on the prospects for a Powell candidacy are analyzed in detail in Smith and Seltzer, *Contemporary Controversies and the American Racial Divide*, pp. 72–76. See also Juan Williams, "President Powell," *Reconstructions* 2 (1994): 67–78; and Henry Louis Gates, "Powell and the Black Elite," *New Yorker*, Sept. 25, 1995.

105. Thernstroms, *America in Black and White*, p. 288.

106. Ibid.

107. Robert C. Smith, *Conservatism and Racism and Why in America They Are the Same* (Albany, NY: SUNY Press, 2010), chaps. 6–8.

108. Ibid., chaps. 2–3.

109. Michael Dawson, *Black Visions: The Roots of Contemporary African–American Political Ideologies* (Chicago: University of Chicago Press, 2001), chaps. 2, 6.

110. Greeley, *That Most Distressful Nation*, p. 226.

111. Stephanie Rains, *The Irish–American in Popular Culture* (Dublin: Irish Academic Press, 2007), p. 8.

112. Ibid., p. 22.

113. Ibid.

114. Alba, *Ethnic Identity*, p. 214.

115. Michael Eric Dyson, *Is Bill Cosby Right? Or Has the Black Middle Class Lost Its Mind* (New York: Basic Civitas Books, 2005). See also Derrick White, "Blacks Who Had Not Themselves Personally Suffered Discrimination: The Symbolic Incorporation of the Black Middle Class," in *Race and the Foundations of Knowledge*, ed. Joseph and Jana Evans Braziel Young (Urbana: University of Illinois Press, 2006).

Chapter 7. Kennedy and Obama: Charisma, Character, and Ethnic Identity

1. These references to Obama are drawn from the following sources: Kate Zernike, "The Charisma Mandate," *New York Times*, Feb. 17, 2008; Jo Becker and Christopher Drew, "Pragmatic Politics Forged on Southside," *New York Times*, May 11, 2008; Charles Krauthammer "Obama's Inaugural," *Washington Post*, Jan. 23, 2009; Lize Mundy "A Series of Fortunate Events," *Washington Post Magazine*, Aug. 12, 2007; Carolyn Lochhead, "Obama Faces Hopes, Expectations," *San Francisco Chronicle*, Jan. 18, 2009, p. xx; Richard Wolffe, *Renegade: The Making of a President* (New York: Crown, 2009), p. 125; David Mendel, *Obama: From Promise to Power* (New York: Harper/Collins Imprint, 2007), pp. 7, 9; and Eleanor Clift, "The Process President: Obama's Cool, Cerebral Style May Be Just What We Need," *Newsweek*, Aug. 8, 2008.

2. The references to Kennedy are from the following sources: Theodore Sorensen, *Kennedy* (New York: Harper and Row, 1965), p. 396; Bruce Miroff, *Pragmatic Illusions: The Presidential Politics of John F. Kennedy* (New York: McKay, 1976), pp. 2–3; Thomas Reeves, *A Question of Character: A Life of John F. Kennedy* (New York: Free Press, 1991), pp. 14–15; William Shannon, *The American Irish: A Political and Social Portrait* (Amherst: University of Massachusetts Press, 1989), p. 396; Andrew Greeley, "John F. Kennedy: Doctor of the Church," in *The Catholic Experience: An Interpretation of the History of American Catholicism*, by Andrew Greeley (New York: Doubleday, 1967), p. 277; Richard Reeves, *President Kennedy: Profile of Power* (New York: Simon and Schuster, 1993), p. 14, W. J. Rorabaugh, *The Real Making of the President: Kennedy, Nixon and the 1960 Election* (Lawrence: University Press of Kansas, 2009), p. 4; James David Barber, *The Presidential Character* (Englewood Cliffs, NJ: Prentice-Hall, 1972), p. 294; and Norman Mailer, "Superman Comes to the Supermarket," *Esquire*, Nov. 1960, http://www.esquire.com/print-this/superman-supermarket.

3. Paul Street, *Barack Obama and the Future of American Politics* (Boulder, CO: Paradigm Publisher, 2009), p. xxxv. "JFK in Sepia" is Street's phrase. The phrase "a Kenyan Kennedy" is attributed to an Obama campaign operative during his race against Congressman Bobby Rush. See David Remnick, *The Bridge: The Life and Rise of Barack Obama* (New York: Knopf, 2010), p. 322.

4. Megan Smolenyak Smolenyak, "The Quest for Obama's Irish Roots," http://www.ancestrymagazine.com/2008/12/features/the-quest-for-obam%E2%80%/99s-irish-roots/. See also Carol Sullivan, "O'Bama? Why Irish Eyes Are Smiling," *Newsweek*, Oct. 1, 2008. In the third year of his presidency Obama paid a sentimental campaign-like visit to the village of Moneygall, the Irish birthplace of his maternal grandparent who immigrated to the United States in 1850. President Kennedy made a similar visit to his Irish ancestral village during his third year in office.

5. Blake Campbell-Hyde, a student in my undergraduate Congress and Presidency class at San Francisco State, made an exacting character comparison of Kennedy and Obama using James David Barber's theories developed in *The*

Presidential Character. See Campbell-Hyde, "The Presidential Character: Comparing Kennedy and Obama," Fall 2009. Although he found Barber's theories wanting, he classified Obama as an "active-positive," the best of Barber's character types. Obama's performance in the presidency in his first two years appears to confirm this classification. Kennedy was, of course, Barber's archetype of the active-positive. Although he does not expressly use the Barber typology, Stephan Wayne's analysis of Obama's personality suggests an active-positive. See *Personality and Politics: Obama For and Against Himself* (Washington, DC: Congressional Quarterly Press, 2011).

6. Mailer, "Superman Comes to the Supermarket."

7. Project for Excellence in Journalism, "Character and the Primaries of 2008: What Were the Media Master Narratives about the Candidates during the Primary Season?" (Cambridge, MA: Joan Shorenstein Center for Press and Politics, Harvard University, 2008), pp. 6–7. The shared cadences with Kennedy are not entirely accidental. Obama's speechwriters carefully studied the speeches of Kennedy and his brother Robert, and the campaign received informal advice from Kennedy speechwriter Theodore Sorensen. See Alex MacCall, "Finding Strength in the Power of Words," *Washington Post*, Feb. 26, 2008.

8. Mundy, "A Series of Fortunate Events."

9. Reeves, *A Question of Character*, p. 420. As far as we know, unlike Kennedy, Obama's books, major speeches, and his substantive and rhetorical styles appear to be largely his own. Kennedy initially was not a good rhetorician and had to undergo extensive coaching in order to become an accomplished orator. And scholars attribute the sophistication, wit, and intellectual and literary prowess of Kennedy's speeches to Theodore Sorensen. Hired initially as "little more than an intellectual valet," according to Shaun Casey, by the time Kennedy became a presidential candidate, Sorensen "was almost a lobe of Kennedy's mind." Sorensen, to whom Kennedy referred "as my intellectual blood bank," did much of the research and writing for *Profiles in Courage*. On Sorensen's role in the making of Kennedy's rhetoric see Shaun Casey, *The Making of a Catholic President: Kennedy vs. Nixon 1960* (New York: Oxford, 2009), p. 26; Reeves, *A Question of Character*, p. 127; and Garry Wills, *The Kennedy Imprisonment: A Mediation on Power* (New York: Simon and Schuster, 1982), pp. 139–42.On *Profiles in Courage* in his memoir Sorensen writes, "JFK worked particularly long and hard on the first and second chapters, setting the tone and philosophy of the book. I did a first draft of most chapters, which he revised with both pen and dictation." See *Counselor: A Life at the Edge of History* (New York: Harper, 2008), p. 146.

10. Wills, *The Kennedy Imprisonment*, pp. 65, 68.

11. Nigel Hamilton, *JFK: Reckless Youth* (New York: Random House, 1992), p. 297.

12. Wills, *The Kennedy Imprisonment*, pp. 68, 73.

13. Ibid., p. 64. We might note that Jackie Kennedy tried anything but to be Irish as well. Arthur Mitchell writes, "Jackie did almost everything to hide her Irish background (both grandparents were famine immigrants) from JFK; to the Kennedys she was French." See *JFK and His Irish Heritage* (Dublin, Ireland: Moytura Press, 1993), p. 39.

14. James MacGregor Burns, *John Kennedy: A Political Profile* (New York: Harcourt Brace, 1960), p. 238.

15. Hamilton, *JFK: Reckless Youth*, p. 206.

16. Ibid.

17. Wills, *The Kennedy Imprisonment*, p. 17.

18. Wills suggests that Kennedy's famous aversion to wearing hats was rooted in the stereotype of the derby wearing Irish politician, ibid., p. 64. See also Shannon, *The American Irish*, p. xiii, 407.

19. Quoted in Mitchell, *JFK and His Irish Heritage*, p. 87.

20. Kenneth O'Donnell and Dave Powers, *"Johnny, We Hardly Knew": Memories of John F. Kennedy* (Boston: Little, Brown, 1972).

21. Mitchell, *JFK and His Irish Heritage*, pp. 3–4, 37–38.

22. Ibid., pp. 37–38.

23. John F. Kennedy, "Address before the Irish Parliament, Dublin," June 28, 1963. http://www.jfklibrary.org/historical+desk/speeches. Kennedy visited his ancestral home several times before becoming president, often seeking distant relatives.

24. Stephanie Rains, *The Irish-American in Popular Culture* (Dublin: Irish Academic Press, 2007), p. 18.

25. Wills, *The Kennedy Imprisonment*, p. 61.

26. Mitchell, *JFK and His Irish Heritage*, p. 36.

27. Ibid.

28. Thomas Carty, *A Catholic in the White House? Religion, Politics and John F. Kennedy* (New York: Palgrave Macmillan, 2004), p. 43.

29. Hamilton, *JFK: Reckless Youth*, pp. 217, 649.

30. Wills, *The Kennedy Imprisonment*, p. 43.

31. Hamilton, *JFK: Reckless Youth*, p. 426.

32. Doris Kearns Goodwin, *The Fitzgeralds and Kennedys* (New York: Simon and Schuster, 1987), p. 392; and Robert Dallek, *An Unfinished Life: John F. Kennedy, 1917–1963* (Boston: Little, Brown, 2003), p. 23.

33. Wills, *The Kennedy Imprisonment*, p. 17.

34. Hamilton, *JFK: Reckless Youth*, p. 28. Kennedy's sex life from his youth until his death is chronicled in detail in, among others, Hamilton, *JFK: Reckless Youth*; Reeves, *A Question of Character*; Reeves, *President Kennedy*; Seymour Hersh, *The Dark Side of Camelot* (Boston: Little, Brown, 1997); and Robert Dallek, *An Unfinished Life: John F. Kennedy, 1917–1963* (Boston: Little, Brown, 2003). Sorensen in his memoir describes Kennedy's sexual behavior as his "one personal weakness," but concludes, "I know of no occasion where his private life infringed on his public duties. . . . There is no requirement in law or logic that solid, thoughtful public officials who make intelligent policy decisions must always be equally solid and thoughtful in their private lives" (see *Counselor*, p. 123). Dallek shares Sorensen's view, whereas Thomas Reeves and Hersh believe Kennedy's behavior did impact his public duties. Wills goes to the heart of the problem when he notes that Federal Bureau of Investigation (FBI) Director J. Edgar Hoover was aware of Kennedy's behavior, which allowed him to blackmail the President; for example, forcing him and his brother to acquiesce

in the FBI's campaign to discredit Dr. King. This, Wills concludes, "makes mockery of any talk that John Kennedy's affairs were irrelevant to his politics." See *The Kennedy Imprisonment*, p. 37. See also James Giglio, *The Presidency of John F. Kennedy*, 2nd ed. (Lawrence: University Press of Kansas, 2006), p. 150.

35. Casey, *The Making of a Catholic President*, pp. 202–03.

36. In 1960 McCarthy quipped, "I'm twice as liberal Hubert Humphrey, and twice as intelligent as Stuart Symington and twice as Catholic as Jack Kennedy." Quoted in Rick Perlstein, *Nixonland: The Rise of a President and the Fracturing of America* (New York: Scribner, 2008), p. 229.

37. Greeley, "John F. Kennedy," p. 289; Hamilton, *JFK: Reckless Youth*, pp. 357, 419; Sorensen, *Chronicles*, p. 164; and Mark S. Massa, *Catholics and American Culture* (New York: Crossroads Publishing, 1999), pp. 127–30.

38. Wolffe, *Renegade*, p. 5. Wolffe was granted unusual access to the candidate during the course of the campaign, and claims that Obama suggested he write a chronicle of the campaign, telling him, "why can't you write a book about it. Like Theodore White. Those are great books."

39. Joan and Clay Blair's *The Search for JFK* (New York: Berkley Publishing, 1976) was the first book to begin to get beyond the Camelot myth and tell the unvarnished truth about Kennedy's life and presidency.

40. Remnick's *The Bridge* is the most comprehensive biography of Obama as of this writing. Based on reading most of the literature and extensive interviews with family, friends, and associates, in the end *The Bridge* remains largely an engagement with Obama's memoir and to a lesser extent his *The Audacity of Hope*; that is, Remnick adds detail and minor corrections to Obama's own books on his life and early career; hence, Remnick's story remains fundamentally Obama's story as told by Obama.

41. Stu Glauberman and Jerry Burris, *The Dream Begins: How Hawaii Shaped Barack Obama* (Honolulu: Watermark Publishing, 2009), pp. 109–11; and Richard Serrano, "Obama's Peers Didn't See His Angst," *Los Angeles Times*, Mar. 11, 2007.

42. Richard Wolffe, Jessica Ramirez, and Jeffrey Bartholet, "When Barry became Barack," *Newsweek*, Mar. 31, 2008.

43. Barack Obama, *Dreams of My Father* (New York: Crown: 1995), p. 116.

44. Wolffe, Ramirez, and Bartholet, "When Barry became Barack."

45. W. E. B. Du Bois, *The Souls of Black Folk*, "Introduction" by Saunders Redding (New York: Fawcett Publications, 1963), p. 17.

46. Quoted from Randall Kennedy, *Sellout: The Politics of Racial Betrayal* (New York: Pantheon, 2008), p. 12.

47. Mary Waters, *Ethnic Options: Choosing Identities in America* (Berkeley: University of California Press, 1990).

48. Kennedy, *Sellout*, p. 14.

49. Glauberman and Burris, *The Dream Begins*, pp. 77–78.

50. Ibid., p. 78.

51. Obama, *Dreams*, p. 91.

52. Ibid., p. 94.

53. Ibid., p. 194.

54. G. Reginald Daniel, *More than Black: Multiracial Identity and the New Racial Order* (Philadelphia: Temple University Press, 2002); and Jon Michael Spencer, *The New Colored People: The Mixed Race Movement in America* (New York: New York University Press, 1997).

55. Obama, *Dreams*, p. 76.

56. Ibid., p. 90.

57. Ibid., p. 46.

58. Janny Scott, "A Free Spirited Woman Who Set Obama's Course," *New York Times*, Mar. 14, 2008; and Glauberman and Burris, *The Dream Begins*, p. 36. See also Remnick, *The Bridge*, pp. 45–62.

59. Obama, *Dreams*, p. 20.

60. Ibid., p. 116.

61. Ibid., pp. 46–47.

62. Barack Obama, *The Audacity of Hope* (New York: Crown, 2006), p. 3. In a 2008 interview Obama said, "I'm pretty well adjusted. You know, you can psychoanalyze my father leaving and this and that but a lot of those things I resolved a long time ago. I'm pretty happy with life." Dan Balz and Haynes Johnson, "A Confluence of Public Mood and Appeal," *Washington Post*, Aug. 3, 2009.

63. Obama, *Dreams*, pp. 46–47.

64. Gerald Horne, "Rethinking the History and Future of the Communist Party," *Political Affairs*, Mar. 28, 2007, 128–47.

65. Glauberman and Burris, *The Dream Begins*, p. 128.

66. Frank Marshall Davis, *Livin' the Blues: Memoirs of a Black Journalist and Poet*, ed. with Introduction by John Edgar Tidwell (Madison: University of Wisconsin Press, 1992), p. 9.

67. Ibid., p. 312.

68. Dudley Randall, "Mystery Poet: Interview with Frank Marshall Davis," *Black World* 23 (1974): 9.

69. Davis, *Livin' the Blues*, p. xiii.

70. Ibid., p. 330.

71. Ibid.

72. Obama, *Dreams*, p. 89.

73. I draw here on the entry on "Blackness" from Robert C. Smith, *Encyclopedia of African American Politics* (New York: Facts on File, 2003), pp. 40–41.

74. Ronald Williams, "Barack Obama and the Complicated Boundaries of Blackness," *Black Scholar* 38 (2008): 55–61.

75. Obama, *The Audacity of Hope*, p. 233.

76. Kennedy, *Sellout*, p. 76.

77. William Cross, *Shades of Blackness: Diversity in African American Identity* (Philadelphia: Temple University Press, 1991).

78. Tommie Shelby, *We Who Are Dark: The Philosophical Foundations of Black Solidarity* (Cambridge, MA: Harvard University Press, 2005), p. 154.

79. Robert C. Smith, *Conservatism and Racism and Why in America They Are the Same* (Albany, NY: SUNY Press, 2010).

80. Obama, *Dreams*, p. 81.

81. Ibid., p. 80.

82. Ibid., p. 106.

83. Ibid., pp. 73–74.

84. Ibid.

85. Mendel, *From Promise to Power*, p. 45.

86. Glauberman and Burris, *The Dream Begins*, pp. 100, 107. On basketball and African American cultural identity, see Reuben May, *Living through the Hoop: High School Basketball, Race and the American Dream* (New York: New York University Press, 2007).

87. Michael Eric Dyson, "His Way with Words begin at Pulpit," *Washington Post*, Jan. 18, 2009.

88. Ibid.

89. Ibid.

90. Nia-Malika Henderson, "Blacks, Whites Hear Obama Differently," *Politico*, Mar. 3, 2009.

91. Dyson, "His Way with Words Begin at Pulpit."

92. Henderson, "Blacks, Whites Hear Obama Differently."

93. Ibid.

94. On various ways to understand the nationalist tradition, see Sterling Stuckey, *The Ideological Origins of Black Nationalism* (Boston: Beacon Press, 1972); Tommie Shelby, *We Who Are Dark: The Philosophical Foundations of Black Solidarity*; James Lance Taylor, *Black Nationalism in the United States: From Malcolm X to Barack Obama* (Boulder, CO: Lynne Rienner,2011); and Robert C. Smith, "Ideology as the Enduring Dilemma of Black Politics," in *Dilemma of Black Politics*, ed. Georgia Persons (New York: Harper Collins, 1993).

95. Obama, *Dreams*, pp. 183–84.

96. Ibid., p. 183.

97. Ibid., p. 184.

98. Ibid., p. 186

99. Hank DeZutter, "What Makes Obama Run?" *Chicago Reader*, Dec. 8, 1995.

100. Ibid.

101. Obama, *Dreams,* p. 123.

Chapter 8. Religion and the Election of 1960

1. Richard Whalen, *The Founding Father: The Story of Joseph P. Kennedy* (New York: New American Library, 1964), p. 461.

2. From 1956 to 1960, Joe Kennedy was the mastermind of his son's quest for the presidency. But because of his unsavory reputation and unpopularity among liberals and party stalwarts like Eleanor Roosevelt and Harry Truman, he operated behind the scenes, was rarely seen in public, and hardly ever appeared with his son. But Shaun Casey writes, "All parties were reporting to

Joseph P. Kennedy." See *The Making of a Catholic President: Kennedy vs. Nixon 1960* (New York: Oxford, 2009), p. 7.

3. The full text of the memorandum is reprinted as an appendix in Victor Lasky, *J.F.K.: The Man and the Myth* (New York: Macmillan, 1963), pp. 587–88.

4. Casey suggests that Stevenson did not wish to select Kennedy and "felt that throwing the vice presidential selection to the convention would give him a way to avoid naming Kennedy to the ticket without offending Joseph Kennedy. He could have the Kennedy money with fewer strings attached." *The Making of a Catholic President*, p. 7.

5. Richard Reeves, *President Kennedy: A Profile* (New York: Simon and Schuster, 1993), p. 15.

6. Joe Kennedy may have intervened with the Pulitzer board in order to get his son the prize. See Garry Wills, *The Kennedy Imprisonment: Mediation on Power* (New York: Simon and Schuster, 1982), p. 141. Among the books that were in competition with *Profiles* were James MacGregor Burns, *Roosevelt: The Lion and the Fox*; Alpheus Mason's *Harlan Fiske Stone: Pillar of the Laws*; and Samuel Flagg Bemis's *John Quincy Adams and the Union.* Wills writes, "It would have been ridiculous to place Kennedy's work in the company of these biographies" (p. 141). And David Stewart concludes, *Profiles* "was replete with factual and analytic errors." See *Impeached: The Trial of President Andrew Johnson and the Fight for Lincoln's Legacy* (New York: Simon and Schuster, 2009), pp. 421–25.

7. Reeves, *A Question of Character*, p. 445.

8. James MacGregor Burns, *John Kennedy: A Political Profile* (New York: Harcourt Brace, 1960), pp. 211–12.

9. Reeves, *A Question of Character*, p. 453.

10. Cited in Casey, *The Making of a Catholic President*, p. 24.

11. Ibid.

12. Robert Dallek, *An Unfinished Life: John F. Kennedy, 1917–63* (Boston: Little, Brown, 2003), p. 581.

13. Casey, *The Making of a Catholic President*, pp. 188–89.

14. Seymour Hersh, *The Dark Side of Camelot* (Boston: Little, Brown, 1997), p. 123.

15. On Lyndon Johnson's use of Kennedy's health as an issue see Dallek, *An Unfinished Life*, p. 261.

16. Dallek, who has conducted the most detailed analysis of the President's health records, writes, his "health troubles were a constant strain on his ability to meet presidential responsibilities. But he concludes that Kennedy courageously surmounted his suffering and his "medical difficulties did not significantly undermine his performance as president on any major question," ibid., pp. 471, 705.

17. Reeves, *President Kennedy*, p. 397.

18. Reeves, *A Question of Character*, p. 449.

19. Mark S. Massa writes that Truman privately opposed Kennedy on religious grounds but was unwilling to alienate the party's Catholic constituency so he expressed his opposition on the basis of age and experience. See *Catholics and American Culture* (New York: Crossroads Publishing, 1999), p. 78.

20. After the election Joe Kennedy, recalling that he had intentionally not appeared with his son during the campaign, declared, "now, I can appear with him any time I want." See "Joseph Kennedy Is Back on Scene after Seclusion in Campaign," *New York Times*, Jan. 8, 1961, as quoted in Thurston Clarke, *Ask Not: The Inauguration of John F. Kennedy and the Speech that Changed America* (New York: Henry Holt, 2004), p. 55.

21. Whalen, *The Founding Father*, p. 436.

22. Dallek, *An Unfinished Life*, p. 256. Always sensitive about the subject of his father's money, at the 1958 gridiron dinner Kennedy quipped, "I just received the following message from my generous daddy: Dear Jack—Don't buy one more vote than necessary—I'm damned if I'll pay for a landslide." Quoted in Theodore Sorensen, *Counselor: A Life at the Edge of History* (New York: Harper, 2008), p. 108.

23. Reeves, *A Question of Character*, p. 449.

24. Lasky, *J.F.K.*, p. 246.

25. Dallek, *An Unfinished Life*, p. 249.

26. Lasky, *J.F.K.*, p. 246.

27. Burns, *John Kennedy*, p. 174.

28. Steward, *Impeached*, pp. 294–95, 308–09.

29. John F. Kennedy, *Profiles in Courage* (New York: Harpers, 1957), p. 103.

30. Ibid.

31. On Stevenson's ambivalence on civil rights see Jeff Broadwater, *Adlai Stevenson and American Politics* (New York: Twayne, 1994), p. 168; and John Bartlow Martin, *Adlai Stevenson of Illinois: The Life and Times* (New York: Doubleday, 1976), p. 554.

32. Mark Stern, "John F. Kennedy and Civil Rights: From Congress to the Presidency," *Presidential Studies Quarterly* 19 (1989): 797–823. See also Nick Bryant, *Bystander: John F. Kennedy and the Struggle for Black Equality* (New York: Basic Books, 2006).

33. Lasky, *J.F.K.*, p. 379. Kennedy subsequently bought Powell's support by offering him $50,000 to make ten campaign speeches. Although Powell had initially requested $300,000, with the smaller sum he became an enthusiastic Kennedy supporter delivering speeches in clerical garb denouncing religious bigotry and equating it with racism. See Thomas Carty, *A Catholic in the White House? Religion, Politics and John F. Kennedy* (New York: Palgrave Macmillan, 2004), p. 83, 91.

34. Lasky, *J.F.K.*, p. 200.

35. Casey, *The Making of a Catholic President*, p. 60.

36. Quoted in Burns, *John Kennedy*, p. 243.

37. Lasky, *J.F.K.*, p. 38.

38. Theodore White, *The Making of the President 1960* (New York: Athenaeum, 1961), p. 40; and Sorensen, *Counselor.*

39. Massa, *Catholics and American Culture*, p. 78; and Andrew Greeley, "John F. Kennedy: Doctor of the Church," in *The Catholic Experience: An*

Interpretation of the History of American Catholicism, by Andrew Greeley (New York: Doubleday, 1967), p. 28.

40. Burns, *John Kennedy*, pp. 249, 97.

41. Greeley, "John F. Kennedy," p. 273.

42. Fletcher Knebel, "A Catholic in the White House?" *Look*, Mar. 3, 1959, as quoted in Massa, *Catholics and American Culture*, p. 98.

43. "Catholic Censure of Kennedy Rises," *New York Times*, Mar. 1, 1959.

44. Quoted in Massa, *Catholics and American Culture*, p. 133.

45. Casey, *The Making of a Catholic President*, p. 23. Al Smith Jr. endorsed Nixon.

46. Donald Robinson, *To the Best of My Ability: The Presidency and the Political System* (New York: Norton, 1987), p. 152.

47. Dallek, *An Unfinished Life*, pp. 229–30.

48. White, *The Making of the President 1960*, p. 55.

49. Casey, *The Making of a Catholic President*, p. 65.

50. Ibid. p. 66.

51. White, *The Making of the President 1960*, p. 95.

52. Casey, *The Making of a Catholic President*, p. 66.

53. For a detailed study of the West Virginia primary see Dan Fleming, *Kennedy vs. Humphrey, 1960: The Pivotal Battle for the Democratic Presidential Nomination* (Jefferson, NC: McFarland, 1992).

54. W. J. Rorabaugh, *The Real Making of the President: Kennedy, Nixon and the 1960 Election* (Lawrence: University Press of Kansas, 2009), p. 54–55; Hersh, *The Dark Side of Camelot*, p. 95.

55. Rorabaugh, *The Real Making of the President*, p. 55.

56. The Kennedy organization also recruited Franklin Delano Roosevelt Jr. to campaign with and for the candidate. President Roosevelt was an iconic figure in the state, and his son's appearances on behalf of Kennedy most likely contributed to Kennedy's margin of victory.

57. John F. Kennedy, "Acceptance Speech Democratic National Convention," July 1960. http://www.americanrhetoric.com/speeches/jfk1960dnc.htm.

58. Philip Converse, "The Concept of a Normal Vote"; and Angus Campbell, "A Classification of Presidential Elections" in *Elections and the Political Order*, ed. Angus Campbell et al. (New York: Wiley, 1966).

59. Converse, "The Concept of the Normal Vote."

60. Kennedy, "Acceptance Speech."

61. Burns, *John Kennedy*, p. 239.

62. 330 U.S. (1947).

63. Ibid.

64. Casey, *The Making of a Catholic President*, pp. 110, 177–78, 184–85.

65. Paul Blanchard, *American Freedom and Catholic Power* (Boston: Beacon Press, 1958), p. ix.

66. Ibid., p. 2.

67. Carty, *A Catholic in the White House?* p. 63.

68. Martin Luther King Jr. "Paul's Letter to the American Church," in *A Knock at Midnight: Inspirations From the Great Sermons of Rev. Martin Luther King, Jr.*, ed. Clayborne Carson and Peter Holloran (New York: Warner Books, 2000), p. 30.

69. Carty, *A Catholic in the White House*, p. 91.

70. Ibid., p. 93.

71. Ibid.

72. Ibid., p. 92.

73. White, *The Making of the President 1960,* pp. 385–87; and Arthur Schlesinger Jr. *Robert F. Kennedy and His Times* (Boston: Houghton Mifflin, 1978), pp. 233–35. A 1959 *Jet* magazine survey concluded "many blacks are opposed to Kennedy because of religion." But on the Sunday before the election the Kennedy campaign distributed at black churches a leaflet describing Kennedy's call to Mrs. King and quoting statements from King senior and junior.

74. Casey, *The Making of a Catholic President*, p. 11.

75. Ibid., pp. 153–56.

76. Ibid., pp. 126, 130, 137, 192; and Carty, *A Catholic in the White House?* pp. 50–57.

77. Massa, *Catholics and American Culture*, p. 4.

78. Ibid., p. 93.

79. Ibid.

80. Philip Converse, "Religion and Politics: The 1960 Election," in *Elections and the Political Order*, ed. Campbell et al., pp. 123–24. See also "The Religious Issue Hot and Getting Hotter," *Newsweek*, Sept. 19, 1960.

81. Quoted in Massa, *Catholics and American Culture*, p. 95.

82. Casey, *The Making of a Catholic President*, p. 175.

83. Ibid., p. 176.

84. Ibid., p. 164.

85. White, *The Making of the President 1960*, p. 313.

86. Massa, *Catholics and American Culture*, p. 84.

87. "Address to Greater Houston Ministerial Association." I am quoting here from the text of the speech as reprinted in White, *The Making of the President 1960*, p. 392.

88. Massa, *Catholics and American Culture*, p. 84.

89. Lasky, *J.F.K.*, p. 482.

90. The Republican Catholic governor of Rhode Island Christopher Del Soto initiated a national campaign on Mitchell's behalf.

91. Carty, *A Catholic in the White House?* p. 56.

92. Students of the election still contend that there is credible evidence of vote fraud in Illinois and Texas sufficient to swing those states and thus the election to Nixon. See Lasky, *J.F.K.*, pp. 495–96; Hersh, *The Dark Side of Camelot*, chap. 10; Rorabaugh, *The Real Making of the President*, pp. 187–90; and James Giglio, *The Presidency of John F. Kennedy*, 2nd ed. (Lawrence: University Press of Kansas, 2006), pp. 19–20. Nixon was presented some of this evidence shortly after the election and advised by some of his staff to challenge the results in court. He declined. In his memoir, Nixon wrote that Illinois Senator Everett

Dirksen, the minority leader, urged him not to concede and request a recount but Nixon said he concluded "a presidential recount would require up to half a year, during which time the legitimacy of Kennedy's election would be in doubt. The effect would be devastating to America's foreign relations. I could not subject the country to such a situation. And what if I demanded a recount and it turned out despite the vote fraud Kennedy still had won? Charges of 'sore loser' would follow me through history and remove any possibility of a further political career." See *RN: The Memoirs of Richard Nixon* (New York: Grosset and Dunlap, 1978), p. 224.

93. Dallek, *An Unfinished Life*, p. 296.

94. Rorabaugh, *The Real Making of the President*, pp. 182–83.

95. Converse, "Religion and Politics," pp. 104–05.

96. William Shannon, *The American Irish: A Political and Social Portrait* (Amherst: University of Massachusetts Press, 1989), pp. 411–12.

97. Ibid., p. 410.

98. Converse, "Religion and Politics," p. 93.

99. Ibid.

100. Ibid.

101. Rorabaugh, *The Real Making of the President*, p. 185.

Chapter 9. Race and the Election of 2008

1. Donald Robinson, *To the Best of My Ability* (New York: Norton, 1987), p. 167.

2. Ibid., and Nelson Polsby, *Consequences of Party Reform* (New York: Oxford, 1983).

3. Robinson, *To the Best of My Ability*, p. 166.

4. Richard Herrera, "Are Super Delegates Super," *Political Behavior* 16 (1994): 79–82.

5. David Plouffe, *The Audacity to Win: The Inside Story and Lessons of Baraka Obama's Historic Victory* (Waterville, ME: Thorndike Press, 2009), p. 5.

6. On the jumpers—the screaming teens and later middle-age women—during the Kennedy campaign, see White, *The Making of the President 1960*, p. 331.

7. Robert C. Smith, "In the Shadows of Ronald Reagan: Bill Clinton and Civil Rights Policymaking," in *Winning While Losing? Civil Rights, the Conservative Movement, and the Presidency from Nixon to Obama*, eds. Kenneth Osgood and Derrick White (Gainesville: University Press of Florida, forthcoming).

8. Ibid.

9. Toni Morrison, "Clinton as the First Black President," *New Yorker*, Oct. 1998, p. 11.

10. DeWayne Wickham, *Bill Clinton and Black America* (New York: Ballantine Books, 2002), p. 239.

11. These polls are referred to in Michael Lewis–Beck, Charles Tien, and Richard Nadeau, "Obama's Missing Landslide: A Racial Cost?" paper prepared

for presentation at the annual meeting of the Southern Political Science Association, February 7–11, 2009, New Orleans, pp. 14–15.

12. In 2008 election year polls and surveys found that whites did not hesitate "to make frankly derogatory comments about blacks," with more than 20 percent describing "most blacks" as "violent," "boastful," and "complaining." See Paul Sniderman and Edward Stiglitz, "Race and the Moral Character of the Modern American Experience," *The Forum* 6 (2008): 1–15.

13. The Gallup poll was conducted in February 2007. http://www.dailykos.com/storyonly/207/2/16/16/154311/206.

14. Lewis–Beck, Tien, and Nadeau, "Obama's Missing Landslide."

15. Obama's Oct. 2, 2002, antiwar speech was strategically efficacious in its appeal to the Illinois primary electorate in 2004, as well as the Iowa and New Hampshire Democratic electorates in 2008. "I don't oppose all wars," he said, just "dumb war, rash war," thus establishing his credentials as a foreign policy realist. Then he burnished his partisan, ideological credentials: "What I am opposed to is the attempt by political hacks like Karl Rove trying to distract us [from the issues of poverty, health and the economy] . . . and the cynical attempt by Richard Pearle and Paul Wolfowitz and other armchair, weekend warriors in this administration to shove their own ideological agendas down our throats, irrespective of the cost in lives lost and hardships bourne [*sic*]." The text of the speech is at http://www.leslig.org/blog/2008/0/baraka_obamas_2002_speech.html.

16. Barack Obama, "A More Perfect Union," Mar. 18, 2008, as reprinted in the *Black Scholar* 38 (2009): 17.

17. Matthew Musk, "Obama Rewriting Rules for Raising Campaign Money," *Washington Post*, Mar. 28, 2008. See also Peter Francia, Gregory Fortelny, and Clyde Wilcox, "The Obama Juggernaut: Presidential Fundraising 2008" in *Understanding the Presidency*, ed. James Pfiffiner and Roger Davidson (New York: Longman, 2011).

18. Federal Election Commission, "2008 Presidential Campaign Financial Activity Summarized," http://www.fec.gov./press/press2009/200900608 presstat.shtml.

19. Plouffe, *The Audacity to Win*, p. 17.

20. Matt Bai, "Is Obama the End of Black Politics?" *New York Times Magazine*, Aug. 10, 2008.

21. Plouffe, *The Audacity to Win*, p. 151.

22. Ibid.

23. I am using data from the cumulative primary exit polls as reported by CNN. http://www.cnn.com/ELECTION/2008/primaries/results/polls.

24. Ibid.

25. James Baron, "9 Jewish Leaders Say E-Mail Spread Lies about Obama," *New York Times*, Jan. 16, 2008.

26. Plouffe, *The Audacity to Win*, p. 228.

27. Plouffe says the campaign did not realize the connection to Kennedy by holding the last night of the convention in a sports arena but "appreciated the connection," ibid., p. 302.

28. "Remarks of Senator Barack Obama: The American Promise (Democratic Convention)," http://www.barackobama.com/208/08/28/remarks_of_senator_barack_obama_108.php.

29. William Julius Wilson, *The Truly Disadvantaged: The Inner City, the Underclass and Public Policy* (Chicago: University of Chicago Press, 1987), p. 117.

30. Ibid., p. 124.

31. Ibid., chap. 10. In his most recent work on the subject Wilson appears to back away from this hidden agenda in favor of more race-specific or targeted policies. See *More than Race: Being Black and Poor in the Inner City* (New York: Norton, 2009), pp. 141–44.

32. Barack Obama, *The Audacity of Hope* (New York: Crown, 2006), p. 247. In *Dreams* Obama quotes Wright as referring to Wilson as that "uneducated brother[s]" at the University of Chicago talking about the "declining significance of race," p. 259.

33. Obama, *The Audacity of Hope*, p. 256.

34. Ibid., p. 255.

35. "Obama Shifts on Welfare" http://blogs.abcnews.com/politicalradar/2008/06/obama–shifts–on.html.

36. Bob Egelko, "Where Candidates Stand on Death Penalty, Crime," *San Francisco Chronicle*, Feb. 10, 2008.

37. Cheryl Harris offers a contextual analysis of Obama's studied ambiguity on affirmative action and race conscious remedies in "An Affirmative Act? Barack Obama in the Past, Present and Future of Race Conscious Remedies" in *The Obama Phenomenon: Toward a Multiracial Democracy*, ed. Charles Henry, Robert Allen, and Robert Chrisman (Urbana: University of Illinois Press, 2011).

38. *Regents of University of California vs. Bakke* 438 U.S. 265 (1978).

39. Jackson's threat was direct and public, telling the *New York Times*, "There is no question about it. My position on it was public, and I stated it to [Clinton]. I had no inclination to run. My choice was, rather, to support him. But if he had taken away the program for equal opportunity, he would have crossed the line." Steven Holmes, "On Civil Rights Clinton Steers a Bumpy Course," *New York Times*, Oct. 20, 1996.

40. Ginger Thompson, "Seeking Unity, Obama Feels Pull of Racial Divide," *Washington Post*, Feb. 12, 2008.

41. Debra Dickerson, "Colorblind," Salon.com, http://www.salon.com/opinion/feature/2007/01/22obama/print.html. On the debate about Obama's blackness during the campaign, see also Brent Staples, "Debating the Debate over the Blackness of Obama," *New York Times*, Feb. 11, 2007.

42. Ibid.

43. Janny Scott, "A Biracial Candidate Walks His Own Fine Line," *New York Times*, Dec. 29, 2007.

44. Jonathan Weisman, "Rev. Jackson Apologizes to Obama," *Washington Post*, July 10, 2008. Jackson made these comments on *Fox News*, unaware that he was being recorded. He was upset by an Obama speech suggesting that

blacks should rely on church-based initiatives rather than the government to resolve their problems.

45. Ibid.

46. Ronald Walters and Robert C. Smith, *African American Leadership* (Albany: SUNY Press, 1999), pp. 7–14, 36–39. Andrew Young reflected this concern when he remarked that he was supporting Clinton because when he called people he knew in Chicago none of them knew anything about Obama.

47. Citied in G. Reginald Daniel, "Race, Multiculturalism and Barack Obama: Toward a More Perfect Union," *Black Scholar* 39 (2009): 51–59. See also David Wilson and Matthew Hunt, "The Eyes of the Beholder: Cross–Racial Perceptions of Barack Obama's Racial Identity," paper prepared for presentation at the 42nd annual meeting of the National Conference of Black Political Scientists, Raleigh, NC, March 16–21, 2011.

48. Frederick Harris, *Survey on Race, Politics and Society* (New York: Columbia University, Center on African American Politics, Sept. 2008).

49. Ibid.

50. "Black spokesmen Title Up for Grabs," http://www.gallup.com/poll/108805/black-spokesmen-title-still-grabs.aspx.

51. Marc Ambinder, "Race Over," *The Atlantic*, January–February 2009, p. 23.

52. Plouffe, *The Audacity to Win*, pp. 124–25.

53. Ibid. Sharpton did not endorse Obama and Plouffe writes that the campaign would have preferred he endorse Clinton. However, as the New York primary on Super Tuesday approached Obama had a well-publicized—including television cameras—lunch with Sharpton at a Harlem restaurant.

54. Ibid., p. 99.

55. Ibid., p. 98.

56. Thompson, "Seeking Unity."

57. Ambinder, "Race Over."

58. Darryl Fears, "Black Community Is Increasingly Protective of Obama," *Washington Post*, May 10, 2008.

59. Raymond Hernandez, "A New Campaign Charge: You Supported Clinton," *New York Times*, July 1, 2008.

60. Ibid.

61. Among prominent African American Republicans or conservatives endorsing Obama was Colin Powell; Armstrong Williams, the columnist and radio talk host; and Rev. Kirbyjon Caldwell, President George W. Bush's long-time spiritual advisor.

62. Joseph McCormick and Charles Jones, "The Conceptualization of Deracialization," in *Dilemmas of Black Politics*, ed. Georgia Persons (New York: Harper Collins, 1993), p. 76.

63. Plouffe, *The Audacity to Win*, pp. 204, 207.

64. Quoted in Richard Wolffe, *Renegade: The Making of a President* (New York: Crown, 2009).

65. Dwight Hopkins, "Race, Religion and the Race for the White House," and John Jackson, "Obama, Black Religion, and the Reverend Wright Controversy," in *The Obama Phenomenon*, ed. Henry, Allen, and Chrisman.

66. Ben Wallace, "The Radical Roots of Barack Obama," *Rolling Stone*, Feb. 12, 2007, p. 19.

67. Plouffe, *The Audacity to Win*, p. 41.

68. Jodi Kantor, "Disinvite by Obama Criticized," *New York Times*, Mar. 6, 2007.

69. Ibid.

70. Ibid.

71. Ibid.

72. Plouffe, *The Audacity to Win*, p. 41.

73. "Preacher with a Penchant for Controversy," *Washington Post*, Mar. 15, 2008.

74. Plouffe, *The Audacity to Win*, p. 211.

75. Ibid.

76. Wolffe, *Renegade*, p. 178.

77. A *CBS News* poll indicated 70 percent of those polled thought that Obama had effectively explained his relationship with Wright and that the controversy would not affect how they voted, CBS.com, Mar. 19, 2008.

78. "Mr. Obama's Profile in Courage," *New York Times*, Mar. 9, 2008.

79. Andrew Sullivan, "The Speech," Atlantic.com, Mar. 18, 2008.

80. Thomas Sugure, *Not Even Past: Barack Obama and the Burden of Race* (Princeton, NJ: Princeton University Press, 2010), p. 118.

81. Houston Baker Jr., "What Should Obama Do about Jeremiah Wright," Salon.com, Mar. 29, 2008.

82. Obama, "A More Perfect Union."

83. Wolffe, *Renegade*, p. 183.

84. There were some tensions around race during the Democratic primaries. Bill Clinton was accused of using the "race card" when he compared Obama's victory in the South Carolina to Jesse Jackson's and for his dismissal of Obama's opposition to the Iraq War as a "fairy tale." Some African Americans also expressed concern about the racial implications of Hillary Clinton's remarks suggesting that Martin Luther King Jr.'s "rhetoric" was not enough to pass the civil rights laws of the 1960s. Rather, she said, it took the "experience" of President Johnson. But these were rare and minor flaps.

85. Tali Mendelberg shows that the race card in U.S. elections historically has revolved around appeals, whether explicit or implicit, to blacks' economic dependency, laziness, and their desire to subjugate whites. See *The Race Card: Campaign Strategy, Implicit Messages and the Norm of Equality* (Princeton, NJ: Princeton University Press, 2001), p. 95.

86. Smith, "In the Shadows of Ronald Reagan."

87. William Kristol, "The Wright Stuff," *New York Times*, Oct. 5, 2008. In this column Kristol reports on an interview with Sarah Palin where she lamented the campaign's failure to bring up the Wright issue. Kristol agreed and used the column to urge McCain to use the issue as early as the next debate, two days away. I had predicted the McCain campaign would run a series of ads connecting Wright with Louis Farrakhan, Farrakhan with Fidel Castro, Gaddafi, Yasser Arafat, and Obama with Wright, with the caption reading, "You are known by the company you keep." Given the way Republican strategists since the 1970s

have relied on race-based communications in presidential elections, it is all the more puzzling that the McCain campaign did not attempt to use the Wright relationships with ads similar to this one.

88. Nickolas Kristoff, "The Push to Otherize Obama," *New York Times*, Sept. 21, 2008. See also Michael Tesler and David Sears, *Obama's Race: The 2008 Election and the Dream of a Post-Racial America* (Chicago: University of Chicago Press, 2010), chap. 7, where they show how the association of Obama with Muslims affected voting in the general election. They suggest the affect was modest because those who believed he was a Muslim were also ideological and racial conservatives who were unlikely to vote for Obama under any circumstances.

89. Stu Glauberman and Jerry Burris, *The Dream Begins: How Hawaii Shaped Barack Obama* (Honolulu: Watermark Publishing, 2009), p. 138.The text of Penn's memo to Clinton can be read at http:/www.theatlantic.com/politics/archive/2008/11penn-strategy-memo-march-19-2008/37952.

90. Ibid.

91. Ibid., pp. 137–38.

92. Nedra Rickler, "Clinton Volunteer Asked to Resign," *San Francisco Chronicle*, Dec. 9, 2007.

93. Jim Kuhnhenn, "Obama Photo Causes a Stir," *San Francisco Chronicle*, Feb. 25, 2008.

94. "Meet the Press," *NBC News*, Oct. 19, 2008.

95. Sara Kugler, "Democrats Outraged over Satirical *New Yorker* Cover," *West County Times*, July 18, 2008.

96. Ibid.

97. Douglass Daniel, "Analysis: Palin's Words Carry Racial Tinge," *West County Times*, Oct. 5, 2008.

98. Randall Woods, *LBJ: Architect of American Ambition* (New York: Free Press, 2006), p. 480.

99. The seminal work is Edward Carmines and James Stimson, *Issue Evolution: Race and the Transformation of American Politics* (Princeton, NJ: Princeton University Press, 1989). See also Robert Huckfeldt and Carol Weitzel Kohfeld, *Race and the Decline of Class in American Politics* (Urbana: University of Illinois Press, 1989); Dan T. Carter, *From George Wallace to Newt Gingrich: Race in the Conservative Counterrevolution, 1963–1994* (Baton Rouge: Louisiana State University Press, 1996); and Robert C. Smith, *Conservatism and Racism and Why in America They Are the Same* (Albany: SUNY Press, 2010).

100. Morris Fiorina, *Retrospective Voting in American Elections* (New Haven, CT: Yale University Press, 1981).

101. Michael Lewis-Beck, *Forecasting Elections* (Washington, DC: Congressional Quarterly Press, 1992).

102. See the symposium edited by James Campbell "Forecasting the 2008 National Elections," *PS: Political Science and Politics*, 41 (2008): 631–96.

103. Lewis-Beck, Tien, and Nadeau, "Obama's Missed Landslide," p. 7. See also James Campbell, "An Exceptional Election: Performance, Values and

Crisis in the 2008 Presidential Election," *Forum* 16 (2008): 1–22. Alan Abramowitz writes, "Obama's twelve-point deficit among white voters was identical to Al Gore's in 2000. However, the fact that white voters favored the Republican candidate by a double-digit margin in 2008 despite the poor conditions of the economy and the unpopularity of the incumbent Republican president suggests racial prejudice did affect the level of white support for the Democratic candidate." See *The Disappearing Center: Engaged Citizens, Polarization and American Democracy* (New Haven, CT: Yale University Press, 2010), p. 115. Other scholars who have found evidence of "ballot-box racism" include Walter Hill (who estimates the race deficit at 2.2 percent), "Should Obama Have Won in a Landslide in 2008 as Did Roosevelt in 1936?" paper prepared for presentation at the 2011 annual meeting of the Midwest Political Science Association, Chicago, Mar. 31–Apr. 2; and Spencer Piston, "How Explicit Racial Prejudice Hurt Obama in the 2008 Election," *Political Behavior* 32 (2010): 431–51.

104. Tasha Philpot, Daron Shaw, and Ernest McGowan, "Winning the Race: Black Turnout in the 2008 Presidential Election," *Public Opinion Quarterly* 73 (2009): 995–1022.

105. Ibid.

106. "Black Politics and Society."

107. Stephen Ansolabehere and Charles Stewart, "Amazing Race," *Boston Review*, Jan.–Feb. 2009.

108. "Behind the Numbers," *Washington Post*, Oct. 24, 2008.

109. Associated Press, "Two Polls Give Obama Edge," *West County Times*, Sept. 28, 2008.

Chapter 10. The Politics of Ethnic Avoidance in the Kennedy and Obama Administrations

1. Thomas Reeves, *A Question of Character: A Life of John F. Kennedy* (New York: Free Press, 1991), p. 228.

2. Robert Dallek, *An Unfinished Life: John F. Kennedy, 1914–63* (Boston: Little, Brown), p. 309.

3. Ibid.

4. Thurston Clarke, *Ask Not: The Inauguration of John F. Kennedy and the Speech that Changed America* (New York: Henry Holt, 2004), p. 55.

5. John Kenneth Galbraith, *Letters to Kennedy*, edited by James Goodman (Cambridge, MA: Harvard University Press, 1998).

6. At the inauguration, Clarke writes, Smith "was the only person to reveal his feelings by leaving his seat and walking back into the Capitol as Cardinal Cushing began his invocation. He watched the ceremony on a television monitor in the rotunda for a few minutes, but when Marian Anderson began singing the national anthem he ambled back to his office, apparently unable to stomach an inauguration showcasing a Roman Catholic Cardinal and a black American singer and culminating in an Irish Catholic president," ibid., p. 185.

7. Milton Cummings Jr. and Robert Peabody, "The Decision to Enlarge the Rules Committee: An Analysis of the 1960 Vote," and Peabody "The Enlarged Rules Committee," in *New Perspectives on the House of Representatives*, ed. Peabody and Nelson Polsby (Chicago: Rand McNally, 1963).

8. James Giglio, *The Presidency of John F. Kennedy*, 2nd ed. (Lawrence: University Press of Kansas, 2006), p. 101.

9. Robert Goldberg, *Barry Goldwater* (New Haven, CT: Yale University Press, 1995).

10. Giglio, *The Presidency of John F. Kennedy*, p. 41.

11. Ibid.

12. The United States did not engage the Northern Ireland problem until the Carter administration, when at the urgings of four of the nation's leading Catholic Irish politicians—Edward Kennedy, Daniel Moynihan, Tip O'Neill, and New York Governor Hugh Carey—the Democratic party platform included a plank declaring "the voice of the United States should be heard . . . against violence and terror, against discrimination repression and deprivation. . . ." President Carter later stopped arms sales to the Northern Ireland constabulary, which was viewed by many Catholics as a repressive force. Later, President Clinton appointed a special envoy who attempted to negotiate a resolution of the conflict.

13. Quoted in Lawrence McAndrews, "Beyond Appearances: Kennedy, Congress, Religion, and Federal Aid to Education," *Presidential Studies Quarterly* 21 (1991): 545.

14. Ibid.

15. Quoted in Hugh Douglas Price, "Race, Religion and the Rules Committee: The Kennedy Aid to Education Bills," in *The Uses of Power: Seven Cases in American Politics*, ed. Alan Westin (New York: Harcourt Brace and World, 1962), p. 23. Catholic clergy sent "pastoral letters" urging parishioners to write their congressmen urging defeat of the legislation unless some assistance was provided to their schools. Kennedy was upset by the stridency of the church hierarchy's oppositions, telling Sorensen that Cardinal Spellman, for example, "never said a word about any of Eisenhower's bills for public schools only, and he didn't go that far in 1949 either"; see Theodore Sorensen, *Kennedy* (New York: Harper and Row, 1965), p. 403.

16. For a history of consideration of federal aid to education in the House from 1945 to 1961 see Richard Fenno, "The House of Representatives and Federal Aid to Education" in *New Perspectives on the House of Representatives*, ed. Peabody and Polsby.

17. Price, "Race, Religion and the Rules Committee," p. 38.

18. Tom Wicker, *JFK and LBJ: The Influence of Personality on Politics* (New York: Morrow, 1968), p. 125.

19. Ibid.

20. Hugh Davis Graham, *The Uncertain Triumph: Federal Education Policy in the Kennedy and Johnson Years* (Chapel Hill: University of North Carolina Press, 1984), p. 21. See also Sorensen, *Kennedy*, p. 404, where he discusses "quiet and informal" meetings he and Secretary Ribicoff had with Catholics regarding the NDEA amendment.

21. Ibid.

22. Quoted in ibid., p. 22.

23. Quoted in Price, "Race, Religion and the Rules Committee," p. 68.

24. Graham, *The Uncertain Triumph*, p. 25.

25. Price, "Race, Religion and the Rules Committee," p. 69.

26. Sorensen, *Kennedy*, p. 406.

27. For a detailed study of the passage of the Elementary and Secondary Education Act, see Eugene Eidenberg and Roy Morey, *An Act of Congress: The Legislative Process and the Making of Education Policy* (New York, Norton, 1969).

28. Russell Renka, "Comparing Presidents Kennedy and Johnson as Legislative Leaders," *Presidential Studies Quarterly* 15 (1985): 806–27.

29. The so–called child-benefit theory of assistance to the children rather than to schools either won over or neutralized the opposition of most of the religious and secular opponents of aid to religious schools, winning endorsements from, among others, the American Jewish Committee, the National Council of Churches, and the National Education Association. Nevertheless, because of his concerns about a Protestant backlash, President Kennedy probably would not have been able to propose this compromise. See James Sundquist, *Politics and Policy: The Eisenhower, Kennedy and Johnson Years* (Washington, DC: Brookings Institution, 1968), pp. 210–13.

30. David Plouffe, *The Audacity to Win: The Inside Story and Lessons of Barack Obama's Historic Victory* (Waterville, ME: Thorndike Press, 2009), pp. 90–91. In an interesting albeit overdrawn account, James Kloppenberg locates Obama's overarching intellectual philosophy in the tradition of American pragmatism, which William James, Charles Pierce, and John Dewey developed. See *Reading Obama: Dreams, Hopes and the American Political Tradition* (Princeton, NJ: Princeton University Press, 2010). Overdrawn because even he concedes there is no "necessary connection between philosophical pragmatism and Obama's politics. The former does not entail the latter," p. 172.

31. Joseph Stiglitz, *Freefall: America, Free Markets and the Sinking of the World Economy* (New York: Norton, 2010), pp. 45–47.

32. David Mendel, *Obama: From Promise to Power* (New York: Harper/Collins Imprint, 2007), pp. 90–91.

33. Quoted in Stu Glauberman and Jerry Burris, *The Dream Begins: How Hawaii Shaped Barack Obama* (Honolulu: Watermark Publishing, 2009), p. 118.

34. Erwin Hargrove and Michael Nelson, *Presidents, Politics and Policy* (Baltimore, MD: John Hopkins University Press, 1984), p. 73.

35. Steven Kull et al., "America's Global Image in the Obama Era," The Program on International Policy Altitudes, University of Maryland, July 2009. http://www.worldpublicopinion.org/pipa/pdf/jul09_usobama_july09_packet.pdf.

36. Clarence Lusane, "We Must Lead the World: The Obama Doctrine and the Re–branding of U.S. Hegemony," in *The Obama Phenomena: Toward A Multi–racial Democracy*, ed. Charles Henry, Robert Allen, and Robert Chrisman (Urbana: University of Illinois, 2011); Andrew Bacevich, *Washington*

Rules: America's Path to Permanent War (New York: Metropolitan Press, 2010, pp. 213–21; and Robert Singh, "Continuity and Change in Obama's Foreign Policy," in *The Presidency: Appraisals and Prospects*, ed. Bert Rockman, Andrew Rudalevige, and Colin Campbell (Washington, DC: Congressional Quarterly Press, 2012), pp. 295–330.

37. Sheryl Gay Stolberg, "Gentle White House Nudges Test the Power of Persuasion," *New York Times*, Feb. 23, 2010. Jonathan Alter writes that in lobbying members of Congress Obama's "style was neither to twist arms or butter them up but to engage on issues, as one Congressman told him in a "comfortable, soothing, soft approach"; see *The Promise: Year One* (New York: Simon and Schuster, 2010), p. 409.

38. Stiglitz, *Freefall*, pp. 62–74.

39. Ibid. The Congressional Budget Office estimated that the legislation increased the inflation-adjusted GDP by between 1.7 and 4.5 percent (after mid-2009), reduced unemployment by 1 percent and increased employment by between 2 million and 4 million full–time jobs. See http://cboblog.cbo.gov/?p=1326.

40. Monte Poen, *Harry S. Truman versus the Medical Lobby* (Columbia: University of Missouri Press, 1979).

41. Haynes Johnson and David Broder, *The System: The American Way of Politics at the Breaking Point* (Boston: Little, Brown, 1997), p. 234.

42. Ibid.

43. Dan Balz and Jon Cohen, "New Poll Finds Voter Anger Drove Results of Mass. Election," *Washington Post*, Jan. 23, 2010.

44. Dan Balz and Jon Cohen, "Public Cooling to Health–Care Reform as Debate Drags on, Poll Finds," *Washington Post*, Dec. 16, 2009.

45. Robert Shapiro and Lawrence Jacobs, "Stimulating Representation: Elite Mobilization and Political Power in Health Care Reform," *Forum* 8 (2010); and Brendan Nyhan, "Why the 'Death Panel' Myth Wouldn't Die: Misinformation in the Health Care Reform Debate," *Forum* 8 (2010).

46. Balz and Cohen, "Public Cooling to Health Care Reform."

47. As a byproduct of use of the budget reconciliation process the administration was able to reform the student loan program, eliminating private student loans with federal subsidies and replacing them with direct government loans. Eliminating the private or-profit middlemen generated $61 billion in savings, half of which was used to increase student Pell Grants.

48. Ricardo Alonso–Zaldivar, "Insurance Rule Was Initially GOP Idea," *West County Times*, Mar. 28, 2010; and Jacob Hacker, "The Road to Somewhere: Why Health Care Reform Happened," *Perspectives on Politics* 8 (2010): 867.

49. David Leonhardt, "In Health Care Bill, Obama Attacks Wealth Inequity," *New York Times*, Mar. 23, 2010.

50. Census data for 2008 indicates that 10.8 percent of whites or 21.3 million persons were uninsured. Among blacks it was nearly double, 19.3 percent or 7.3 million persons. U.S. Bureau of the Census, "Income, Poverty and Health Insurance Coverage in the United States, 2008," news release, Sept. 10, 2009. A November 2009 Pew poll found that blacks were much more likely (67 percent) to support the health reform bill than whites (37 percent).

51. Barack Obama, *The Audacity of Hope* (New York: Crown, 2006), p. 207.

52. Sheldon Albert, "Obama Rejects Charges He's Ignoring Black People," Canada.com, Dec. 22, 2009. http://www.canada.com/business/story.html?id=2371848.

53. Presidential Press Conference, Apr. 30, 2009, Transcript, *New York Times.*

54. Howard Kurtz, "Color of Change," *Washington Post*, Dec. 23, 2009.

55. Ronald Walters, "Obama Rejects Special Needs of the Black Community," Black Commentator.com, Dec. 3, 2009.

56. Michael Shear and Perry Bacon, "Black Lawmakers Call on Obama to Do More on Behalf of Blacks," *Washington Post*, Dec. 9, 2009; and Steven Greenhouse, "NAACP Prods Obama on Job Losses," *New York Times*, Nov. 17, 2009.

57. Jim Kuhnhenn, "Panel OKs Key Regulatory Measure," *Washington Post*, Dec. 2, 2009.

58. Kurtz, "Color of Change."

59. Zenitha Prince, "Muffled Criticisms Reflect Racial Pride, Pragmatism," *Washington Afro-American*, Mar. 19, 2010.

60. "Obama's Report Card: One Year Later," Black Enterprise.com, Jan. 20, 2010, http://www.blackenterprise.com/business/2010/01/20/obamas-report-card-one-year-later/pr.

61. Jeffrey Jones, "Obama's Approval Slide, Poll Finds Whites Down to 39 percent," Nov. 24, 2009, http://www.gallup.com/poll/124484/obama-approval-slide-finds.

62. Obama at the NAACP Convention," transcript, July 27, 2009, http://www.cbsnews.com/blogs/2009/07/17/politics/politicalhotshee.

63. Ibid.

64. In what might be viewed as efforts to help blacks, the President created by executive order the Office of Urban Affairs and tasked its director—Latino Adolfo Corrion—to develop a new national urban policy to address on a metropolitan basis problems of poverty, crime, housing, and transportation. At the end of its third year, the office had not issued a report and the President had not proposed any new urban policy initiatives. The Attorney General in his first year substantially increased the Justice Department's civil rights enforcement budget and staff, and enhanced enforcement of racial antidiscrimination laws with a new focus on public and private policies that have a disparate impact on minorities. See Robin Shulman, "New White House Office to Redefine Urban Policy," *Washington Post*, July 3, 2009; and Charlie Savage, "Justice Dept. to Recharge Enforcement of Civil Rights," *New York Times*, Sept. 1, 2009.

65. Michael Tesler and David Sears, *Obama's Race: The 2008 Election and the Dream of a Post-Racial America* (Chicago: University of Chicago Press, 2010), pp. 144, 182. At the end of Obama's first year, 65 percent of Republicans said they thought his policies favored blacks.

66. Michael Fletcher and Michael Shear, "Obama Voices Regret to Policeman," *Washington Post*, July 25, 2009.

67. Henry Louis Gates, "An Accident of Time and Place," *The Root*, http://www.theroot.com/print22416.

68. "Obama's Ratings Slide across the Board," July 30, 2009, http://people-press.org/report/?pageid=1540.

69. Bob Herbert, "Anger Has Its Place," *New York Times*, Aug. 1, 2009.

70. Eric Knowles, Brian Lowery, and Rebecca Schomberg, "Racial Prejudice Predicts Opposition to Obama and His Care Reform Plan," *Journal of Experimental Psychology* 46 (2010): 420–23. On the racialization of attitudes toward health policy, see also Tesler and Sears, *Obama's Race*, pp. 155–56. See also Tesler, "The Spillover of Racialization into Health Care: How President Obama Polarized Public Opinion by Racial Attitudes and Race," *American Journal of Political Science* (forthcoming).

71. "Poll on Birthers: Most Southerners, Republicans Question Obama Citizenship," http://www.usnews.com/blogs/robert-schlesinger/2009/07/31 poll-0.

72. Ibid.

73. Ewen MacAskill, "Jimmy Carter: Animosity towards Barack Obama Is Due to Racism," http://www.guardian.co.uk/world/2009/spe/16/jimmy-carter-racism.

74. Ibid. In interviews on each of the Sunday talk shows (except Fox) the following week, Obama insisted that the vitriolic opposition to him was based on his policies not his race. See Mark Silva, "In Media Blitz, Obama Says Vitriol Isn't Racism-Based," *Los Angeles Times*, Sept. 19, 2009. Privately the President reportedly told friends at a May 2010 dinner that "race was probably a key component in the rising opposition to his presidency from conservatives, especially right-wing activists in the anti-incumbent Tea Party movement . . . a 'subterranean agenda' in the anti-Obama movement—a racially biased one." He went on to say this was "unfortunate," but "there was nothing he could do about it." Quoted in Kenneth Walsh, *Family of Freedom: Presidents and African Americans in the White House* (Boulder, CO: Paradigm Publishers, 2011), p. 223.

75. Kathleen Hennessey, "Tea Partyers Get Together in Nashville," *West County Times*, Feb. 6, 2010. Studies show a predisposition among Tea Party supporters toward racial intolerance or "racial resentment." See "2010 Multi-State Survey on Race and Politics," University of Washington, http://dept.washington.edu/uwiser/racepolitics.html; and Alan Abramowitz, "Partisan Polarization and the Rise of the Tea Party Movement," paper prepared for presentation at the 2011 annual meeting of the American Political Science Association, Seattle, Washington, Sept. 1–4, 2011. See also Ronald Walters, "Tea Party Racism," *Oakland Voice*, Feb. 14, 2010.

76. Jeff Zeleny, "Liz Cheney, Gingrich Rally Republicans," *New York Times*, Apr. 8, 2010. In a little-reported remark, Oklahoma's Republican senator Tom Coburn told an Aug. 2011 town hall that Obama wanted to "create dependency" because "as an African American male" he had received "tremendous benefit" from government programs, painting him as *New York Times* columnist Maureen Dowd wrote as "something akin to a welfare queen and an affirmative action president." See Dowd's "Advice to Obama from Alpha to Be More, Well, Alpha," *West County Times*, Aug. 23, 2011.

77. Daily Kos/Research 2001 Poll, http://www.dailykos.com/statepoll/2010/1/30us/437.

78. Jeffrey Jones, "Obama Averages 57 percent Approval in First Year in Office," http://www.gallup.com/poll/125096/obama-averages-approval-first-year-office.asxp.?v.

79. See Michael Barone, *The Almanac of American Politics, 2010* (Washington, DC: National Journal, 2009), pp. 28–29.

80. Samuel Kernell, "Presidential Popularity and Negative Voting: An Alternative Explanation of the Midterm Decline of the President's Party," *American Political Science Review* 71 (1977): 44–66.

81. James Campbell, "The Midterm Landslide of 2010: A Triple Wave Election," *Forum* 8 (2010); and Costas Panagopoulos, "The Dynamics of Voter Preferences in the 2010 Congressional Elections, *Forum* 8 (2010). Both of these preliminary studies suggest that the health insurance debate contributed to the size of the Democratic Party's defeat in the election.

82. James A. Stimson, *Public Opinion in America: Moods, Cycles and Swings* (Boulder, CO: Westview Press, 1999), p. 129.

83. Mark Smith, *The Right Talk: How Conservatives Transformed the Great Society into the Economic Society* (Princeton, NJ: Princeton University Press, 2008); and Catherine Rudder, "Transforming American Politics through Tax Policy" in *Congress Reconsidered*, ed. Lawrence Dodd and Bruce Oppenheimer, 9th ed. (Washington: Congressional Quarterly Press, 2009). The nation's debt was about $11 trillion when Obama took office. In his first two years, about $3 trillion was added, mainly due to the recession, the stimulus package, and other anti-recessionary expenditures.

84. For a recent examination of this research, see Lynn Vavreck, *The Message Matters: The Economy and Presidential Elections* (Princeton, NJ: Princeton University Press, 2009).

85. Alan Abramowitz, *The Disappearing Center: Engaged Citizens, Polarization and American Democracy* (New Haven, CT: Yale University Press, 2010); and Matthew Levendusky, *The Partisan Sort: How Liberals became Democrats and Conservatives became Republicans* (Chicago: University of Chicago Press, 2009).

86. "The Senate: A Crisis in Leadership," *Newsweek*, Nov. 18, 1963. The deadlock in Congress over Kennedy's program was part of the inspiration for James MacGregor Burns's classic, *The Deadlock of Democracy: Four Party Politics in America* (Englewood Cliffs, NJ: Prentice-Hall, 1963). Between 1964 and 1966, Lyndon Johnson broke the deadlock and enacted Kennedy's liberal reform agenda and more. But in his first midterm election in 1966, Johnson saw his party lose forty-eight seats in the House and six in the Senate.

87. Robert C. Smith and Richard Seltzer, "Red, Blue, Black and Gray: Polarization and the Presidency from FDR to Obama," paper prepared for presentation at the annual meeting of the National Conference of Black Political Scientists, Las Vegas, Nevada, Mar. 14–17, 2012. See also Michael Tesler and David Sears, "President Obama and the Growing Polarization of Partisan Attachment by Racial Attitudes and Race," paper prepared for presentation at the annual meeting of the American Political Science Association, Washington, DC, Sept. 4–7, 2010.

Chapter 11. Conclusion

1. Theodore Sorensen, *Counselor: A Life at the Edge of History* (New York: Harper, 2008), p. 317

2. In 2010 an indicator of the irrelevance of Catholicism and religious considerations generally in U.S. political life: the Supreme Court with Obama's appointment of Elena Kagan was constituted by six Catholics and three Jews.

3. Andrew Greeley, *The Ugly Little Secret: Anti-Catholicism in North America* (Kansas City: Sheed Andrews and McMeel, 1977), p. 11.

4. Ibid.

5. Ibid., p. 103

6. Mark S. Massa, *Anti-Catholicism in America: The Last Acceptable Prejudice* (New York: Crossroads Publishing, 2003), p. 41.

7. Ibid., pp. 43–44.

8. Ibid.

9. "Abortion views by Religious Affiliation." http://pewforum.org/docs/?DOCid=384 and "Public opinion on Gay Marriage: Opponents Consistently Outnumber Supporters." http://perforum.org/docs/?DOCid+424.

10. Massa, *Anti-Catholicism in America*, p. 198.

11. Abby Goodnaugh, "Rep. Kennedy and Bishop in Bitter Rift on Abortion," *New York Times*, Nov. 12, 2009.

12. Theodore Sorensen, *Kennedy* (New York: Harper and Row, 1965), p. 407.

13. Tim Rutten, "Kennedy's Catholic Legacy," *Los Angeles Times*, Aug. 29, 2009.

14. W. J. Rorabaugh, *The Real Making of the President: Kennedy, Nixon and the 1960 Election* (Lawrence: University of Kansas Press, 2009), p. 7.

15. Randall Kennedy writes, "Obama's principal contribution to race relations will derive not from any policies or decisions he makes but from the symbolic power of his example as a black man who became president." See *The Persistence of the Color Line: Racial Politics and the Obama Presidency* (New York: Pantheon, 2011), p. 277. Symbolism is for sure important in society and politics as Murray Edelman shows in his classic *The Symbolic Uses of Politics* (Chicago: University of Chicago Press, 1965). But I am reminded of the words of the apocryphal Harlem street corner man when told of the symbolic benefits to the race of Ralph Bunche winning the Nobel peace prize: "I can't eat Ralph Bunche for lunch." On how symbolism in politics may operate to undermine a group's substantive demands, see David Easton, *A Framework for Political Analysis* (Englewood Cliffs, NJ: Prentice-Hall, 1965), p. 127.

16. Ronald Walters with the assistance of Robert C. Smith, "Civil Rights and the First Black President: Barack Obama and the Politics of Equality," in *Civil Rights, the Conservative Movement and the Presidency from Nixon to Obama*, ed. by Kenneth Osgood and Derrick White (Gainesville: University Press of Florida, forthcoming). See also Frederick Harris, *The Price of the Ticket: Barack Obama and the Rise and Decline of Black Politics* (New York: Oxford University Press, 2012): 170–92. Andra Gillespie concludes that even in "low cost symbolic

gestures such as recognition in proclamations, executive orders and signing statements in his first six months President Obama's rhetoric and actions were no more racialized than those of Presidents Clinton and George W. Bush. See "Judged by His Actions: How President Obama Addressed Race in the First Six Months of His Administration," *Journal of Race and Policy* 6 (2011): 8–22.

17. Hope Yen and Liz Sidoti, "Figures Expected to Show Record Rise in U.S. Poverty," *Contra Costa Times*, Sept. 12, 2010.

18. http://www.census.gov/hhes/www/poverty/data/historical/people.html. See also Associated Press, "After Decades of Hard-Fought Progress, Black Economic Gains Were Reversed in Great Recession," *Washington Post*, July 10, 2011; and Pew Research Center, "Wealth Gap Rise to Record Highs Between Whites, Blacks and Hispanics," http://pewsocialtrends.org/2011/07/26/wealth–gaps–rise–to–record–highs–between–whites–blacks–hispanics/.

19. Richard Riley, *The Presidency and the Politics of Racial Inequality: Nation-Keeping from 1813 to 1965* (New York: Columbia University Press, 1999), p. 10.

20. Some suggest that in a second term Obama might become more attentive to the interests and concerns of blacks. Speaking at a Congressional Black Caucus sponsored town hall on the jobless crisis in the black community Frederica Wilson said, "If he comes out and speaks for black people in the middle of this, he will lose reelection, and you know it. We have to temper this in such a manner as we can get him reelected, and once he's a lame duck president, I think we will see lots of changes and lots of movement toward the black community." The imperatives of party and the incentive structures referred to by Riley, however, make it unlikely that the cautious, pragmatic Obama would even in a second term abandon the politics of race avoidance. Wilson is quoted in Peter Wallsten and Krissah Thompson, "Obama Faces Uncomfortable Questions from Back Community, Lawmakers," *Washington Post*, Aug. 25, 2011.

21. Barack Obama, *Dreams of My Father* (New York: Crown, 1995), p. 212.

22. Ibid. p. 123.

23. Kathleen Flake, "Mormons on Broadway Could Bring Them to the White House," *Washington Post*, Apr. 3, 2011. On Huntsman's equivocating on his religion, see also Timothy Egan, "The Reluctant Mormon," *New York Times*, June 9, 2011` and on how other prominent Mormon politicians attempt to downplay Mormon "otherness" in practicing the politics of ethnic avoidance see Walter Kirn, "Mormons *Rock*!" *Newsweek*, June 5, 2011.

About the Author

Robert C. Smith, professor of political science at San Francisco State University, is the author most recently of *Conservatism and Racism and Why in America They Are the Same* also published by SUNY Press.

Index

www.ingramcontent.com/pod-product-compliance
Lightning Source LLC
LaVergne TN
LVHW040758070826
844660LV00025B/1185

* 9 7 8 1 4 3 8 4 4 5 6 0 1 *